# Growth and Culture

# Growth and Culture

## A PHOTOGRAPHIC STUDY OF BALINESE CHILDHOOD

by Margaret Mead
and Frances Cooke Macgregor

BASED UPON

*PHOTOGRAPHS BY GREGORY BATESON*

ANALYZED IN

*GESELL CATEGORIES*

G. P. Putnam's Sons New York

MANUFACTURED IN THE UNITED STATES OF AMERICA

TO LAWRENCE K. FRANK

*to whose scientific vision, unflagging enthusiasm, commitment to man's obligation to assume responsibility for his own destiny, and constructive planning for research, the fields of child development and personality in culture are deeply indebted.*

# *Acknowledgments*

THIS BOOK is the second extensive publication based upon the combined research by Gregory Bateson and Margaret Mead in Bali. The first publication was *Balinese Character: A Photographic Analysis.* New York: Special Publications of the New York Academy of Sciences, Volume II, ed. by Wilbur G. Valentine, 1942. While this study draws heavily on the theoretical framework of *Balinese Character* and is based on an analysis of 4000 pictures selected from Gregory Bateson's collection of 25,000 still pictures made in Bali between 1936 and 1939, the present analysis is entirely the responsibility of the two authors, made with the help of Dr. Arnold Gesell, Dr. Frances Ilg, and Dr. Louise Ames, formerly of the Yale Child Development Clinic and now of the Gesell Institute of Child Development.

As this volume represents one cross section of the material collected and draws, in background if not explicitly, on the entire research, acknowledgment is due to all the persons and organizations who have contributed to any part of the expedition or to the subsequent organization of the materials, to all those collaborators in Bali, New York, and New Haven upon whose concrete data or theoretical insights we have drawn, and to our research assistants, without whose patience, devotion, and industry the work could not have been done.

For general field funds and maintenance in the field, acknowledgment is due to the Department of Anthropology of the American Museum of Natural History (and in particular to the Voss Fund and the South Seas Exploration Fund), to St. John's College, Cambridge, England, and to the William Wyse Foundation of Trinity College, Cambridge, England. For special field funds and for funds directly devoted to the preparation of this monograph, acknowledgment is due to the Social Science Research Council and to the Committee for Research in Dementia Praecox supported by the Thirty-third Degree Scottish Rite,

Northern Masonic Jurisdiction, and the Institute for Intercultural Studies. For the imagination that made possible the publication of *Balinese Character,* and indirectly, therefore, the conception of this volume as a practical venture, we are indebted to Mrs. Eunice Thomas Miner, Executive Director of the New York Academy of Sciences, who believes that scientific work can be published in a form that is beautiful, inexpensive, and practical. Acknowledgment is also due to the New York Academy of Sciences for permission to reproduce some of the photographs used in *Balinese Character*. Those reproduced are noted on the copies of the photographs. To the then government of Bali, the Government of the Netherlands East Indies, we owe thanks for many courtesies and for substantial assistance. With the new government of the Republic of Indonesia we can rejoice in the widened horizons that are now opening before the children of Bajoeng Gedé, and indeed all the children of Indonesia.

For collaboration in the field, thanks are due to Katharane Mershon, C. J. Grader, R. Goris, the late Walter Spies, and our invaluable Balinese assistant, I Made Kaler; for collaboration in the field and subsequently in working up the material, thanks are due to Jane Belo and Colin McPhee.

For some of the general theoretical insights used here, thanks are due to Erik Erikson and Lawrence K. Frank and to the Macy Foundation Cybernetics Conferences. For the special theoretical insights used in this volume, we have to thank, in addition to our principal collaborators of the Gesell Institute of Child Development, Drs. David Levy, Margaret Fries, Myrtle McGraw, and Harry S. Shapiro. Finally, thanks are due to those who have worked untiringly over the details of preparing this volume: to Dorothy Kraus Davis, who indexed the records of child behavior in Bajoeng Gedé; to Eva Lulinsky, who made the first series of 4000 photographic enlargements from which we worked; to Thane Bierwirt and Alexander Rota, who prepared some of the final prints; to Frederick Scherer and Ernest A. Nielson, who prepared the plates; to Maurice Richter, who extracted from records the preliminary background data for each figure; to Mary G. Cacciapuoti for assistance in integrating the group-conference material with the plate captions; and to Isabel Ely Lord, Rose Wax, Maryat Lee, and Elizabeth Krom for help in the final preparation of the manuscript.

MARGARET MEAD
FRANCES COOKE MACGREGOR

# *Preface*

THIS STUDY presents a series of group researches, brought to bear finally in the analysis of 4000 pictures of a group of children and their parents who lived from 1936 to 1939 in the village of Bajoeng Gedé in the mountains of the island of Bali in Indonesia. It is an attempt to focus different lines of research and different clinical and diagnostic skills on a carefully selected body of concrete nonverbal materials—photographic records of motor behavior in which a particular child is represented by a series of still photographs, usually but not always taken in sequence, and the cultural regularities in the behavior of the children are represented by the consistencies that can be found, in spite of wide individual difference among the children, when the behavior of the Balinese children as a group is contrasted against a group of American children from New Haven and its environs who have been studied during the last twenty years by Dr. Arnold Gesell and his associates. The fifty-eight plates have been arranged, first, to illustrate the individuality of each of the eight children who form the core of this presentation; second, to carry them through the particular Balinese version of the developmental progression from sitting with support to walking; and third, to present in detail those forms of motor behavior in which Balinese children differ most conspicuously as a group from the New Haven series.

This research has involved a series of antecedent pieces of teamwork, the first of which was two years of research in Bali (extending over the period from March 1936 to March 1938 and a period of six weeks in February and March 1939) by Gregory Bateson, myself, and our American and Balinese collaborators. This field work provided the knowledge of Balinese culture, the photographic and the cinema records, the detailed records of the life of the village of Bajoeng Gedé, its calendrical round, the place of each family in the social organization, and long, detailed observational records in English and in Balinese, combined with film and still records, in which individual children were followed over time, in their own courtyards, in our courtyard, on the street, at ceremonies, when they were ill, learning to walk, being weaned, and so on.

The second long series of team researches that have been focused on these materials are those of Dr. Gesell's and his associates' intensive analysis of individual children, followed over time, with still and film records and detailed periodic data on their behavior. We have drawn on these researches in two ways: by an initial use of the published materials, especially *The Atlas of Infant Behavior,* to organize our materials in a form suitable for communication with the members of the Gesell group, and by invoking the experience of Dr. Gesell, Dr. Ilg, and Dr. Ames through having them examine intensively the series of photographs, which were successively organized in response to their comments so as to invoke further comment.

The third contributor to this research, upon whose analytical sensitivity to posture and gesture the whole study rests, is Frances Cooke Macgregor, who devoted ten months to studying the 4000 photographs that were specially enlarged for this project, learning to know the distinctive motor patterns of each child, to translate the Gesell categories into a selection from the Balinese pictures, and, from what she saw in the photographs of motor behavior, to illuminate the Gesell formulations further on the one hand, and on the other, to illuminate previous formulations about Balinese character formation. Frances Macgregor has contributed to this study an unusual sensitivity to the underlying rhythms and expressive continuities of motor activity, strong native empathy and kinesthetic imagery, and a cultivation of athletic skills that has made possible the extensive work she has done in training young people in sports and in the correction of postural deviations. She has brought to this study a complex background of experience. As a documentary photographer, she made photographic studies of cultural contrasts for her books *Twentieth Century Indians* and *This is America.* She has analyzed sequences of behavior in the field of medicine from detailed photographic records she made of surgical procedures. Finally, the study has benefited from the research she was doing at the time she began the analysis of the Balinese pictures, and is now engaged in, a study of the social and cultural implications of facial disfigurement and plastic surgery.

The research was directed toward a series of questions: 1. Do these Balinese children from the village of Bajoeng Gedé appear to go through the same general developmental stages as the American children from New Haven? 2. What are the identifiable differences—if any—in the forms these developmental sequences take? 3. What clues does this analysis of motor behavior provide to the way in which Balinese culture is modeled, to the way the expectations and practices of child-rearing lay emphasis on one developmental path rather than another among those developmental paths that have been found to differ from child to child among the New Haven children? 4. What illumination is provided by the *specific* ways in which Balinese adults and older children communicate with infants and young children so that those specific learnings occur that result in each child who is born and reared in Bali, by Balinese parents, having an identifiably Balinese set of motor habits, associated with an identifiably Balinese character?

This was an experiment in teamwork, in group research. It has resulted in the preparation of the plates and the development of a series of hypotheses about the way in which human growth patterns express themselves in different cultures. Such a study is exploratory, hypothesis-forming, preparatory to more intensive, differently designed research on these particular problems.

It is not designed to prove that Balinese children go through a given sequence of development, but rather to form new hypotheses about the way in which human beings develop, on the basis of suggestive contrasts provided by the Balinese field work.

M. M.

# *Contents*

## Part I

by Margaret Mead



## Part II

## *Contents*

## *Contents*

*Contents*

## *Note on Orthography and Pronunciation of Personal Names and Balinese Words*

IN THIS BOOK I have followed the conventions used in previous publications on this Balinese field work, adhering to the spelling of our Balinese assistant, I Made Kaler, which was based upon Dutch orthography. A change to the modern Indonesian spelling would make it very difficult for the reader to use previous publications. The principal peculiarities for the American reader are the use of *oe* for the *u* (as in *sure*) and the use of a *j* where we would use a *y*. Terminal vowels, with the exception of the terminal *a* which is pronounced like the French *eu,* are long as in Italian. I have written the name of the village, Bajoeng Gede, as Bajoeng Gedé to facilitate pronunciation. The word *Bajoeng* is to be pronounced as if it were written *Baiyung,* with even accent. Personal names in Bajoeng Gedé are prefixed with an I (pronounced *ee*) until an individual becomes a parent, and then the word *Nang* (father of) or *Men* (mother of) is prefaced to the name of the oldest child. So I Wadi becomes Men Diasih when her first child is named I Diasih. The Balinese often name successive children in a series with small variations, so I Marti has a younger sister, I Marta.

I have used real names throughout. The people of Bajoeng Gedé knew that we were studying and photographing their children; indeed, they often helped set the stage for an afternoon's photography. Very cautiously, but quite definitely, they gave us permission to live among them, and there is no need to blur their contribution by disguise or subterfuge.

The eight key names are accentuated as follows: I Kárba, I Kenjoén, I Mártí, I Mártá, I Tongós, I Râoeh, I Ngendón, I Sĕpék.

CHAPTER I

# *The Need for Awareness*

THIS IS AN age of awareness. When we stand as parents or teachers, as physicians or philosophers, beside the crib of a newborn child, we are aware, as never before, of the extraordinary complexity of the life that child will live. It has become a moral imperative to know this complexity, to understand it, and to act upon our understanding of it. There are no longer any rules to follow with simple humility and obedience; it is no longer enough simply to try to do right as one learned the right at one's mother's knee. We live in a world which has discovered—in horror— that those who do what they believe to be right often do great harm to themselves and to others. Simple conformity and uncritical righteousness have both proved to be outworn ways of finding meaning in life.

This new age demands instead that we be aware—aware of the period in which we live, aware of the culture we embody, aware of the nature of the mammalian inheritance that we share with other mammals, and aware of the special potentialities that are the birthright of our humanity. And even more than that, we are also required to be aware of our particular situations and of our idiosyncratic bents. Are we the children of immigrants from Europe, or of a mixed Eurasian marriage? Were we born as the only representative of one race in a community of another race? Were our parents self-satisfied and overly complacent, desperate and bewildered, harmonious or in conflict? These circumstances—we now know—will be reflected in the way we live our lives and rear our children.

As we work for a world in which we do not punish any individual for anything beyond his control, in which we try to make race and place of birth and social position of parents factors that will neither handicap a child nor determine his future, we have at the same time introduced a new imperative—that this is only possible if each of us who works for such a world is aware of how he himself carries the marks of his particular situation. As a class is released from stigma, the individual member of it assumes new responsibilities. So society once punished the illegitimate child indiscriminately, as well as the mother; now, as we free the child altogether and try to deal with each mother in terms of what lay back of her failure to assume responsibility, we also take responsibility ourselves for recognizing and allowing for in ourselves the same potentialities that led to her failure. The dutiful and the righteous man, the moral hero of an earlier age, has been replaced by the man who is aware, the one who assumes responsibility not only for "all foreseeable results of his actions," but also for the complex effort involved in foreseeing them.

Nowhere has this change in moral climate been felt more sharply than in the field of child development, in the new methods of child care, and in the new styles of parenthood. The last twenty-five years have seen an enormous venture in understanding: understanding the nature of growth, the nature of the parent-child relationship, the nature of individuality, the nature of culture. The term "nature" is used advisedly here, for this inquiry has been pursued within the framework of science, of man's explicit search in *nature* for truth. To understand about growth, we have set up institutes in which real children are measured and studied; to understand parenthood, we have set up clinics to explore the failures, and institutes and nursery schools to explore the regularities, in parent-child relationships. To understand the nature of human culture, we have gone out to remote tribes and made detailed studies, on the spot, of just how differently human beings could live together and still fulfill the demands of their humanity, of just what is given by being human and just what is learned by growing up in different cultures.

We have done least, so far, with the study of individuality, and perhaps this is not surprising, for young sciences work first to reduce to order what seems like an irregular mass of observations, studying convergence before divergence, uniformities before uniqueness.

With this increasing knowledge of the human organism, of the way human beings learn and the consequences of learning in different ways, has gone a responsible sense that this knowledge must be put into effect. Each new advance in knowledge has meant an attempt to translate into child-care practices our newest insight. Thus as physiologists measured the time required to empty an infant's stomach, pediatric emphasis focused upon scheduled feeding; as psychiatrists reported the effects of too rigid scheduling, pediatrics shifted to more relaxed schedules. This rapid, sensitive response of those charged with the care of little children to the findings of the clinic and the laboratory has increased the difficulties of parents reared in an age of unquestioning following of tradition or conscience. They must now learn to change, to bring up one child differently from its elder brother or sister. They must learn, above all, to look outward at the child and then inward at themselves, rather than simply to ask, "Is the child the right age to be weaned?" or "Am I doing the right thing?"

This new style of parenthood is frequently one-sided. When the parents look only at the child, treating it as a sort of end product in an assembly plant, using it as a measure of their success, we get a distortion of this new approach. Then, instead of the following of rules and the fulfillment of one's own early inculcated sense of righteousness, one gets a dependence upon the applause of others because one's child is taller, brighter, or "better adjusted" than the neighbors' children. This solution, falling back upon outward success as a sign of moral grace, is the uncomfortable residue of our Puritan past, in which parents, no longer able to rely either on an immutable set of standards or upon their own individual sense of being right, turn instead to mass-production standards and seek to estimate their parenthood by the product. The price of this interim type of parenthood, this unrewarding dependence upon others and upon comparison for certainty, is *anxiety.*

But this exclusive preoccupation with the neighbors, with the standards set by the group, is only the pathology of our present age, widespread as it is. There is another group of parents, especially among the marriages of young veterans of World War II, among whom we are beginning to see not a pathology but a viable new form of parenthood, where the prevailing mood is not anxiety, but awareness. These young parents have learned that a mother or a father must look not only at the baby as it compares with the other babies on the block or in the tables of the book, but inward at themselves, at their relationship to each other and their relationship to the baby. When the eye is turned thus inward, although it may sometimes be anxiety that sends it there, the parents become aware, newly aware, of themselves as individuals, as sentient, percipient creatures, not as lay figures in a line of "good parents." They look back again at the baby and back into their own hearts, and it is from this looking back and forth—noticing the responsive stomachache and the responsive smile of child to parent or parent to child, or the way a child raises its arms to be included in a smile one parent has given the other—that our awareness is born.

This book, then, is a contribution to our awareness of the world we live in, of the period in which we live, of the ways we are going about studying that world so that we may know at which points we are able to affect the future, especially in the care and education we give our children. The discussion that follows is divided into a number of parts:

First: A description of some of the problems of growth in culture.

Second: A description of the immediate conditions within which eight Balinese children grew up, illustrated with 58 plates showing the way in which children are treated in Bali, the special ways in which they learn, the ways in which their bodies respond to that learning, and the conclusions we can draw from these materials.

Third: A description (Appendix 1) of the series of steps by which this book came to be: how the decision was taken to write it, how the materials were collected, and how they were analyzed in co-operation with the research staff of the Yale Clinic of Child Development (then directed by Dr. Arnold Gesell).

These three parts do not look as if they were parts of the same book, because they are on three quite different levels, designed in a sense for the interests of different audiences. Part I will interest parents and teachers in our own culture, and they may want to turn immediately to the pictures of these eight distinctive Balinese children, mainly as contrasts to sharpen their perceptions of American children. In Part II the details of the way in which Balinese children are reared and cared for will be interesting chiefly to those who are students of comparative culture or who delight in the details of other ways of life, especially today, when the peoples in the far reaches of the world are astir. The appendix is primarily for the student and the research worker. Yet in a sense all the parts are for each of these, because only if the research worker sees the research in the context of a changing world, only if those who wish to understand and participate in the changing climate of opinion really understand how the research that contributes to that climate of opinion is done, and only if those who must put these attitudes and research results into immediate practice in the nursery, the clinic, the nursery school, and the playground understand something of both—only then can we hope to have a world in step with itself, a world that can make awareness its strength.

In the human sciences, what we know and what we are, what we find out and what we are able to believe and use of that which is found out, are inextricably interwoven. When human beings must serve in the twin roles of subject and observer, of those who are watched and those who watch, we must take into account the understanding that the baby has of why he is presented with an experimental paper pellet or that the child has of why he is asked to respond to the picture of a boy with a broken violin, as well as the understanding the scientific observer has of the behavior that he is attempting to study. Even after this hurdle is overcome—after we have learned to recognize what adult and child each contributes to the observation, and that the cultural and personal preoccupations of the observer determine what it is that he observes, so that we arrive at observations with some reasonable claim to a limited precision—there is a second hurdle: the acceptance of the findings. A new discovery in physics may be so esoteric that while a huge majority of the world's literate population can make nothing of it, it may nevertheless be used to construct an atom bomb and destroy a city. But a new discovery in the field of human behavior has no efficacy at all until it is diffused, absorbed, and made part of a way of life by human beings, by physician and patient, by teacher and pupil, by writer and reader.

Research in child development is no exception to this rule. Twenty-five years ago Lawrence Frank, helping to inaugurate a long-term project in the field of child development, planned three steps: (1) institutions for research in which groups of individual children could be followed over time, could in fact be watched grow; (2) teacher-training facilities in which students could be trained in such a way that they would be able to use the research findings of the child-development institutes; and (3) programs for lay organizations, in order that lay people and parents could be stimulated to a receptive and supporting interest in the new subject matter so that they would provide a climate of opinion within which the teachers and other professionals who work with children would be able to put into practice what they had learned. Within such a tripartite approach the child-development movement in the United States has flourished and grown.

In this book, I propose to preserve this association between research, training, and a receptive climate of opinion, and to go one step further and include systematically a discussion of what our American culture beliefs are that enable us to accept one research finding but not another that is equally well documented, to accept a research finding in one context and reject the same finding in a different one, in a climate of opinion in which certain inventions like "self-demand feeding," "rooming in," or the ideas expressed in the terms "psychosomatic" and "group dynamics" are changed and distorted.

As those who will use the research findings of child-development studies, we must ask not only: Is this or that so? How were the data gathered? What other explanations are there? We must also ask: Why do I, as an American parent, or pediatrician, or psychiatrist, want to believe that such and such findings are factual, and why do I welcome some and reject others? Why do the very research workers themselves contradict themselves and one another, so that the whole field appears to be in confusion? Why do we who are research workers introduce self-defeating contradictions into our own material so much of the time, and why do our readers who are given these ideas select some and reject others?

Our problem becomes not only the questions: What do we know about human growth and development, about the extent to which sequences of development are fixed or alternative, about the way in which periods of rapid growth are followed by periods of consolidation, about the importance of individual differences and the way they manifest themselves within the general human growth pattern, about the extent and the ways in which learning in different cultures is interwoven with human growth, and with the idiosyncratic nature of the particular human organism? It includes also the question: To what extent is the research worker so bound by the premises of his own culture that he will ask only certain questions and make only certain observations? And even more, if the research worker succeeds by some feat of the imagination, some deviance of imagery, or some device for broadening his experience, in noting that which is not acceptable to his culture, to what degree can this finding really be useful?

In the ferment of the modern world, psychologists trained in Berlin come to teach in Iowa, Greek-born physicians learn to be psychoanalysts from German-born psychoanalysts and conduct analyses in English in New York on Swedish-born patients. Small children are transplanted in the course of a few years from loving homes to the nightmares of German concentration camps to the therapeutic ministrations of Bull Dog Bank; boys and girls from American towns and cities are trained to go out and learn the language and the culture of Eskimo and Batciga, Alorese and Kangiang. American boys parachuting down into some central-Asian jungle learn in spite of themselves of other cultural ways.

In such a world, the capacity to see new things, things to which we were previously impervious, has been greatly developed. We have been able to perceive those common human elements in the behavior of people of different races and levels of civilization to which before we were blinded, and likewise to perceive much of our own behavior, which we once thought of as universal, as exceedingly patterned and local. We have been able to recognize that all peoples do not seek happiness or success, feel shame in their foreheads, express "no" with a shake of the head, feel jealousy unless they have exclusive sexual possession of a mate, think that it is worth while to consume less today in order to have more tomorrow. Such perceptions as these are not easy. We have been asked to perceive first that children of the same chronological age are not physiologically identical (thus breaking down the earlier tendencies in American age typing) and then by a further, and perhaps more difficult, act of perception, to perceive that nevertheless chronological age is an important factor. We are asked to perceive that culture can provide extraordinarily different settings for the growth process or for any physiological state, such as puberty or menopause, and still further, to perceive that nevertheless there are physiological regularities that can be discriminated even when cultural differences are most sharply contrasting.

Within each of these perceptions it is possible to see two steps: first, the imaginative act of recognition that something could be different than the way we have been taught to think about it, and so the development of the initial research stage by asking a new question; second, the even more difficult task of correcting for the overacceptance of the first new perception. It seems probable that the more difficult the first percepion was, the harder it was for an individual to give up his cherished belief that his peculiar cultural habits had been specially ordained—or that his racial or sex or class membership represented innate superiority over others, or that the calendrical date of a baby's birth was not the only relevant statement about its development—then the harder any change in this first perception will be fought. So we may look at the history of new insights to see which have been accepted very easily and almost uncritically and which have been resisted most sharply, and so get an estimate of the degree of cultural deviance involved in the idea.

As an example of an idea that obtained very facile, rapid acceptance, we might take the Watsonian ideas of conditioning, in the 1920's. The idea that the child started out with a few very simple innate responses, which could be endlessly manipulated and combined, was thoroughly congenial to Americans, who are accustomed to fix rather than to cope, and are anxious to produce babies of superlative superiority. The baby was regarded as quite flexible. It was only necessary to arrange the scene and provide the right set of stimuli and a perfectly trained baby would emerge.

Ideas of sterilization and pasteurization obtained an equally wide acceptance. Here again good results could be obtained by manipulating the environment, keeping dirt away from the baby; if it was clean, it would be well. The danger, like the potentialities for good, lay in the outside world; the parent could, by behaving properly, control it. Furthermore, all the emphasis was active—on what the parents could do to train, condition, sterilize, nourish, exercise, and in general work *on* the child and *at* becoming successful parents.

Here the suggestions based on research that were being presented to American parents and teachers had a high degree of congeniality, because they dealt with manipulation of the external world. We can contrast them with the fate of the insights that have grown out of the therapeutic practices that have been more introspectively oriented. For example, what has happened to the idea that it would be better to feed each baby on a schedule that was adapted to its own individual rhythm rather than to force on all babies identical schedules that were adjusted to nothing more individual than age and weight? This idea drew on three sets of research materials: (1) observations made by psychiatrists that extremely rigid feeding schedules seem to be one of the identifiable negative factors in the case histories of some neurotics and psychotics; (2) observations made by students of child development that however regular the general pattern of human growth, each child has its own peculiar rhythm and style; and (3) observations on the way in which infants are fed in other cultures where breast feeding is the rule.

Consideration of these three sets of research findings suggested that by carefully observing the new suckling relationship of her own child each mother could work out an individual pattern of mutual adaptation more felicitous than any pattern based on a rigid interpretation of the clock, and designed, after all, not for breast feeding but for the regulation bottle-given formula. From this a genuinely *new* idea was born, the idea that each infant should be carefully studied during its first weeks in order to find out what its rhythm was, and that on the basis of this recorded rhythm a schedule, differing for each child, could be established that would give the mother freedom to plan her day. It was further hoped that such a way of feeding an infant would ensure that the child's first learning would be, not that *this is a hard world in which food comes seldom,* but instead, that this is a world in which impulse and satisfaction can be so fitted together that patterned behavior actually gives the organism freedom from the imperiousness of its own inchoate impulses.

We may look at what happened to this new idea as a sample of how any idea may founder on the rocks of traditional cultural attitudes. First, what happened to the name for this new method of child feeding? It was called "self-demand," a term that put all the emphasis on what the infant *demanded,* and simply reversed the dictatorship from that of clock and mother to that of cry and baby. This reversal is one with which we are familiar in those areas of American life in which democracy has not yet been established; attempts to introduce the mutuality of democracy are likely to result instead in nothing more than reversals of autocratic behavior. So when Kurt Lewin started his experiments in autocratic and democratic leadership of children's groups by adults, he found that autocratic leaders responded to requests for changed behavior not by becoming democratic, but by becoming laissez-faire, yielding all control to the child. This is, of course, a self-defeating type of behavior; in no situation where the greater knowledge and responsibility of an adult are needed can the child be made the sole arbiter of what it wants. So the new method of child feeding was rephrased as a system that turned the child into a dictator, was described as feeding the baby whenever the baby wanted to be fed. The careful attention to keeping a record and establishing a schedule was abandoned, many mothers became worn-out and frantic, and pediatricians who had been initially friendly to the method became doubtful and sometimes hostile.

As a second example of nonacceptance, consider the method described as "going back to the way Grandma fed the baby" or even by the more sophisticated as "going back to the primitives." An overly enthusiastic exponent of breast feeding as the cure for all psychological ills made a film of a South Sea island filled with terrifying scenes of skin disease and painful treatments, alternating with occasional shots of mothers suckling their babies, and the fact that the babies were suckled was supposed to account for the stolidity of the adults in undergoing pain. This was in complete disregard of an enormous mass of well-established knowledge: (1) that babies are breast-fed in every known culture except those in which modern bottle feeding has been introduced and (2) that breast feeding is therefore associated with the entire range of stoicism and abandoned resentment of pain. Going back to either Grandma or primitives is not a congenial American activity, and the introduction of these considerations decreased the acceptability of the idea. The newness of the idea—the fact that nowhere before in the history of the human race had it been possible to combine together record keeping, time keeping, and the will to observe the individual child and adjust to it—was lost sight of. This argument was given a final double twist by the comment of a grandmother who said to me:

"There is a wonderful new way of feeding babies now called 'self-demand.' No bother with schedules any more. The baby just eats three meals a day like anybody else."

The third device of nonacceptance was also a familiar one—that of atomization, of failure to generalize. The original observations, especially observations such as lay behind the recommendations made by Dr. Gesell, were that a child has its own rhythms about everything it does—waking, sleeping, eating, eliminating, watching, manipulating, walking, resting. But the psychiatric observations were focused inevitably upon areas of American child rearing where conflict seemed more traumatic for the child, the areas of feeding and toilet training. So observation of the rhythms of the child became atomized into two areas: the feeding area and the toilet-training area. A conspicuous omission was the whole area of sleep. It was forgotten that the basic premise hadn't been about eating or about toilet training as such, but about the ways in which cultural learnings were to be made more easily assimilable by the child, ways that would work less violence to the child's own unique growth rhythm. So we now have the report that babies fed on self-demand have sleep problems, which, being interpreted, means that inconsistencies in child rearing, based on complete dictation by the child in some areas and attempts to dictate by the parents in other areas, have confused the child, who refuses to go to sleep on a different premise than that on which he eats and eliminates.

A fourth device of rejection was the transformation of a problem of physiological rhythm into a problem of the will. American culture is outstandingly a culture in which very small children are expected to exercise will power to a degree that appalls Netherlands mothers, who supervise each minute expected duty, and English mothers, who lightly but physically prevent the baby from hitting them with a waving jam spoon instead of exhorting the baby not to "hit Mother." Feeding a baby congruently with its own physiological rhythm was conceived of originally as establishing a relationship between an innate metabolic rhythm and the nurturing practices of the mother. It was related to the particular rate at which a particular infant's stomach and digestive system function, not to the question of training or hardening or yielding to the baby's will. Such phrases as "The baby knows when it is hungry" did not apply to fully developed moral beings making a morally justifiable demand on the world, but to the ability that the child had to indicate, by cries of hunger or smiles of repletion, its particular bodily state.

By all of these devices, an idea that held, many of us believe, great promise as a way of rearing children who would have the flexibility and the knowledge of themselves they will need so sorely in the years ahead of us—that idea has been diluted and often lost entirely. By the devices of reversal, relegation to the past and the primitive, atomization, and moralization, cultural selectivity has been exerted and the original idea denigrated and distorted. I have gone over these steps in considerable detail because in this book we are to be concerned with a related series of problems that should result in new insights—from the findings of the child-development clinic and the anthropological study of children in other cultures—and we should also be concerned with the types of cultural resistance that such attempts have met and will continue to meet.

Recognition of the extent to which our American heritage patterns our ability to accept or even to perceive the new, and predetermines us to distort and select from any set of new ideas, will provide no automatic guarantee that we will be able to act in such a way that we use our culture as a tool of understanding, instead of ourselves remaining, unconsciously, tools of cultural processes that we do not understand. Cultures may be transformed, they may be raised to new levels of abstraction and inclusiveness, but we who live by them must remain bound to some culture. Our freedom lies always in transforming the culture rather than in attempting to escape from it into a cultureless limbo of relativity and cynicism. If we had succeeded in incorporating the original idea of a mother who adapts to her child's observed physiological rhythms and so builds a special little two-person subculture through which her baby has a gentler and more strengthening path into his society, then our culture would have been enriched and deepened, but it would not have been less a culture by which and through which we live.

We may now consider what the problem of acceptance may be expected to be in the presentation of the material with which this study is specifically concerned. This book is a study of the way in which human growth rhythms are patterned within human cultures. It focuses on three areas of research: (1) the nature of the human growth process, (2) the degree of individuality within the human growth process, and (3) the way in which these growth processes, the generally human and the idiosyncratic, are interwoven in the process of learning to be a human being in a given culture. The first series of difficulties that will be encountered will be in the tendency to think in either-or terms. If a certain type of behavior, such as walking, is to be attributed to the unfolding of an innate human capacity, then walking is due to growth, not to culture. In thinking this we are ignoring the importance of the way in which walking is taught or learned, encouraged or discouraged, in any given culture.

Conversely, those readers—scientific or lay—who have accepted the findings of anthropologists that children do learn different things, and learn them differently, in different cultures are inclined to go all the way in the other direction, and say that everything is learned and the innate unfolding capacity is so plastic that it can simply be taken for granted. These latter resistances have many curious facets, such as a willingness to accept the findings of the Gesell Institute on infants but a tendency to reject the findings on older children, a willingness to believe that chronological age may be a factor in the way the head is held—somehow assumed to be entirely free of culture—but an unwillingness to believe that chronological age may equally play a role in whether children of middle-class New Haven families want to be read to before instead of after supper.

Then there is a third area of all-or-none response, which manifests itself in the question of individuality as compared with general tendency, whether the general tendency discussed is regarded as referable to laws of growth or to laws of culture. The argument runs that since each infant is different, it is not possible to establish *any* general laws of growth and development, or if there is a general set of laws of growth, then individuals are to be regarded as conforming to them or deviating from them, as advanced or retarded, so that the central tendency that was originally derived from a study of individual cases is converted into some Frankenstein monster of normalization. The fine recognition of individual differences that used to be expressed in more stable times by saying, "John walked a long time before he talked, just like Uncle Henry," is converted into statements of retardation to be lamented or precocity to be boasted about.

The analogue of this particular set of resistances to growth studies runs like this when anthropological material is considered: Anthropologists describe a culture in terms of those behaviors that are to be attributed to learning, stressing, for example, not the ability to make patterned sounds, but what particular sorts of patterned sounds the members of a particular culture who speak a particular language make. As the emphasis is upon the uniformities and regularities within a culture —that all sane and full members of a given culture will recognize a given word, understand a given gesture, regard sitting in a given way as appropriate for persons of a given sex or age or status—this means, the argument runs, that anthropologists think everyone is alike, and don't recognize individual differences. But it was only by observing and allowing for individual differences that the patterns which the anthropologist describes were derived. If stammering and lisping were not regarded as individual idiosyncracies, the anthropologist might well emerge with the statement that several languages were spoken instead of one. If each relevant detail of the life history of each individual on whose behavior the generalizations are based were not allowed for—

such as a foreign-born mother, or residence abroad—deviations in pronunciation might be regarded as intrinsic to the pattern of variation in the particular language, or postural aberrances classified as etiquette for widowers.

None of these matters are either-or matters. The greater the respect for the innate growth pattern, the greater the respect also for the way in which cultural patterns make it possible for human beings to become in one culture dancers of incomparable grace and in another, air pilots of absolute reliability and trustworthiness, in one culture modern physicists and in another, sculptors of beautiful statues. The more the process of growth is seen as having its own regularities, the greater the significance of the differences between cultures. And the anthropologist, who specializes in the regularities of human cultures—the extent to which human behavior that is shared by a group is systematic and patterned because it is related to these innate patterns of growth and development and to the properties that human nervous systems have in common and that human communication demands—the anthropologist must also respect fully those patterns of physiological functioning to which the regularities of his own cultural material are related.

And each specialist in growth and specialist in culture who has derived his uniformities and regularities from a study of individuals, fully recognized and appreciated as individuals, must continue to recognize and include within his systematic approaches a recognition of the uniqueness of each human individual, who is not to be seen as more or less representative of a stage of growth or of a particular culture but, if his whole individuality is taken into account, as a full representative —of his particular sort—of his own stage of growth and his particular culture. A three-year-old dwarf is not a retarded three-year-old, but a three-year-old dwarf. An illiterate American is not a subcultural creature, but an American who has not learned to read. A general understanding of the hereditary and endocrine conditions that underlie dwarfing can be derived from the study of the dwarf only if he is seen to be a dwarf, not a retarded normal, and an understanding of the social conditions that still make illiteracy—even of individuals with adequate intelligence—possible in the United States will be arrived at only if we are willing to study the individual in his uniqueness and not refer him to some classification which assumes that Americans who can't read are either mentally subnormal or racially destined to that condition.

This, then, is the first set of expectable resistances that will arise as the reader approaches this material. Ideally, each sentence should take them into account, but such a method of presentation would be intolerable and unreadable, and would very soon set up a new set of resistances. Instead, by outlining the expected resistances here I hope to persuade the readers to set up a code of warning signals, of ways of catching themselves, of saying to themselves (as students do in response to an instructor's frown at a one-sided statement): "*But* it is also recognized that human growth and the functioning of the human organism have their own regularities. *But* it is also recognized that the human being always grows and functions within a culture and that each culture has its own particular pattern. *But* it is also recognized that each individual, though partaking of our common humanity and of his own culture, is unique."

There are, however, another set of cultural susceptibilities and resistances that have to be taken into account. This book is a study of parents and children, of the way in which parents and children communicate with each other and reinforce certain types of behavior. To the extent that it demonstrates how differently Balinese babies, with the same original capabilities as American babies, learn to behave differently, this is congenial to Americans. American culture is a culture of choice; millions of people have come to this country as adults electing to become United States citizens and to turn their children into "real Americans." The idea that the grandchild of European peasants can be so reared as to be indistinguishable from the grandchild of Maine farmers is a precious tenet of the American ethic—an ethic that flounders when major racial differences in skin color or facial configuration interfere with this basic tenet of indistinguishability.[1] As long as anthropological material underlines plasticity—and by indirection the power of parents, teachers, and public men to make foreigners into Americans—it is acceptable.

But the other side of the anthropological analysis is far from acceptable. For the other part of the story is that cultural learnings are very deep and complete, and that the grandson of European peasants has not only become indistinguishable from the grandson of the Maine farmer in superficial ways, but in ways so deep that they are part and par-

[1] Numbered footnotes will be found on pages 209-10.

cel of his being. He cannot go back to the land of his ancestors and ever become what he would have been if he had been born and reared there by parents who had never emigrated. While the demonstration that members of the same human group can grow up to be savages in a G-string or doctors in a consulting room is reassuring, this statement of limitations is repugnant to Americans, whose optimism often overflows into a belief that one can have one's cake and eat it too. We want to believe both that we can, by the proper educational methods, make anything we like of our children and that we can, by taking thought, make any alteration we like in what our parents did with us. Fluctuations in theories of child care over the last half-century reflect this dilemma, the eager acceptance of Watson on the one hand, acceptance of Freudian teaching seen as a doctrine of susceptibility of the child to parental good and bad deeds, the lack of interest in Jungian analysis, which stressed intractable constitution as well as the determinative effects of nurture.

Rejection of the finality of cultural learning not only conflicts with the desire of American parents to produce whatever new and better children they desire, but also with the effort of the foreign-born to take hold of the American heritage that American political thought has assured them is theirs by right. So it is not surprising that some of the most impassioned repudiations of the anthropologists' stress on the importance of cultural learning come from first-generation Americans who are unwilling or unable to come to terms with their own pasts. The circumstance that these pasts were so often lived in countries that have become politically closed to them, although often still deeply loved by them, makes the dilemma even greater.

Where there is such a deep-seated cultural desire to believe in an open-ended system, a system in which we ourselves can do what our parents could not do, shape our children as they did not shape us, give them freedom while being ourselves unfree, give them security while being ourselves anxious and unaware—where all this is true, mere logical argument is not sufficient. I could argue, most cogently, that if parents in any culture can profoundly alter their children by the way in which they are reared, then those parents themselves must also be referable to what their parents did. Such arguments have little effect even on people who claim to be scientists, and still less on those who work in other fields. Human cultures are not logical systems: that is, they are not built in accordance with the laws of nature that can be elaborated on the basis of a careful observation of the external world. Rather, they are mediating systems by which human beings are able to combine ways of thought and feeling modeled upon looking inward with ways of thought and acting modeled upon looking outward, at the external world, or at the self viewed as if it were part of the external world. As mediating systems, cultures are also infused with the logic of inner and outer worlds.

So it seems the better part of wisdom, at least for the anthropologist whose subject matter is the wholeness of any cultural system, to recognize that Americans will accept with fair alacrity any statement about the plasticity of human childhood except one that conflicts with racial prejudice; that Americans, especially first-generation and immigrant Americans, will reject any statement that suggests that they themselves are bound by what they learned during this plastic childhood period; and that to reconcile this contradiction we will need some new research on how adults learn a new culture. If we can demonstrate, as practical experience suggests that we can, that there is a different order of learning, so that the more perfectly an adult has learned one culture, knowing it to be one among many cultures, the more perfectly he can learn another—so that learning as a child to eat with chopsticks with ease and skill can be seen as a possible prelude to learning to eat with knife and fork as an adult with comparable ease and skill—then we may expect to reduce this area of rejection.

Such research does not yet exist. All I can do is to warn the reader that the material in this book will be viewed, either with aware acceptance or with anxious rejection, as it is related to one's own children's future or to one's own past. If outbursts of disbelief are encountered, they may be examined in the light of this discussion; if the examination proves illuminating, one more step toward awareness will have been taken.

But even this does not exhaust the difficulties. An examination of the response of American parents to Dr. Gesell's books provides material on another area of difficulty. As new research develops in the field of human relationships, there is a tendency to use it to counter some other tendency that has gone too far. Nowhere has this been truer than in the field of child development, where scientific theory and pediatric and educational practice have swung back and forth between an overemphasis on environmentalism and an overemphasis on innate capacities and physiological regularities. The research worker who takes responsibility for the use to which his researches are put is inevitably and rightly involved in these swings of opinion, but such involvement carries its own penalties. Dr. Gesell's work and the studies that Dr. Myrtle McGraw made in the 1920's were begun in an era of environmentalism, in which the human infant was conceived as extremely subject to external manipulation. The re-establishment of some recognition of human-growth process that might be stunted but could not be hurried was important. As in the case of anthropological work, this significance of the growth process could be stated in terms of regularities, such as the age at which, plus or minus a few days or weeks or months, the child learned to focus its eyes, or to sit alone, or to walk. Broad statistical statements, based on the study of individuals but constructed as generalizations—just as the anthropologist states the pattern of a language or a house form or a method of gardening without each time emphasizing the individual variations—were congenial to American forms of communication. Too congenial, in fact.

So, by a painful irony, the work of Dr. Gesell, the impassioned champion of the right of children to grow at their own pace, with a partisanship so complete that the main raison d'être of a culture, in his opinion, is to provide the setting for such a development of each individual child, has often been transformed instead into an instrument through which mothers rob their children of this very right. Books that were designed as guides to help the mother know what to expect, so that she might take care not to hurry her child on the one hand, and to take full advantage of its need for new experiences on the other, are used instead as ways of comparing one's child with other children, simply to establish how well one is doing as a mother. If a child walks early by the Gesell norms, the mother concludes not that the child is the type of individual on which the lower range of the Gesell series was based, but that the child is vindicating her success. The statement that at a given age some children like to kick, and so it may be better to let them wear soft shoes to the table, becomes converted into a norm through which the mothers of kickers can comfort themselves that their children are "normal" and the mothers of non-kickers worry as to whether it is after all "good" or "bad" not to "kick normally."

But this frequent misunderstanding by American mothers of what the Gesell norms meant would not in itself be so serious if the best thought in American educational practice, at the pediatric and nursery-school level, had been there to correct and advise each proud or overanxious parent as to what those norms really meant, and that, while useful for sorting out extreme cases of mental deficiency in young infants, they were primarily designed not to test for normalcy, and certainly not to test for successful nurture, but to provide a framework of expectation within which a mother could guide a child through its particular version of normal growth and development. But here again the cultural factor entered. The majority of pediatricians and nursery-school teachers were as unsophisticatedly American, as fully members of their own cultures, as were the parents who classified their children according to the Gesell norms. On the one hand, they were happy to take credit for children who were advanced, and on the other, to disown responsibility for the children who were retarded. So we find, reflected in another area, the same cultural contradiction found in a willingness to believe one can shape one's children and an unwillingness to accept that one was shaped oneself. When the norms underwrote a self-regarding self-approval, the Gesell norms were used to support environmentalism; when a child fell below the norms, heredity was invoked.

But here, to explain further what happened, we must invoke history, as well as cultural regularity. While Gesell was documenting the extent to which *growth* has its own patterns and cannot be forced or hurried, another group of child educators began to focus on the importance of individual differences, and the inadequacy of chronological age as a way of classifying children together for educational purposes. The principal impetus to this investigation came from the study of adolescence, from the recognition of the enormous difference between individual children in physiological, social, and intellectual maturity, and how maturation in these various ways seemed to be completely discrepant. Like Gesell in his study of infants, the students of adolescence whose work informed the Adolescent Study[2] of the mid-thirties were animated by a desire to protect, support, and facilitate the unique growth process in the individual. But ironically, it looked, and still looks, to many specialists in the field as if the two approaches contradicted each other. Were not the opponents of classification by chronological age saying that "being ten or eleven or twelve" is *not* the point, and was not the Gesell school saying, "There is a state of development that can be described as 'ten-ness' even when found in children who mature at astonishingly different rates"? It sounded like a complete contradiction, and the circumstance that both sets of researches, the Gesell work beginning with the infants and the work that centered on adolescence, were reactions against current cultural trends did not clarify the situation.

The students of adolescence saw American adolescents made horribly miserable by discrepancies in their rates of maturation. Indeed they conceived the major problem of adolescence as "Am I normal?" They tried, but often failed—for our techniques of communication between anthropologists and members of other disciplines were rudimentary in those days—to hold in mind that they were talking about *American* adolescents, and to recognize the value to Americans of uniformity in all externals, the need to devalue individuality in a country in which each individual's experience differs so much from that of all others. They ended up, however, with a belief that any emphasis on chronological age meant somehow a negative valuation of individuality, the particular value that they were fighting a losing battle to defend. It was not too apparent that the same mothers who seized the Gesell norms to support their own deep cultural preoccupation with producing a successful child also seized on the studies on adolescence as demonstrating the importance of letting their children do "what the others do" so as to feel "normal." Both sets of researches, each valid, each based on a recognition of the innateness of the growth process, were misinterpreted and misused, and incorrectly treated as contradictory. A similar mishap befell my initial work on adolescence,[3] which was interpreted to mean not that puberty *need* not be a time of such great stress as it is in our culture, but rather that puberty does not matter at all.

A disciplined attention to the way in which a climate of opinion is dependent not only upon the insights and the researches of individuals, but also upon the pattern of the culture within which they occur, is one way of preventing these contretemps. By recognizing that Americans will reach for solutions that are optimistic and open-ended, will repudiate suggestions that are limiting, will tend to see things in black-or-white terms, often simply reversing a past position rather than arriving at a higher level of abstraction—by recognizing all this we can build a new climate of opinion in which we shall be able to include, simultaneously, the recognition of the regularity of the growth process for all human beings, the regularities of the cultural process within each culture, and the individuality with which each human being has grown with his particular physical endowment within his particular culture, his particular period of history, and his particular life situation.

We can then ask, out of the knowledge of these processes, and out of our twentieth-century American hope for an open-ended and improving world, whether we can devise pediatric and educational procedures that will make it possible for adults who understand their culture and the limitations it lays upon them to bring up children who will be as much stronger, as much more aware, than their parents as they will need to be if they are to carry the load of developing a world community.

CHAPTER II

# *The Significance of Growth in Culture*

THE SIGNIFICANCE of this minute analysis of the behavior of eight small children in a remote Indonesian village may perhaps be conveyed by thinking about the problem that confronts the parent or the educator in the presence of an individual child of seven months old who is clapping its hands. How are we to think about this hand clapping? What are the sets of systematic knowledge about human behavior that can be invoked? Should we ask, Does clapping its hands prove the child is bright, or perhaps musical? Should we assume that the child would never have clapped its hands unless someone had taught it, so the question is: Who taught it to clap? Is it enough to say that this is a traditional form of behavior in the child's society? Should we remember that its older brother also clapped his hands at the same age, and so refer the hand clapping to heredity? Or remember that its mother was a teacher who clapped her hands to get order in the classroom, and somehow connect this up with the tendency of her children to clap their hands? Is the hand clapping something that should be discouraged or encouraged, ignored or elaborated? And how would one go about getting the necessary information to answer such questions?

When we set about the task of analyzing such a very simple act as hand clapping, it is immediately apparent that the matter is very complicated. If we want to refer it to the growth process, as delineated by Gesell and his coworkers, we need to use such concepts as symmetry and asymmetry. We would have to ask whether the child was at a stage of development in which its behavior was primarily symmetrical, so that the stage of growth reinforced and facilitated the hand clapping, or in an asymmetrical phase in which hand clapping had to be learned in opposition to the prevailing bodily tendency. Similar questions would have to be asked about the amount of co-ordination involved, the degree to which the eyes were involved in the co-ordination of palm to palm, the extent to which the sound of the impact of one palm on the other palm appeared to be important in keeping the clapping going—whether the sound of one clap is the stimulus to the next one. For a knowledge of how the hand-eye co-ordination fitted together, and how the auditory stimulus was involved, we would go again to material on the normal course of development.

From an exploration of this small piece of behavior in Gesell categories, we would be able to place this isolated bit of symmetrical palm-to-palm eye-co-ordinated, auditorially stimulated behavior in a setting of a systematic conception of growth. The extent to which the details vary from the performance of the many other children on whom the study by Gesell was based would give us a picture of the individual child's manual dexterity, type of co-ordination, and so on. The exact age at which the clapping came would give a clue as to the particular pattern of development this child had followed, and was likely to follow, as it alternated between periods of symmetry and consolidation and periods of asymmetry and expansion, for example, or as it used opposition between the essential character of a stage and an act as a tension-producing situation indirectly facilitative of the act.

There would, however, still be aspects of the situation to which an application of the Gesell categories would give no clue. Was the clapping "natural," a regular spontaneous expression of a period of physical development that might be expected in any child of the same developmental level, or was it taught or reinforced, and if so how and by whom? The first two are cultural questions, the last is a situational question that can be answered only by actual knowledge of particular events. The question whether the clapping was a "natural, spontaneous" human response can only be answered by making studies in different cultural settings. If we find whole cultures in which babies never clap, and other cultures in which they are taught to clap, and other cultures in which there are isolated untaught cases of clapping, then we can assume that clapping is something that all human babies can learn and which can be completely inhibited by other learnings, but which may, under still another set of cultural circumstances, appear occasionally as a possible, but not an inevitable, form of human behavior.

The assumptions on which this study is based are that we may expect (1) that the over-all growth process will be the same for all human children, (2) that wide variations will occur among individual children in the details of the process, (3) that there may well be developmental types within which these individual variants may be grouped, and (4) that cultures will differ from each other in the way in which the growth process is interwoven with learning. Thus, the existence of a sucking reflex at birth, of varying degrees of strength, will be taken advantage of in some cultures by putting the baby at once to the mother's breast, so that the infant's sucking is used to stimulate the flow of the mother's milk while the infant itself remains hungry, or the infant may be put at the breast of a wet nurse with a well-established flow of milk, in which case the infant's sucking behavior is reinforced but the mother is left without the stimulation it would have provided. As another alternative, the infant may be starved until the mother has milk, and as still another, the infant may be given a bottle with a different type of nipple, combining satisfaction with a learning that will interfere with rather than reinforce the establishment of breast feeding. The student of child development will concentrate on the sucking reflex, its strength, the child's differential response to sweet and salt and bitter, treating the establishment of sucking behavior as an autonomous process that the mother and other environmental persons can either facilitate or inhibit. But the anthropologist will be concerned from the start with the relationship between child and others as a system of intercommunication, affecting the mother as well as the child. The existence of a culture pattern that calls for giving the newborn child the unflowing maternal breast or the flowing breast of a wet nurse, and a pattern that calls for a period of starvation, will be seen as ways in which infant capacity and early growth pattern are interwoven in both child and maternal behavior.

Furthermore, the anthropologist will assume that each detail of behavior involving mother and child may both refer to and reinforce other behaviors in the culture. The effort to have a wet nurse present at birth may be either congruent with and reinforce other forms of cherishing and punctilious care, or it may contrast with general negligence and carelessness in other areas. In one case the effect on wet nurse and mother will be reinforcement of a general set, in the other it may result in a singling-out of the suckling situation as having a special character, which may carry over into the way in which mothers suckle their own children. A host of other behaviors about carrying, lulling, bathing the child may center about the suckling experience and so be inextricably interwoven with it, in such a way that differences between children in vigor of sucking, or between mothers in ease of flow of milk, may be crucial to the establishment of certain types of individual differences in character formation within a particular society. Or the suckling experience may be much less tightly interwoven, so that there will be little expression of such individual differences between children or in maternal behavior.

Cultural analysis of the child-rearing process consists in an attempt to identify those sequences in child-other behavior which carry the greatest communication weight and so are crucial for the development of each culturally regular character structure. Knowledge of the age ranges within which children sit, stand, walk, balance, or develop opposition of thumb and forefinger, give an extra depth to such an analysis, since it indicates whether the regular cultural practice demands more than the organism is usually capable of, or less, or actually is in opposition to the central tendency of a given phase of development.

A further dimension can be provided by a knowledge that in a particular culture, for example, any relaxation of a new skill is frowned upon as backsliding. The Gesell analyses of growth and development hypothesize that growth follows a spiral course, so that often a period of apparently lowered efficiency—the down sweep of one round of the spiral—is to be seen not as regression or loss, but as a different type of organization, in which some skills may temporarily lessen, in preparation for the next upsweep. In those cultures in which there is relentless expectation of the maintenance of gains, like that of the Manus of the Admiralty Islands, or in our own culture, where such low swings of the spiral are classified indiscriminantly as "regression," there may be said to be an opposition between cultural practice and the nature of the growth process. Or there may be a neglect in a given culture of the moment when most of the children would learn a new skill most readily, so that a human potentiality is left unexplored and undeveloped.

Placing the expected spiral of development in detail beside any set of cultural practices gives us a means of describing the learning-teaching practice of that culture, and a means of delineating one aspect of the way in which members of one society grow up to be graceful, flexible, and tireless, those of another, tense, controlled, and purposeful, those of a third, poorly co-ordinated, easily fatigued, and aimless.

In this discussion, I have emphasized motor behavior and motor learning, since it is motor behavior that can best be presented pictorially, and it is upon motor behavior that the Gesell categories have been refined. It is assumed, however, that human behavior is so integrated that the same type of generalization can be drawn in the end from any carefully defined set of sequences, verbal or motor, zonal, modal, or total.

There are other ways also in which an understanding of the human developmental sequences are important in the analysis of culture. Through the centuries of human history man has been able, by taking clues from his own body, from relationships among human beings, and from the observation of the world around him, to elaborate complex traditions within the defining forms of which human beings can reach new heights of intellectual and artistic achievement. This is what is meant when it is said that art comes from art, not from nature, that a long series of imaginative steps, each one based on previous imaginative steps that have been culturally elaborated, is a necessary prerequisite of a great art. It is what is meant when we talk of great periods in art and literature, or in scientific exploration and invention.

An understanding of this whole process through which imaginative and gifted individuals draw on their culture in such a way that other men who come after them can use their new insights and their new culturally embodied skills, is partly dependent upon a study of the clues that are used. So the beginnings of literature in primitive folklore can be analyzed to show how they draw on the plots of life in the human family, and upon the cosmic plots of the rhythms of the sun and the moon and the tides. The human reproductive and growth processes have provided some of the abiding and fruitful imagery for the religious leader, the poet, and the philosopher, as one civilization after another has drawn upon these clues. So the Polynesians speak of the command that "Darkness become a light-possessing darkness" so that the waters and the heavens were separated, "and at once the moving earth lay stretched abroad."[1]

The Gospel says, "Except ye become . . . as little children,"[2] and speaks of being born "of the water and of the spirit."[3] And in early Buddhist teaching, "life span" is used as a symbol in the developmental sense of a completed reproductive cycle within a long or a short number of years, so that when men do evil, the generations fall on evil days and "maidens of five years will be of marriageable age," while when men do good, "because of their getting into this good way they will increase again both as to their span of life and as to their comeliness."[4] But in addition to the use of the imagery of human growth as a basis for poetry and religion, cultures also may be said to use models of human growth that provide models for many aspects of the culture. So it makes a great deal of difference whether the child is regarded as complete, but small and for some reason physically incapable of exercising his full role, or as only partially human until something has been done to him—he has been "broken in" or "educated"—or as still embryonic at birth, so that great qualitative changes have to occur within the organism. So also it matters whether the child is conceived of as originally evil, to be gentled by society, or originally innocent, to be corrupted by wisdom, or hardened in the ways of the world. Whether learning is seen as a way in which a child does "naturally" that which he sees others do, or something that must be cultivated by the most excessive and continuous application on the part of the child, accompanied by supervision and reward and punishment from the teacher, or one of the many combinations of these, will be important in determining how a society handles questions of social mobility, yielding gracefully to "nature's gentleman," condemning to irreversible low status regardless of origin those who have missed the proper initiatory steps in learning, or believing—as do Americans, who tend to use not growth models but manufacturing models in thinking about change in human beings—that one can begin all over as an adult, acquiring a new skill, or making oneself into a success, or an American.

The Balinese attitude toward growth was primarily a passive one. The same human soul or cluster of souls (the theory is obscure) is born over and over, every fourth generation, into the same family, carrying with it from life to life no accretion of skill or knowledge, but only occasionally compromising debts—incurred in heaven or on earth—that may result in extra burdens during the new sojourn in this world or in the other world. The child at birth is very close to his recent holy dwelling place; he is addressed with honorific terms, and treated with reverence. As he grows older, he becomes earthly enough to enter the temple —at 210 days in Bajoeng Gedé—and takes part in the rites in which man's earthly life and heavenly life meet, and from which injury or breaking of taboos or temporary states of taboo may exclude him at certain periods in his life—as when he is just married, has an open wound, has touched the dead. In old age, when he becomes a great-grandfather, he is again too close to the other world to mingle freely with mortals. He must pay his great grandchild a copper coin if he meets him on the street, since he and his great grandchild, being one and the same, should not be on earth together.

This theory of reincarnation will be recognized as a special version of widespread Asiatic beliefs in which the idea of ascent and descent in accordance with spiritual progress is missing. The Balinese of Bajoeng Gedé have instead a simple belief in changes of good and bad fortune within the same social level. In this theory, with its emphasis on the unchanging human soul that moves in and out of life in a never-ending round, bodies become garments worn by the soul, and it is even possible, by certain magical rites at death, to attempt to influence the appearance of the next body. Only the body grows and only the body decays, and there is no idea of a self that has only one embodiment, unskilled in childhood, skilled and efficient in middle life, deteriorating in old age, which is the model on which our American attitude is at present built. And congruent with this, there is much more latitude in the way the culture institutionalizes learning. Small children and old men, as long as the hand of one can grasp at all, although with a weak ulnar grasp, and as long as the hand of the other does not, in a senile tremor, let the mallet drop on the keys, can play the xylophone. Growth is a change in ceremonial and religious status as strength and size increase and reproductivity takes its course. This theory is consonant with a view of life in which that which is to occur is already determined, but not yet clear, and the individual moves, sometimes in urgent situations looking for clues from a seer or a diviner, but most often simply moving like a dancer to music that has not yet been heard but is familiar in style, foot ever poised for the next perfectly anticipated note.

But besides the way in which the whole course of development from birth to death is viewed, there are other and more detailed ways in which human developmental states are embodied and elaborated in cultural form. Clues taken from models based on the bodily orifices, or from stages in the relationship between parent and child, have been explored,[5] but we still know very little of two ways in which the Gesell type of analysis could give us further illumination: the extent to which any culture may take a particular age as its model either of the whole of childhood or of the peak of life.

No people of whom we have any record are equally sensitive and articulate about each change through which children go as they develop from birth to whatever may be regarded—in that society—as physical maturity. Some peoples treat an infant in almost exactly the same way until it is six months or a year old, swaddling or binding it with little recognition of expanding capacities to grasp, crawl, sit up, and stand. Others begin standing a newborn baby up at birth, modeling its early infancy on a stage that it will be ready for months later. Some peoples set four-year-olds to herding alone in the mountains and others think that an eighteen-year-old cannot be trusted with a house key. Tasks that are accounted appropriate for a ten-year-old in one part of our own historical tradition—such as writing Latin verses—may be regarded as too difficult for college students in another.

These blurrings and extrapolations and condensations of the readinesses and unreadinesses of different stages of growth are all exceedingly significant in character formation in different cultures. If we are to make the kind of detailed analysis on the basis of which we can acquire real knowledge of the steps involved, then we must be able to answer, for each culture, and for each class, and for each individuel studied in detail, the questions: How do the way in which a child or an adolescent is treated, the expectations to which he has to conform, and his learned capacity to behave in a certain expected way at a certain age, correspond with the rhythms of the growth cycle, and with the individual variations that occur within them? When, how, and how much is each infant, each child, and each youth being forced into behavior modeled on a different age, or a different stage?

The choice of particular ages for elaboration, either as ideals, such as "courageous youth," "serene old age," or "maturity," will also be reflected not only in the tone in which other ages are thought of—as just approaching, or having forever passed, as the most desirable point—but also in the emphasis upon some earlier stages of development rather than upon others. A people who admire contemplation and the capacity to feed the imagination through the beauties of the landscape can be congruently more tolerant of the period of early childhood, when the child is looking at the world, and less insistent on the child's acquiring sphincter control and motor autonomy. Cultures like our own, in which motor control is exceedingly important, will congruently begin demanding control at a very early age from children, and show less permissiveness toward dependency and dreaming. In periods of culture change, as in modern Russia and modern China, the attempt to transform a culture with one set of values into a culture with a very different set of values, to change from peasant adaptation and acceptance of the cyclic rhythms of the earth and sky to the machine's irreversible sequence and demands for punctuality, accuracy, and control, is reflected in attempts to change the way in which children are cared for and educated.[6]

American culture has been moving steadily toward giving more consideration to the special needs and capabilities of children at different ages and at different stages of maturity, and congruently this increase in sensitivity to the needs of different-aged children is now being accompanied by a growing sensitivity to the special needs and capabilities of the aging. First came the nursery furniture—chairs and tables, towel racks, toilet seats, washable books adapted to little children—and now we begin to hear also about forms of stairs and household equipment that are safe and possible for failing steps and faltering hands. This is a vivid example of the dynamics of cultural change, and how increasing sensitivity to one part of the growth cycle—in terms of itself, not of some imputed relationships as prelude or postlude to "maturity" —generates a sensitivity to other periods also, to their intrinsic characteristics, until we are at least able to conceive of a culture in which each age would have an equally dignified, different, and appropriate place.

We may now turn to the problem of what kind of question we should ask about the environment of a child if we are primarily concerned with the development of motor patterns of behavior. When the focus is on the emotional development of the child, an analysis of the interplay between child and others in zonal-modal terms has proved rewarding and instructive.[7] When to an analysis of emotional development we wish to add an analysis of thought processes, then attention is usefully centered on the extent to which the child's early experience is inward-turned or outward-turned, and how continually it is mediated by cultural interpreters, who may be either persons or objects.[8] If we are primarily concerned with the learning of cultural behavior, then the situations of learning can be classified in terms of sanctions underlying certain types of behavior.[9]

But in this study we are primarily concerned with the extent to which the cultural setting facilitates or inhibits, deflects or specializes, the orderly processes of growth of motor behavior. From this point of view, it is possible to place the environment of the very young child on a number of continua: the extent to which the child is in active contact, as contrasted with passive contact, with other objects or persons, the extent to which the child is insulated from contact with the world around it, experiences it directly, or experiences it as mediated by other persons; the differential play allowed to different parts of the body, the extent to which those who care for the child, or the ways it is wrapped or fed or bathed, emphasize one part of the body, either negatively or positively. An analysis of the environment of the infant and the young child in these terms seems to yield significant results.

First, how much is the child in contact, and in what ways? Is it clothed, or wrapped, or left naked, or are parts of the body wrapped and others left free? When it reaches out, what does it find—only its own body, only the smooth side of a crib or the smooth surface of a mattress, or the feel of another human body? Or are its hands bound on a cradle board, or by a swadding band, so that instead of reaching with its hands, it "reaches" with its eyes? Is it strapped or held so that the upper part of the body is free but the legs are constrained? Is the head fastened to a backboard, propped against a pillow, or allowed to settle lightly into an unsupported position as the child sleeps in arms?

If the child is held, what is the nature of the holding? A child can be carried like an object, as it is if strapped to a cradle board; it can be taught to hold on so that there is continual tension between carried child and carrier; it can be treated as part of the self, well attached but lightly attended to—as the Balinese treat it. Or it can simply be propelled about, the mother sometimes substituting for the baby carriage or the kiddy cart, in which her body approximates the movements of a supporting piece of furniture.

Are the earliest experiences of movement experiences of being moved or of moving, so that moving becomes either a sign of active autonomous life or a plastic adjustment to the outer world? Are these experiences active or passive in the sense that the child watches things move into which he feels himself moving, or himself rides in a car, or propels himself along on a velocipede, or with a tiny car model in his hand, himself provides the impetus that will later be provided by an animal or an engine? One implication of such questions as these is reflected in two current crazes among American children, the small boy's passion for guns and the passion of slightly older girls for horses. Both may be seen as a compensatory response to the mechanization of life, a desire to feel master, or mistress, of power, expressed in the small boys as a power to kill—and bring to life—in the girls as riding on a large obedient living creature. Comparative exploration of the cultural experiences of movement—especially in cultures in which movement is crucial, as it is in Bali as plastic rhythmic adaptation, as it is in America as control and autonomy—should give us much greater understanding of what is happening to our children.

An understanding of the human growth process and of the way in which one's own culture patterns that process is also an essential background for understanding a particular child, for giving to it the kind of protection and stimulation it needs. A hastily outflung arm, throwing the whole body out of kilter, may be the beginning of a new phase of development, may be the sign of severe emotional disturbance, may be an inappropriate practice of some new form of nursery-school jujitsu. It is necessary to know. Just as all of us correct all the time for gross age, accepting comments from a young child for which an older child would be rebuked and an adult sued, judging a broken cup as the result of imperfect co-ordination, bad temper, or a senile tremor, it should be possible, especially when dealing over time with individual children, to learn to make much more minute judgments, to catch the moment of readiness, to hold our hands during periods of nonreceptivity or transition, to recognize when a piece of unharmonious behavior is a symptom of disorder and when it isn't.

But if as parents and grandparents, pediatricians, teachers, and clinicians, we are to develop such awareness, then we need not only a detailed experience with the growth process in children but also a tremendously heightened sensitivity to individual variants of the process. Such sensitivity can be learned particularly well by observation of children from other cultures. By attentive scrutiny of unfamiliar systems of posture and gesture, those differences among individual members of our own culture which we have reduced to common categories and ignored again become discriminatable.

So the plates that follow may serve different uses for different readers. For me, and for all students of culture, they have served as one way of exploring a cultural patterning of the growth experience, and they have given me new understanding of how the regularities in Balinese culture are perpetuated generation after generation. For the students of child development they should highlight the participation of the adult and the older child in the younger child's development, and make it possible to discriminate the major abstractions, such as "greater emphasis on upper half of the body," from the culturally embodied behavior of "sitting at school desk with one arm sprawled out." To those who wish to understand better the children whom they are rearing or teaching or treating, they should give a new awareness of what the relationship between one finger and another may and can mean.

In the next chapter, I will give what seems to me the necessary background for an intelligent study of these pictures, enough about the cultural setting, the social context, the individual situation of these eight children so that the reader may, in imagination, follow the camera into the mountain village of Bajoeng Gedé, experience, just for the moment, the relaxation of the people who after hours of industrious activity "walk about forgetting."

## CHAPTER III

# *Childhood in the Village of Bajoeng Gedé*

### THE VILLAGE IN A WIDER WORLD

THE CHILDREN about whom this study is centered were all born within two years of each other in the humblest quarter of one of the most old-fashioned villages on the island of Bali. At this period in history, Bali was part of the Netherlands Indies, under Netherlands rule, and this small mountain village was part of the subdistrict of Kintamani, in the district of Ganjar, South Bali. The governmental structure within which these babies were born, therefore, had its headquarters in the Netherlands, where Netherlands administrators in turn were reacting to the world policies of the Great Powers, then the United States, Great Britain, France, Nazi Germany, the Soviet Union, and Japan. China was torn by civil conflict, India and Pakistan were not yet free, and revolutionary ideas had not yet penetrated the minds of the Balinese, who just ten years later were to be playing an active role in the establishment of Indonesian independence.

If one looks backward in time from the period of these babies' birth, one can place the village of Bajoeng Gedé in Indonesian history by the earthworks around the village, which date back many centuries, and see the present inhabitants as descendants of the original Indonesian population, whose life had been modified through the last thousand years by waves of influence from Hindu and Buddhist cults, by the flight from Java to Bali of the Javanese aristocracy before the Mohammedans in the fifteenth century, and finally by the conquest of Bali by the Dutch. That ended in the *Poepoeptan* in 1906, when Balinese aristocracy, dressed in beautiful ceremonial garments, walked out unarmed to be mowed down by the advancing Dutch soldiers, and when the hands of the soldiers faltered as the unarmed soldiers fell beneath their fire, the Balinese turned their creeses of tempered steel against their own breasts. During the fifty years of Dutch rule, Bali had become a port of call for tourist ships, and even though tourists did not penetrate to the village of Bajoeng Gedé, motor carloads of them, staring, wondering, buying, rolled over the mountain road that ran through Kintamani, the market town for the people of Bajoeng Gedé, from North Bali to South Bali, stopping for lunch to see the view from the high mountains.

Children born in Bajoeng Gedé were subject to all of these influences: to political decisions made in Holland, to the price of rubber or rice in the world market, to the public-health act which decreed that every Balinese baby was to be vaccinated at the age of three months—so roughly and thoroughly that it left a scar on the arm as big as a fifty-cent piece. Although no Dutch official ever entered the village except in the role of an archaeologist interested in temple forms, the tax collectors came, and the village citizens took turns sitting in the office of the Poenggawa in Kintamani in case some message from the higher levels of government should need to be brought to the village.

The cloth in which the children were wrapped, the cloth of the slings in which they were carried, their mother's and father's sarongs, gay when new with Javanese designs copied in the mass-production industries of Europe and Japan, were cheap cotton imitations of the old handwoven local fabrics. The little tight jackets of the women were sewed in the local market by Balinese or Chinese tailors on modern sewing machines, and sometimes oddly modern children's hats or dresses, jackets, or a pair of ready-made cerise-colored pants would be brought home from market for a child. The knives with which the women cut up palm leaves to make the complex designs of traditional offerings were no longer made by the caste of smiths; they were imported from overseas, although the traditional little tinkling bells were fastened to their handles. It took about 1750 of the worn old Chinese coins, which children were given to buy a tiny drink of *cake* from the local venders, to make a ringgit, the Dutch 2½ guilder piece in which larger transactions were now carried on and the treasure of the village was kept.

The life of each Bajoeng Gedé baby was thus affected by events half a world away, directly in the vaccination mark on its arm, and indirectly as its parents and other adults reacted to some change that reached them only as a ripple from the world outside. In the village, Bajoeng Gedé babies lived a public life, attended marriages and funerals, slept or waked through nightlong theatricals, rode on their mothers' hips in processesions to temples miles away in the fields, sat on their fathers' lap during club meetings or orchestra practices, slept or waked safely relaxed as their child nurses played rough running games. Passers-by stuck flowers in their hands, bits of carelessly spat blood-red betel spittle spattered their hands, acrid incense tickled their noses, the rough edges of fresh-cut palm leaves scraped the backs of their necks. Holding babies is one of the things that every woman and girl and many men and boys like to do, so on a crowded occasion a popular baby may change arms forty times in an afternoon. People tickle them and tease them, ask where their mothers are, making them cry, threaten to send them away among strangers, to put another baby on their head (*Balinese Character,* Plate 12).

Furthermore, the infant itself has a ceremonial existence from the time of birth, when the midwife addresses it with honorific terms as a being still so close to the gods, through the series of ceremonies—42nd day for a first baby, 12th day for the later-born, 105th-day and 210th-day ceremonies—and sometimes at subsequent 210th-day anniversaries, when it is dressed, given holy water, censed, and made to receive the essence of the offerings, its hands are folded into appropriate gestures, and correct phrases toward the gods, toward adults, toward strangers, are recited in its name. So at the same time that a child watches others go through ceremonial,[1] it is itself put through comparable ceremonial, making the prayer gestures over again, exploratorily, with remembering fingers, reaching for the holy water that had recently been cool on its forehead.

The whole tempo and rhythm, smell and taste, of life is open to Balinese children, and it would be artificial to draw a line and say that one part of Bajoeng Gedé life is significant in the upbringing of children, another not. But with the imposed limits of this particular volume, I shall give in detail only those aspects of life that directly affect motor behavior: the physical setting, methods of handling and teaching, amounts of latitude and restriction. This is comparable to what is known in a child-development clinic as the routine questioning when the mother checks off such items as "number of naps," "has playpen," "uses slide," and so on.[2]

The life of the children of Bajoeng Gedé was also subject to the weight of the whole religious tradition of India and Southeast Asia, marked not only by what had been accepted (holy water, flower offerings, the names of Hindu gods), but also by that which had been rejected, by the local ceremonies in which a people who still buried their dead in the cemetery, and refused to cremate, nevertheless made an effigy of the dead, paralleling the post-cremation ceremonies of the Hinduized plains; and by the stubbornness with which the villagers clung to such prohibitions as that against Brahman priests' entering the village. The little wooden watchhouses at the entrances to the village were no longer officially guarded, but families took turns supplying a guard, often a small girl with a baby on her hip, to watch over the storehouse in the center of the village, where the rice paid as tribute to the village temple was stored. Each *Galuengan* (210-day period) for almost every day for a month, clubs of players, presided over by the *barong,* a Balinese version of the Chinese dragon, enter the village and give theatrical productions that stem from classical Javanese drama, from the epics of the Ramayana and the Mahabharata, and also include skits and jokes on the most recent events in the two cities of Bali, where there are now modern hotels, ice plants, and moving-picture houses.

In the glen between Bajoeng Gedé and the little entrance village of Peloedoe, where lived the citizens who had been expelled from Bajoeng and the newcomers who were trying to get in, there were illegal cockfights to which strangers came. There was one woman in the village who had spent several ambiguous months in Den Pasar, returning with fine lace jackets, and so discontented with peasant life that she scarcely raised a finger to hold back her three-month-old baby from death. An occasional high-caste man who had lost his wife and fortune might wander into the village; a disgruntled native of the village might wander away to become a pig buyer. People moved up from villages lower in the valley, and for a generation worried when their children showed the characteristic goitrous development of the mountains, but after that ceased to care.

The village itself lies half a mile off the Kintamani road and can be reached only by a steep footpath cradled in the hills across which the morning light falls slantingly. It is dominated by the temple, an enclosed space with a series of terraces, small shrines, and large meeting pavilions. All of these eight babies lived to the west and south of the temple, where the people of less standing lived, in the section where the village authorities had been willing to rent a large banana garden for the temporary residence of anthropologists who had been introduced by the Netherlands authorities in Buitenzorg, through the Governor of Bali, the Controlleur of Ganjar, the Raja of Bangli, the Poenggawa of Kintamani, to the village heads of Bajoeng Gedé. The village could be entered by any one of the three unwatched gates, and those who were impure because of recent contact with birth or marriage or death entered and left by the two lower-status gates.

The village ground plan, and that of each small courtyard which contained one or two dwelling houses, a storehouse, a pigpen, and a family temple, are polarized between the high gods, the gods of life, whose place is the center point of the island, and the low gods of earth and death, whose place is toward the sea. Temple and burying ground, family shrines and pigpen, repeat the pattern, and when people sleep, they sleep with head toward the center of the island, and the children are told to brush flies off "the seaward side of your nose." The head takes precedence over the feet, village officials who have been purified over those who have not been, visitors with caste over the casteless inhabitants of the village (when the intricate turns of speech that are appropriate to relationship between members of different castes are successfully remembered).

Yet though the parents of these eight children were among the poorest and humblest people in Bajoeng Gedé, a poor mountain village on a tiny island with a total population of less than a million people, the children were growing up in a world that not only registered the inspiration and the art styles and the inventions of several thousand years, symbolized by the intricate Sanskrit characters in which names were traced by the few literate persons on books whose pages were cut pieces of lontar palm, but also in a world in which any one of them might someday play a world role. For thousands of years Bajoeng Gedé had been a backwater, maintaining a core of solid, stolid, hypothyroid citizenry, a firm unwritten but intricate code of village organization, calendrical ritual, rules and sanctions for the acceptance of newcomers and the temporary or permanent exclusion of offenders. Ripples of influence, Chinese coins, music bred from contact with the West, cattle-branding for registry for a wider market, cotton cloth, dances based on European gymnastic models, drifted in to them, brought them by fugitives, by slight memories of something seen on the road or in the market, by members of their own community who ventured out to the large cities. But very likely never in all of the hundreds, perhaps thousands, of years of its history had anyone born in Bajoeng Gedé ever traveled outside the little island of Bali. The citizens of Bajoeng Gedé had passively received, or stubbornly rejected, the currents of world religious and political and economic movements, reducing ceremonies to simple terms, muddling and forgetting many of the elements, keeping their pattern by breaking the invasive elements into bits that could be fitted in or rejected piecemeal.

Today the new movements that are sweeping Southwest Asia, the new aspirations of the young Indonesian Republic, mean that one of these children born in Bajoeng Gedé in the mid-thirties may perhaps lead a delegation to the United Nations fifteen years from now. In the past the children whom an anthropologist studied in such a village would live on, perhaps immortalized by the camera in a static and unreal fixity like the figures on a Grecian urn, symbol and statement of a way of life that was perhaps vanishing altogether, and that had little place in a world scheme. Today I can look at the pictures of young Karba, who might have died like all his elder brothers and sisters if I had not been there to nurse him through the fevers of teething, and wonder, as one may when one looks at the picture of a child born in New York or San Francisco, Buenos Aires, Peiping, or New Delhi, Istambul, Odessa, or Timbuktu, "What will you be when you grow up? How may you not affect the future of the world?"

## SOME CHILD-REARING PRACTICES

The Balinese child's chief physical environment is the arms or the hip of another human being who is lightly conscious of its presence. This is a statement of a very different order from saying that the most important person in an American baby's life is its mother. The most important *person* in an American baby's life is of course its mother, or mother surrogate, but an American baby's physical environment consists of objects: crib, kiddy coop, baby carriage, high chair, swing, walker. Its mother moves it about among these various objects. But the Balinese baby, from birth until well after it can walk alone, lives most of its waking hours in the arms of another person. Here the plates will give a false impression, because we made every effort to photograph children whenever they were *out of arms,* as this was the only time when any whole body activity could be observed. I took balls and marbles and dolls into their family courtyards to stimulate them to play, and to entice the parents to put them down. A great proportion of the pictures reproduced in this book are from scenes where I had somehow set the stage with "Put him down so I can see whether he *can* creep," or "Can he pick up these marbles, do you think?" The only way in which we can present material on feet as well as hands, on balance and bodily flexibility, is to select from these induced scenes. But in interpreting them, in placing the life of Balinese children within its natural setting it is necessary to keep continually in mind that the usual life of a Balinese child is in arms.

For this tiny baby, life in the arms of another means that it is carried, very loosely wrapped in a cloth—a piece of which is sometimes laid over its face when it is carried outdoors—and suspended in a sling around the shoulder of mother or father, or of young adolescent—for the small five-year-old child nurses are not trusted with very young babies. The infant sleeps and wakes without moving out of the mother's arms.

When it is about two months old, it is set astride the hip, still in the sling, and now securely fastened to the carrier's body. The mother is free to pound rice or carry on her head without further attention to the infant, which learns to adapt with plastic passivity to her every movement. If it falls asleep, it may be laid down on the bed platform inside the house, but it will be immediately picked up if it wakens. Its bath is practically the only occasion when a child under five or six months is out of arms when it is awake. Habitually carried on the left hip, its right hand is pinioned under the carrier's arm, or extended around the carrier's back, but as it reaches out with the left hand for something offered it, the carrier pulls the left hand back—for it is forbidden to receive things in the left hand—and pulls the right hand out. Thus the child's reaching behavior occurs in a supervised, culturally patterned situation. As in the course of the first year of its life it is carried by all sorts of people, male and female, young and old, skilled and unskilled, the child has as wide an experience of the human world, of different skin surfaces, different odors, different tempos, as it has a rather narrow experience of objects. The only objects that it habitually touches are its own ornaments, a necklace of beads with a little silver box attached, on which it teethes, which is customary for all but the poorest children, and its own silver bracelets and anklets. With the bracelets the child can pound as its carrier stands near a platform, or against a pillar. People give children flowers to play with, and occasionally a weary little child nurse lays a baby down and fastens a flower above it, which she waves before its eyes, transforming the position on the bed into a watched position in her arms.

So the child learns life within human arms. It learns to eat, with the exception of the experience of being fed in its bath, to laugh, to play, to listen, to watch, to dance, to feel frightened or relaxed, in human arms. It urinates in the arms of its carrier, and feels the urination disregarded; it defecates, and feels the low concern with which a dog is summoned to tidy up the scene, the baby, the sling, and the body of mother or nurse. It teethes, and bites on its own necklace. It spends many hours on its mother's hip as she pounds rice, so that it is not surprising that Colin McPhee has found that the basic tempo of Balinese music is the same as the basic tempo of the women's rice pounding.[1] Only in an occasional temper tantrum, on the part of infant or the child nurse, is the body of the child actively at odds with the carrier, although it may experience the impatience and fatigue of a child nurse who has not fully accepted her role. The father playing a musical instrument, the child nurse playing a running game, the mother pounding rice, are all experienced by the child in motor kinesethetic terms given their special quality by the fact that the child is passive and relaxed, and the carrier habitually inattentive.

As I go on to describe the physical care of the child under more conventional headings, to describe the house in which it lives, the clothes it wears, the way it is bathed and fed, it will be both important and difficult for the reader to keep in mind this central fact—that the normal place during waking hours for any child under fifteen to eighteen months is human arms.

A Bajoeng Gedé child has two homes, the more formal home set in a walled courtyard in the village proper, where houses stand in neat rows along straight streets, and a cottage outside the village, where the domestic animals are kept and some gardening is done. In addition, its parents will plant and harvest their shares of annually divided village land, and the child will be taken along on these occasions. There are temples in different parts of the village and scattered about in the fields, and there are ceremonies in these, and at various sacred places, to which a child is carried after it is seven months old. Relatives often live close together, and neighbors form close ties; most courtyards have side openings into the next courtyard, and groups of women and child nurses flow back and forth, babies in arms, between adjacent households. The child gets its sense of the strangeness or the familiarity of the environment from the carrier's arms rather than from the look or the sound of the scene. So the children of people who were frightened when they entered our courtyard cried, but brought by someone else who was not apprehensive, the same child was placid and accepting. And as adults, people who are terrified to go any distance alone will enter the presence of a Raja or the court of a strange temple with quiet assurance if they are accompanied by a group from their own village. The human environment is definitive. When a child in the arms of a child nurse cries, people say, "Go and find its mother" rather than, "Take it home."

Houses themselves vary little in Bajoeng Gedé. Every family has at least one enclosed house, almost entirely occupied by a platform that serves as a sitting and work place by day and a bed by night. Most households have also an unwalled pavilion, sometimes well constructed of wood, sometimes poorly constructed of bamboo, in which many of the daylight hours are spent. Within the house, which is lit only by the light from a low doorway and the flicker of the fire, children are sometimes set down on the mat-covered platform, where they learn to sit placidly. At night the whole family sleep side by side on the platform, the youngest baby, wrapped in a cloth, on the mother's arm. But children are not put down to sleep; they are put down after they have fallen asleep. The place to go to sleep is the mother's arms. Older children lean against other people and fall asleep, and in a tight-packed audience that is watching some theatrical show adults sometimes sleep standing, relaxed, swaying a little. When people go on religious pilgrimages, they have to sleep in layers on narrow platforms in a way that can sometimes be painful if the pressure is too great. But the expected environment for sleep, with adults as with children, is the close proximity of other bodies. During ceremonies, at a wake, or during a birth, a dozen people may be crowded together on a space the size of a large double bed, sitting, sleeping, dozing.

The child sees the world always, except as a very tiny infant, from a vertical position, carried high on the hip or up in the arms of the carrier, looking out at life. When there are interesting events going on in the courtyard of a neighbor, fathers will set their children high on their shoulders to watch them over the wall. In crowds children are held high, and slightly older children are allowed to sit along the front edge of any audience, from which their guardians rescue them if the action gets rough or frightening. The phrases "Watch a dance" and "Listen to the orchestra" are used continually to divert crying children, not as a promise but as an invocation of remembered pleasure.

The child's first experience of clothing is of something that binds him and the mother together; her sling, which is also her shawl against the cold, is also his wrapper and his diaper, and when he is bathed she takes the sling she has been carrying him in and wraps it into a pillow that she places under his head. Cloth thus becomes not something that separates the child from contact with others, but something within which, under which, he is in contact with others. When he is frightened, his mother draws the cloth over his face; when he sleeps, she may also do this. Small child nurses inept at fastening the sling are always readjusting it so that it again becomes part of a relationship with another human being.

With the exception of the cloth in which the child is wrapped and carried, other clothes come under the heading of ornament. For ceremonies, its own anniversaries, and after it is seven months old temple feasts, the baby is dressed up, someone's bright sash being turned into a sarong for it, a father's large headcloth being set on a boy baby's head. Odd pieces of foreign clothes, little cloth hats, knitted caps, little shirts, are brought from the market and put on and off as whim dictates. When children begin to run about, they are naked most of the time between one year and three or four years; girls gradually learn to keep a sarong on, and boys that is is more important to cover the lower part of the body than the upper. Instead of being routinely dressed and undressed every day, in clothes that are its own and which are put on it and taken off it, as an American baby is, the Bajoeng Gedé child is attached to its mother or its carrier by a cloth that is neither distinctly its own nor hers, and occasionally is dressed up, treated like a doll rather than a human being.[4] Thus neither costume nor sleeping habits differentiate night from day for the Balinese, who develop no internalized time pattern, but wake and sleep at any hour, practice in an orchestra or watch a play all night, sleeping and waking as their immediate impulse and the interest of the situation dictate.

Bathing is important to Balinese. They measure the heat of the day by the number of baths one feels moved to take, and bathing pools are important and often highly elaborate spots. In Bajoeng Gedé the spring is a very long way from the village, and only babies and little children are bathed with the precious water that has been carried so far on the heads of women and girls. A little baby is bathed twice a day in lukewarm water in a container made of areca-palm bark, sometimes just the sheath supported on four sticks, sometimes shaped into a container (Plate XX). A few pieces of onion are floated in the bath water for magical medical purposes, and at the end of the bath a bit of onion is often placed on the baby's fontanel. Very young infants are also powdered with grated turmeric. During the bath, the mother or the father splashes and plays with the baby, and flicks and manipulates the genitals of a male baby, so that the bath becomes a situation of heightened bodily experience. During infancy the child is also fed in the bath (Plates XIX, 1; XX, 2).

At about six months, or earlier if the child sits easily alone, a round earthenware container is substituted for the bark bathtub, and the child sits, and as it learns to stand, stands in this tub, while the parent splashes water over it. A bath can be a pleasant occasion in which there is much teasing and interchange, or a hasty scrambling affair if everyone is getting ready for some ceremony, when the children are likely to wail and resist. Bathing, like feeding solid food, originally associated together, is definitely something that is done *to* the child, during which a manipulative handling, as if the child were a puppet capable of obstructive but not human movement, is substituted for the relationship between child and carrier characteristic for suckling and for eating snacks in arms also. From the time the child is old enough to walk to the spring, it bathes itself, and bathing becomes from then on a solitary pleasure, performed in company but in a withdrawn fashion.

Feeding babies falls definitely into two categories: (1) suckling, in which the infant, after it is a few weeks old, is held high above the mother's breast and nurses down (Plate XVIII), and (2) giving solid food to the infant, which is done in the bath (Plate XIX, 1). The mother prechews a mixture of rice and banana and builds a mound on the baby's face. When it opens its mouth to protest, she pushes some food in. When older children are given food, they display related behavior, pushing the food into their mouths with the flat of their hands, or turning their coconut shell plates straight over their faces (Plate XIX, 4). Feeding is something done *to* a baby, and later something that one does to oneself, while bathing, first done *to* one, later becomes something that one does oneself.

Learning formal gestures is part of the very early experience of a Balinese child. At its various anniversary ceremonies its hands are cupped to receive and hold water, its palms pressed together in prayer, its arms shaped to receive the essence of the offerings. Whenever anything is offered it, its mother pulls out its right hand from under her arm, and if a gift is given, she will cup one hand in the other, repeating on behalf of the child a formal thanks—literally, "I ask." Words are put into the child's mouth from its first days, elaborate phrases coupled with "I am just a little baby," "I have as yet no name," so that in verbal and postural terms the child is fitted passively into the etiquette long before it would be able to enact it without these initial cues. But at the 210th-day birthday, babies sit and repeat over and over the gestures through which they have just been put, the hands of the parents occasionally playfully reinforcing them.

Dancing is taught by alternately pressing the child's hands into position and making the gesture oneself, inducing the child to imitate it as the adult hums a dance tune. Hand dancing is learned in arms, before the child can walk, and a child may be set down to go through a beginning dance routine before it can keep its balance. Walking, like dancing, is taught by holding the child from behind, or with the aid of a walker, a single bamboo rail set up in the middle of the yard.

One of the most striking aspects of Balinese child rearing is the specific objection to creeping. The crawling stage, of infant struggling along with abdomen to floor, is given no opportunity to occur, and knee-creeping and creeping on all fours are frowned upon as animal-like. Children learn to creep or go on all fours or hitch themselves along by very small excursions on platforms, usually only moving a very short distance. They are very occasionally set down in the yard before they can walk, but much creeping is usually a stimulus to someone to pick them up and hold them, high and human, above the level of the pigs and the scavenger dogs that frequent the ground.

Elimination is treated very lightly. No fuss at all is made over urination by an infant; children urinate playfully into their baths, little boys learn to make elaborate patterns in the dust. Adults simply turn aside from a group to urinate. Eating, standing up, urination, and defecation are strictly forbidden within temple groups, and children slowly learn to regard defecation as mildly shameful. Little babies experience only the shout for the dog that is to clean them up, or the attention of the dog when they are placed on the ground. As they learn to walk steadily, they toddle a little away from a group and squat, and the distance gets greater as they get older. So one solemn little four-year-old once remarked to me, of a three-year-old over in the corner of our yard, "I Anoe is defecating." "And don't you defecate?" I answered. "Yes, but not in your yard!" was the proud and superior answer. Within the family courtyard, the pigpen, placed at the extreme seaward diagonal from the house temple, is the latrine. During the night and early morning adults use the streets as latrines, which the dogs clean up by daybreak. A child's chief learning from the culturally imposed elimination habits is to watch where it is and to move away from inappropriate spots. It never has to go far, so that the emphasis on foresight and self-control, which American children learn and generalize to other areas of life, is missing.

Contact with animals is another way in which children learn about their own movements in many cultures. Significantly, the Balinese have very little feeling for animals, with the exception of those which men take individual pride in, fighting cocks, oxen in Bajoeng Gedé, water buffalo on the plains. Dogs are regarded as unpleasant necessities, to scavenge and to guard against thieves, and children are given puppies to play with without any training in gentleness or empathy. They push and pull them around or even bounce them like balls. The focus on the animal as a feeling creature is quite absent, although occasionally small children of three or four may treat a puppy, a chick, or an insect on a string as an extension of themselves, as their mothers and sisters treat babies and their fathers and brothers treat their fighting cocks.

Toys tend to be almost entirely extensions of parts of the body, and only occasionally a wooden carving of a human being may be given to a child as a doll, or little girls may make dolls out of fruit or vegetables. Pinwheels, sticks, flower wands, are the forerunners for children in arms and toddlers of the kites and the musical instruments of older boys. A toy is thus something that extends the body, either the arm or occasionally the penis, as when a small boy marches about with his father's machete at a steep angle. Or a toy may extend both hands and voice, as the whirring pinwheel does. This emphasis is interesting in view of the amount of hyperextension found in their postures also. Occasionally some object, such as a fruit or a foreign ball, will be used in playing out swallowing, or defecation, and even more occasionally, a puppy or another baby will be treated as the self (*Balinese Character,* Plates 38-44).

Infants and young children experience a patterned treatment that recognizes their change in age in rhythm with the time when a new baby is expected, but not dependant upon the time when a younger sibling actually arrives. A child's social experience as the welcome inhabitant of the arms of others steadily expands from about the fourth month, and reaches its height between the seventh and the ninth. It is teased and tickled, then the teasing mother or nurse looks away and breaks the teasing sequence, leaving the child to turn its attention back to its own body; but the teasing is light. At about fifteen to eighteen months the child is treated as if it had a younger sibling, though if there is no younger sibling it will not be weaned. The teasing bid for a response, which is cut by the teaser turning away when the child responds and permitting no climax, becomes harsher; mothers borrow babies and provoke their own children to jealousy, but demand the most loving treatment of an own younger sibling. As the teasing bids and threats become harsher, the child withdraws more and more from them, and children of three are characteristically withdrawn, unresponsive, and sullen. They grow out of this stage as the little boys accompany the older boys to the fields to care for the cattle and the little girls are drawn into the child-nurse group. This habitual change in the child's position in relation to other people appears to be a setting within which the difference between the more outward-rotated and the more inward-rotated children is expressed at different ages.

Bajoeng Gedé children are part of the adult world from birth, completely named individuals who can enter the temples from seven months on, although not entitled to adult burial if they die before they have their second teeth. Wherever they are too young, or too inexperienced, to play any necessary role, it is played out for them, on ceremonial occasions or on meeting a stranger. No one worries if a child is slow to learn to walk or to talk, although a boy or girl of seven or eight who remains overly dependent will be a cause of concern. But the small children live in a world in which the fully adult gesture—of playing the xylophone, or praying to the gods—is available to them, effortlessly, so that little girls pass imperceptibly from having their fingers flexed backward so as to make them more graceful in the dance to sitting inattentively flexing their own.

The limits of life beyond which one must not venture are defined. Children are recalled by their mothers or nurses mimicking fright, and child nurses keep their charges from touching things by exclaiming, "Feces!" or "Scorpion!" Toddlers who venture away from sheltering arms to get mixed up under the feet of the actors in a play are smiled at, but pulled implacably and gently back. But they come back to the familiar human environment, the known arms of parents and siblings, where fright and comfort, interest and sleep, have already been experienced. Bodies are always there, other peoples' bodies to lean against, to huddle together with, to sleep beside. One's own body remains plastic and flexible, each part felt as separate, but the whole moving together in such a way that any casual group of Balinese seem to compose themselves like a ballet.

## THE EIGHT CHILDREN AND THEIR FAMILIES

Two plates have been devoted to each of the eight Bajoeng Gedé children, and the captions contain accounts of their parents and siblings. But it is necessary to place them here within the village and within Bali. All the inhabitants of Bajoeng Gedé were peasants, living by agriculture—the cultivation of dry rice, sweet potatoes, and maize—and raising domestic animals. All were members of that section of the population to which most of the Balinese belong, the casteless people, the "outsiders." All were illiterate. Three of the fathers were immigrants into the village, and two of them, the fathers of I Raoeh and I Ngendon, were very poor. The father of I Sepek was a more prosperous immigrant. Two of the children, I Karba and I Kenjoen, were the grandchilden of people who had been of considerable consequence in the village, but whose eldest son, in despair over being childless, had gambled away much of their propery in recent years. The grandfather of I Marti and I Marta, and the actual father of I Tongos, was a member of the *Saih anam blas,* the group of sixteen at the top of the religious hierarchy of the village. I Karba's father, Nang Oera, held a government appointment as *klihan,* official intermediary between the village and the next highest level of government.[5] I Kenjoen's father, Nang Karma, was one of the most interesting and tempermentally deviant men in the village, father of six living children, only son of a mother who kept some specially important gods in her house temple, and who was also the village innkeeper. He himself was an expert tuner of musical instruments, in return for which he was exempted from heavy work for the village. He was the originator and the priest of the *sangiang* club (a club for giving child-trance dances) and had also started a *djanger* club (a modern form of dance that had been influenced by European gymnastics). His wife had the type of hair that is called *bok gempel* (elflocks), and this disqualified him from membership in the main temple.

Of the other five children in the household of I Kenjoen, I Karma, the eldest, a boy of about fourteen, lived with his father's mother and does not appear in the plates; I Karmi, a young girl in early adolescence, was the eldest at home; I Ridjek, a girl younger than I Karmi, lived with her mother's parents and only appears occasionally (Plate LV). The family at home consisted of Nang Karma, Men Karma, I Karmi, I Gati, I Kenjoen's child nurse, and I Gata, her brother, the dispossessed knee baby. The sibling constellations of the other seven children are given in the captions to the plates.

These eight children have close relationships among themselves. I Karba and I Kenjoen are the children of sisters, and the children of four of their mothers' other sisters appear in some of the pictures, I Karsa, I Meres, I Doemoen, I Baroek, and I Riboet. I Karsa, a slightly older child, and I Karba are double cousins, sons of two sisters who had married two brothers. I Marti and I Marta, I Karsa and I Karba, form another grouping of first cousins through their three fathers, who are brothers. The mothers of I Ngendon and I Sepek are sisters. I Raoeh alone is unrelated to any of the others by any tie that was currently recognized. He and I Sami appear frequently with the other children as close neighbors.

Two of the children seemed to me to be physically defective. I Raoeh, who developed a swelling on his face that never disappeared and which his brother also showed, and I Ngendon, whose extreme flaccidity and dullness seemed more attributable to some physical state than to any family situation. Children of immigrants sometimes showed a more aggravated hypothyroidism than did the descendants of those who had lived for many generations in Bajoeng Gedé, where simple goiter was endemic.

None of these families belonged to the most prosperous element in Bajoeng Gedé, although this was due to the number of children in the case of I Kenjoen's family, to immigration in others, to recent downward turns of fortune in the case of I Karba's maternal grandparents and paternal widowed grandmother. Bajoeng Gedé itself is one of the most archaic villages in Bali; its ceremonial, its music, and its dancing have none of the polish and style of the plains. Yet the people of Bajoeng Gedé are sturdy, self-sufficient people, and might be regarded in some ways as comparable to the inhabitants of a very remote English village of wholly Anglo-Saxon stock that had never been directly affected by the Norman Conquest. There was one difference, however; as population pressure was increasing in Bali, due to the elimination of smallpox, which had kept the population down, people were moving up into the mountains in search of land. So Bajoeng Gedé, although it was a very old, very old-fashioned, and backward village, was also receiving new blood, immigrants, some of whom were drifters like the father of I Raoeh, others of whom were well-established men like the father of I Sepek, who had come to seek economic betterment.

Observation in other parts of Bali, on children of high castes as well as low castes, in North Bali as well as South Bali, does not suggest that these Bajoeng Gedé children differ essentially from the children of other areas. Although their parents were peasants, clumsy in speech, deficient in artistry, the essential Balinese grace that was elaborated to such a high degree in the courts and on the plains is clearly present in the postures and gestures of these children and in the characteristic way in which they are carried and taught.

# Part II

# *Introduction to the Plates and Captions*

BY MARGARET MEAD

THESE 58 PLATES present 380 pictures, mainly of the eight Balinese children of the village of Bajoeng Gedé around which this study has been built. They are designed not to prove, but to illustrate, those aspects of the motor development of children which emerged during the year Frances Macgregor spent intensively examining the 4000 photographs that had been enlarged as the basis of this study. The pictures all represent close-ups of the children—there are no general landscapes or contextual pictures; for these and for thematic description of Balinese culture and a succinct note on Balinese ethnography the reader must turn to the earlier publication, *Balinese Character*.

This book is a detailed study of a few children. The pictures from which these photographs were finally chosen formed the basis of communication among the members of the research group. Frances Macgregor would identify some special flexibility in a child's hand and study it beside other photographs of the same child taken the same day, taken on other days, taken when the child was sick or convalescent. She brought to the task a long experience of studying, photographing, and analyzing bodily movement—but these Balinese children were strangers, and she had never been to Bali. Her understanding of the way they moved, of the individuality of each child, and of the distinctive Balinese character of each movement grew out of minute, empathic scrutiny of the hundreds of pictures of the children. What she found, she presented, first to me and then, in complex classified selections, to the Gesell group, not in words but in mosaics of photographs, which by juxtaposition and sequence conveyed the first, nonverbal stages of a formulation.

To these patterned arrangements, partly in Gesell categories and partly in her own, the Gesell group could respond quickly, comparatively, the first response often being a postural one, as Dr. Gesell lightly threw his shoulders into an amazing imitation of a Balinese child's dancing posture, Louise Ames experimented with what difference it would make to extend the knees in the Balinese frogging position, and Frances Ilg tested the complexities of touching the middle of the back with an outwardly rotated arm. From the hundreds of pictures spread out on table after table, Frances Macgregor would select still other pictures that would clarify the developing idea or raise a new question. From my knowledge of the individual children and of Baliness culture, other questions would arise, which she discussed again by arrangements of pictures, one picture, twenty pictures, which showed just what did happen to the second finger in a certain type of grasping or just how persistent certain types of low tonus were. Only her hours of working with the pictures, comparing, cross-comparing, and absorbing the motor images they conveyed, made it possible to do this study, to work from the singleness of 4000 individual pictures to the integrated presentation of the 58 plates.

## THE GENERAL PLAN OF THE PLATES

| | |
|---|---|
| Plates I-XVI | Two plates are devoted to presenting each of the eight children, so that their individualities will become familiar to the reader. For pronunciation and explanation of personal names, see note on page 2. These children are, in order, I Karba, I Kenjoen, I Marti, I Marta, I Tongos, I Raoeh, I Ngendon, I Sepek. |
| Plates XVII-XX | Traditional ways of sleeping, suckling, feeding, and bathing. |
| Plates XXI-XXVIII | Peculiarities of the maturational path taken by Balinese children, the distinctive sequence through which children progress from frogging to walking. |
| Plates XXIX-XXXVIII | Whole-body postures that are distinctively Balinese. |
| Plates XXXIX-XLI | Handling children. |
| Plates XLII-LIII | Hand and foot postures that are distinctively Balinese. |
| Plates LIV-LVIII | Aspects of behavior that reveal definite relationships to the patterns of motor development. |

## ARRANGEMENT OF THE PLATES

The plates were arranged by Frances Macgregor and rearranged in response to theoretical considerations raised by the rest of us, but she is responsible for the original choice and the final juxtapositions, even sometimes placing a photograph from later in a sequence earlier on the plate because it makes the presentation more telling. The final selection from among the photographs was based: first, on the accuracy and representativeness of the picture, and second, on the photographic quality for reproduction purposes; but the former consideration was never sacrificed to the latter. Enlargements were made in those cases where small details showed adequately in the prints but would be lost in reproduction and enlargement was also technically possible, but enlargement was limited to increasing visibility and not carried to the point where other individuals in the picture would be cut out. Experience has demonstrated that a picture of one individual is the more meaningful the more it can include the relevant human surroundings, and a part of the body more meaningful if the whole body is included. This is especially true for the Balinese, who live their lives among people as either actors or audience, and often as both. The photographs were retouched in four instances where the reproduction process was expected to lessen the sharpness of an image that was either referred to or was too important to leave obscure. The following pictures were retouched:

| | |
|---|---|
| Plate XLVII, Figure 5 | The outside thumb line of I Tongos' right hand |
| Plate XLIV, Figure 6 | The forefinger of I Karba's right hand |
| Plate XLIX, Figure 7 | The forefinger of I Marti's right hand |
| Plate LII, Figure 7 | I Sepek's left heel |

For further technical data concerning the actual taking of the photographs by Gregory Bateson, information about cameras, lenses, films, and processes, the reader is referred to his own description in *Balinese Character.*[1]

## THE DESCRIPTIVE CAPTIONS

The captions represent a long period of integration of notes made by Frances Macgregor as she worked with the pictures, flashes of insight or comparative comments made by the Gesell group during conferences, and discussions of the most exact phrasing appropriate to a particular hand or foot, stance or distortion. The vocabulary used is that of the Gesell group, plus a few words added to meet the needs of the Balinese material: *flexibility* to cover the special Balinese versions of *symmetry* and *asymmetry; premonitory grasping* to describe the way in which American children adjust their fingers in advance of a grasping act in contrast to Balinese children, who characteristically do not do this; and the descriptive phrases *cupping hands or feet* and *fanning hands.* The basic Gesell use of terms like *flexion, extension, inward* and *outward rotation, eversion* and *inversion, ulnar* and *radial, volar* and *mesial,* has been followed throughout.[2] These terms are used not only descriptively, but with explicit reference to the Gesell analysis. The need for new words comes at the point where the behavior of the Bajoeng Gedé children is so strikingly different from that of the New Haven children that the Gesell analysis had to be expanded to contain it. Occasionally references to other aspects of Balinese culture have been included in the captions, but on the whole, we have kept the captions close to the actual subject matter of the plate, a contrast to the complex, analytical juxtapositions used by Gregory Bateson in the captions of *Balinese Character.*

Each figure is accompanied by a caption that identifies the others included in the photograph in relation to the central child figure. So an individual is classified as "father's brother" or "neighbor." The other children whose ages are not known exactly can, however, also be followed sequentially through the use of the index.

The circumstances under which each picture was taken have been inspected in the notes in the photographic sequences from which these stills were taken,[3] and from Cine films, when films exist of the same scene,[6] so that the full context of the particular photograph presented has been taken into account, although only when this context is immediately relevant has it been included in the caption. For example, in Plate XL, Figure 8, it is relevant to know that I Sami, now limp in I Sambeh's limp, inattentive hands, has just dozed for a minute after a period of very active play, or that on Plate XXXIX, Figure 7, I Kenjoen is being set down by her mother, against her will, during a scene in which I had presented stimulating toys to evoke more activity. But in the case of Plate XIX, Figure 3, it is sufficient to know that this picture was taken while the mother who had been carrying the child about was standing in our yard. It is also important to realize that all the recorded photographs of these particular children were printed, a final selection was made from them, and only after this was the background material looked up. In the 380 finally selected by Frances Macgregor, there are a few cases where the full identifying data are missing for pictures taken in 1939, when I was ill, when the Balinese text recorded by our secretary merely records which child was photographed and does not list the other children, some of whom had altered greatly during the year we had been away. Samples of the types of contextual running notes that were kept in Bali, by me and by I Made Kaler, can be found in Appendix 1, page 189.

The ages of the central children are given, and the age of any other child in a photograph is included if its age is exactly known. In the case of children born during the Balinese field work, or just before, I have sometimes specifically added "age unknown." Very often I know the age to within a few days, but in an analysis such as this, where chronological age is a significant variable, an age is either known or not known. The ages have been given to the nearest week up to thirty weeks, and after that to the nearest half month, rather than in days, as in *Balinese Character,* because this seems a more useful method for comparison with Gesell publications.

In the captions, remarks are included that invoke Gesell categories, for which the pictures were originally selected or upon which members of the Gesell group commented particularly. These are *contemporary* comments (made in 1948 or 1951), although in many cases the notes indicated that this particular behavior was also commented upon in the field in different phraseology. The *place* where the picture was taken is identified, without, however, repeating the name of the village each time, as, unlike *Balinese Character,* this book draws entirely on the material from Bajoeng Gedé, with the exception of one picture, Plate XLI, Figure 6, of a dancing lesson in Tabanan. The exact location within the village of Bajoeng Bedé is given as *own yard*—that is, the family courtyard of the central child—*our yard,* specified further as *our veranda* if too little of the scene shows to make this clear (but not specified as to which of our verandas, although this information exists), or other location, such as *Men Sama's yard* if the central child is not her child, or *the ramp in front of our house.* The date is given in all cases, but the exact hour of the day is not included, although I habitually record it in terms of intervals of five to ten minutes, nor are there references to small units of time unless these are significant, as, for example, the length of time I Karba left his hand against the wall (Plate LV), which is based on I Made Kaler's text record, in my absence. Finally, the Leica number is given, the first figure referring to the alphabet, the letter to the sequence within the alphabet, the third number to the frame;

e.g., 1 A 1 is the first frame in the first film in the first alphabet taken in Bali.[5]

Minimal data in this type of research must include complete identification of the individual within the social context, which means knowing the relationship, blood, affinal, or situational, of each person to the central figure within a particular context.

The reader will find that some scenes recur over and over again. There is I Sepek's delayed 210th-birthday ceremony (*otonin*), where we waited for three hours for the ceremony to begin while the whole family had nothing to do except let the children play about actively, so that we could photograph them.[6] There is the afternoon when their two mothers enjoyed the game of making a flower wand for I Tongos and I Raoeh to play with. There are numerous occasions when marbles or balls, doll or Australian toy bear, cup and spoon had been used by me as a stimulus to get the smaller children out of their parents' arms and moving about. These occasions repeat themselves because they were deliberately evoked to show motor behavior, which is hard to see among children who live the first two years of their lives almost entirely in arms or seated. They are essentially laboratory situations, although free ones—interspersed with traditional situations of children in temper tantrums, children expressing shyness or embarrassment, children being bathed or washed.

For fullest enjoyment of the plates, the reader will want to learn to recognize the eight children, not to come to know them with the precise knowledge of the way they flexed their hands or the exact degree of tonus they showed when they relaxed, as Frances Macgregor knows them, and not, of course, with the memory of their laughter and the touch of their fingers, as I know them, but well enough so that each snapshot will be informed by a sense of the child's individuality that has been built up by looking at many pictures. In this way, each reader can make for himself a portrait of the motor behavior of each of these eight children from another way of life, can experience something of the feeling of having painted a portrait, not merely appreciated one painted by another.

Frances Macgregor has provided the visual arrangement for such creative participation by each reader. The Index gives the children's names, the references to plates being arranged chronologically, making it possible to follow a child from plate to plate and to find other pictures taken the same day. As in a museum, there is a sequence, but the sequence is not enjoined as it is in a film or a sound recording. Instead, each reader may turn the pages as he wishes, seeking for the same child, or discovering a thousand details in posture and gesture that are unnoted in the captions—making his or her own thematic arrangement of the complexities of Balinese child behavior.

## *The Eight Children*

# PLATE I – I KARBA

I Karba, the only surviving son of Nang Oera and Men Oera, was the gayest baby in the village of Bajoeng Gedé during the entire period in which we lived there. His home was nearest to our camp, his young uncle worked in the house, and his father, Nang Oera, did our marketing in the Kintamani market. All of of this meant that he was in and out of our house a great deal, and I often carried him about while I was watching a ceremony. There are more pictures of Karba than of any other child, but this is not entirely a result of circumstances, but partly because of his liveliness, intelligence, and responsiveness, which made him the most actively interested participant in scenes where other children were supposed to be the center of observation.

Karba was a strong, symmetrically organized child, with a physical development more like New Haven children, but he combined with this the characteristic Balinese flexibility of hands and feet, and fluidity in taking any position. As an only child he had no child nurse sibling and was cared for by his mother's sister, Men Singin (fig. 5), whose own son, I Karsa, was too heavy to be carried except in emergencies. Men Singin was the wife of Karba's father's brother, so Karsa and Karba are double cousins, and in many of the scenes where the two children occur together, Karsa's behavior, which is reaching the sulky, withdrawn stage, foreshadows the type of behavior that Karba will show later. Neighboring little girls, particularly I Djeban, whose only sibling was about five, used to care for Karba a great deal. Very possibly being cared for voluntarily by his aunt, a lusty, high-spirited, energetic young woman, rather than by a child nurse who was burdened by the task, may have contributed to Karba's high spirits.

1. I Karba, 8 months, in the hands of his father (Nang Oera) on a mat in our yard.
9/30/36. 2 U 26.

2. I Karba, 12 months, in the arms of his father (Nang Oera), pointing at the toy koala (Australian teddy bear). Our yard.
2/5/37. 4 R 19.

3. I Karba, 14½ months, in a tub on platform in his yard. A bit of the dress of his mother (Men Oera) shows in the background.
4/29/37. 7 M 12.

4. I Karba, 14½ months, and I Sami, 7 months. Own yard.
4/29/37. 7 N 38.

5. I Karba, 15 months, wearing paper hat, in road in front of our house, with Men Singin (mother's sister) and I Karsa (his double cousin).
5/7/37. 8 H 8.

6. I Karba, 15½ months, and *togog* (native carving made as a semitoy). The *togog* was made by Nang Dakta, a deaf-mute. In front of the main temple during a theatrical performance.
5/18/37. 9 C 15.

1

2

3

4

5

6

# PLATE II – I KARBA (continued)

This plate carries I Karba from a period of active happy exploration, carrying off the mallet, exploring the drum of a visiting orchestra (figs. 1 and 2), exploring the legs of the photographic tripod (fig. 4), through the period when his parents' teasing, his mother's borrowing a baby to make him jealous (fig. 6), begin the period of withdrawal, which is shown in the photograph taken a year later (fig. 7), when Karba no longer responds to teasing efforts to provoke him, but sits, sulkily, among the other children. But even in this period of withdrawal through which Balinese children characteristically go, his gaze is level and appraising; he is withdrawn into himself, but still presents a picture of a well-integrated child. In this picture (fig. 7) he is still unweaned, and if his mother does not become pregnant, may wean himself gradually, as he becomes old enough to follow his father out to the fields and spend long hours away from his mother.

1 and 2. I Karba, 16 months, with his father (Nang Oera) and a musician, left, from an orchestra accompanying a *djoget* (girl dancer with whom villagers dance). The road in front of our house. Karba plays with the drum (fig. 2).
6/9/37. 11 M 20, 11 N 2.

3. I Karba, 17½ months, with his mother's sister (Men Singin) and I Karsa, left (Karba's double cousin, son of Men Singin). Taken in our yard under the banana tree.
7/15/37. 12 Q 29.

4. I Karba, 20 months, playing with legs of our tripod and a cup. Nang Sama's yard.
10/9/37. 16 X 21.

5. I Karba, 20 months, standing alone. Our yard.
10/11/37. 17 H 15.

6. I Karba, 24½ months, being suckled by his mother (Men Oera), who is teasingly dandling I Marta, 14 weeks, daughter of Karba's father's brother. Marta's father (Nang Marti) in background.
3/1/38. 21 R 15.

7. I Karba, 36 months, with I Ridjek, I Riboet, age unknown, and I Gati (his back to camera), in Nang Karma's yard. Ridjek is Gati's next oldest sister who lives with her maternal grandparents and cares for Riboet, Karba's half sister and half double cousin.
2/12/39. 36 E 31.

1

2

3

4

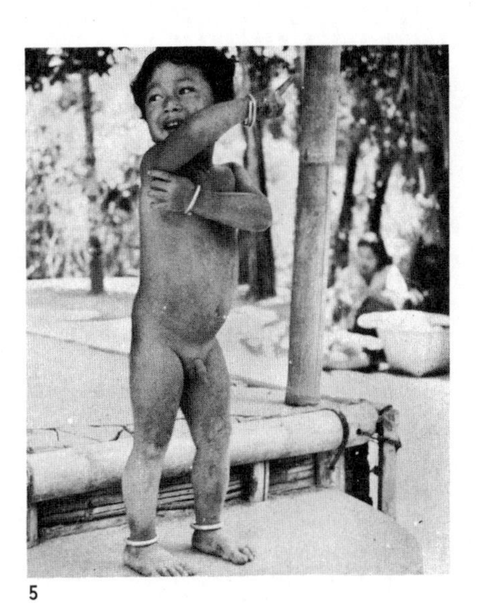

5

6

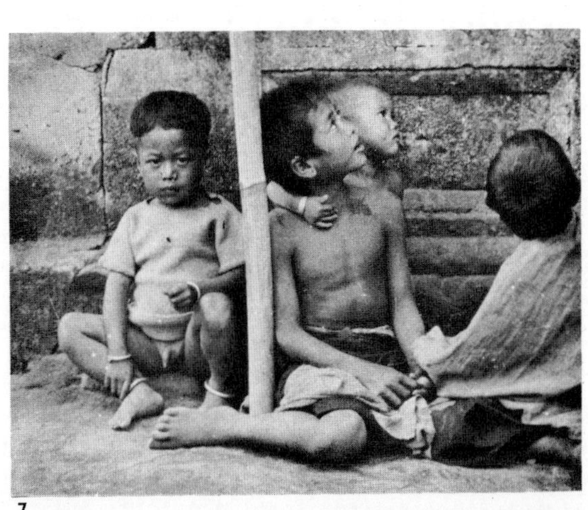

7

# PLATE III – I KENJOEN

I Kenjoen was the youngest daughter of a family of six, and her mother, Men Karma, was the oldest sister of Men Oera, I Karba's mother. Kenjoen was just six weeks younger than Karba, but her family situation was very different. She was cared for most of the time by her sister, I Gati (fig. 3, in gateway), who was initially inept and continuingly impatient. Her brother, I Gata, the knee baby, was still an active contender for his parent's attention and slipped back into his mother's arms and attempted to nurse whenever Kenjoen was temporarily out of the way. As a little baby she was so gay that she was named Smile at her 210th-day birthday, but it became a village joke that she hardly ever smiled. She was a stubborn, jealous, and possessive child, holding onto both of her mother's breasts (figs. 2, 4, 6), grabbing at anything which her child nurse had, unresponsive to suggestions, but reacting vigorously whenever anyone else had something. Her mother, Men Karma, was a warm, competent, busy woman, and her father, Nang Karma, whose intelligence was somewhat confused by the violence of his ambition, for which the placid life of Bajoeng Gedé offered little outlet, was devoted to his children, even giving Kenjoen his breast to comfort her.

When she was about four months old, Kenjoen became covered with scabies and had to undergo a long period of palliative treatment until her 210th-day birthday when her hair could be cut off. But however painful the treatment, she always stopped crying the minute the treatment stopped. Physically she was unusually flexible, and many of the pictures of extreme contorted positions (cf. fig. 3) are of Kenjoen.

1. I Kenjoen, 22 weeks, in the arms of Nang Karma (father). I Gati (Kenjoen's child nurse sister), standing beside him on our steps.
8/26/36. 2 I 26.

2. I Kenjoen, 7 months, in the arms of her mother (Men Karma), at her 210th-day birthday, *otonin,* before she was dressed and had her hair cut.
10/13/36. 2 Z 5.

3. I Kenjoen, 15 months, seated on ground. I Gata (her brother), with his back to us. I Gati (her sister child nurse), sitting in gateway, eating rice. Own yard.
6/20/37. 11 W 42.

4. I Kenjoen, 15 months, being suckled by her mother (Men Karma). I Gata (her brother) on ground and I Karsa (her maternal cousin), standing beside pediment. Own yard.
6/20/37. 11 T 41.

5 and 6. I Kenjoen, 17 months, standing at Men Karma's knee, while Men Karma holds her older brother, I Gata, the knee baby. Later (fig. 6) Kenjoen climbs up and begins to nurse, covering the other breast with her hand. Own yard.
8/19/37. 14 I 9, 29.

1

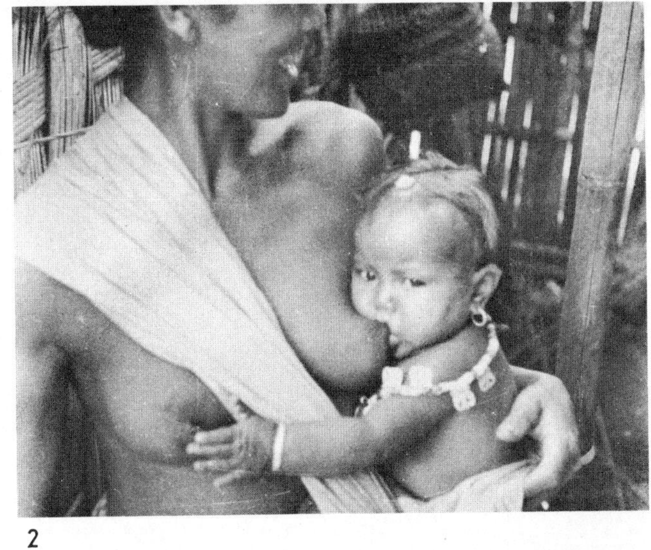

2

3

4

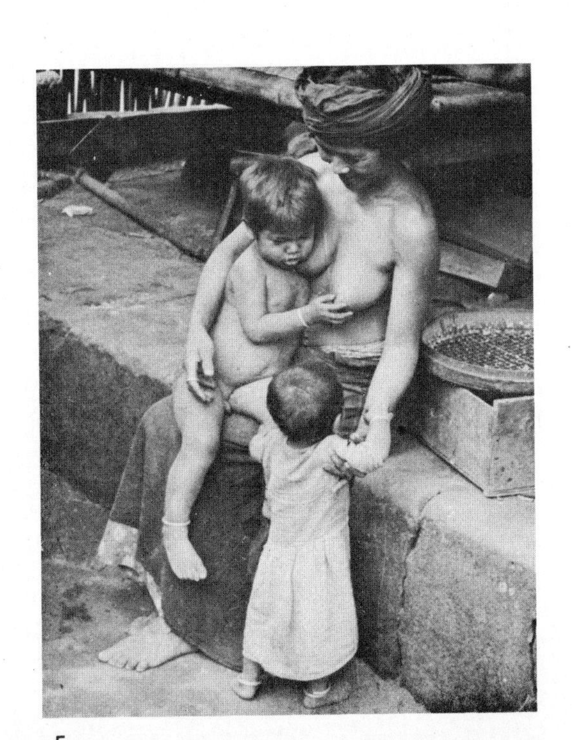

5

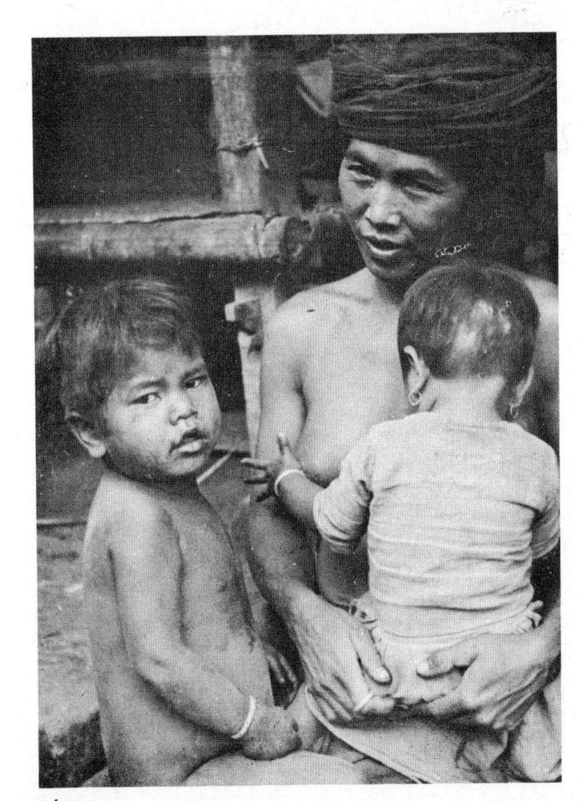

6

# PLATE IV – I KENJOEN (continued)

Although I Kenjoen almost ceased smiling at seven months, very occasionally, especially when her father was concerned, a particularly coy, winning smile would break out (fig. 2). When we offered toys, Kenjoen would initially refuse them, but then if I Gati (her child nurse) showed an interest, as in the doll (fig. 3), Kenjoen would go after it again. Gati was still at the temper-tantrum stage herself, pathetically left out of the attention of both parents, often to be found leaning against her father's back, or sitting, disassociated and withdrawn (fig. 5). A less vigorous child than Kenjoen might have come to parallel her sulkiness, but Kenjoen responded with aggressive competitive vigor.

During her third year she became exceedingly heavy, too heavy for Gati to carry about, and her oldest sister, I Karmi, who had earlier taken over Gata, when Kenjoen was born, now became Kenjoen's nurse (figs. 6 and 7), just as Kenjoen reached the period when Balinese children begin to withdraw. Kenjoen was the fourth younger sibling whom Karmi had carried about. Karmi was a patient good-humored girl, well knit into the group of young girls who served in the temple, and treated Kenjoen's sulks and tempers with a lighter indifference than had Gati. From the picture which Kenjoen presented in 1939 (figs. 6 and 7), it would have been very difficult to have reconstructed the smiling little baby that she had been, or the gay young girl which she will—if she follows characteristic lines of development—someday become.

1 through 3. I Kenjoen, 18½ months, on Men Karma's lap (fig. 1). In fig. 2, Kenjoen leans against the leg of her father (Nang Karma). I Gelis, a neighbor boy, sits on the pediment. Kenjoen, her hand on mother's arm (fig. 3), reaches for doll held by her sister nurse, I Gati (doll presented as standard experimental stimulus). Own yard.
10/10/37. 17 B 20, 17 D 26, 5.

4 and 5. I Kenjoen, 20 months, climbing up beside mother. The back of her brother (I Gata) can be seen, and I Gati (her sister child nurse) is kneeling in between. Kenjoen (fig. 5) sucking at the breast of her mother (Men Karma). Gati thoughtful. Own yard.
11/23/37. 19 B 39, 19 C 39.

6. I Kenjoen 34½ months, in arms of her older sister (I Karmi). She is now too heavy for I Gati, her former child nurse. Own yard.
2/9/39. 35 P 17.

7. I Kenjoen, 34½ months, seated on lap of her sister (I Karmi).
2/12/39. 36 D 22. Own yard.

1

2

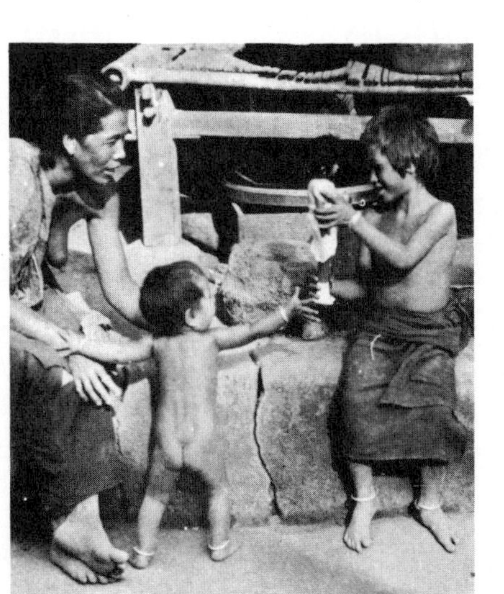

3

4

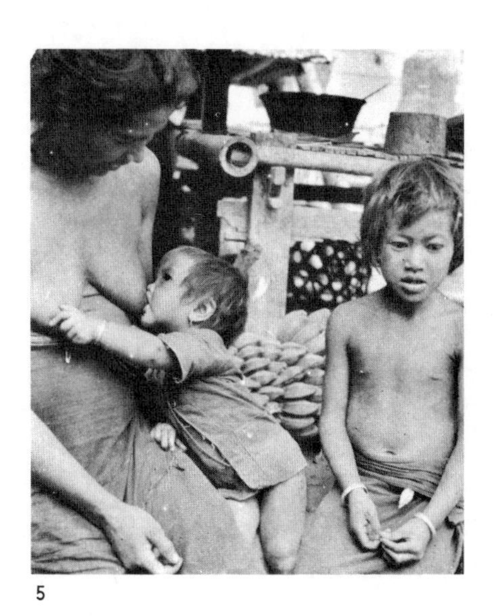

5

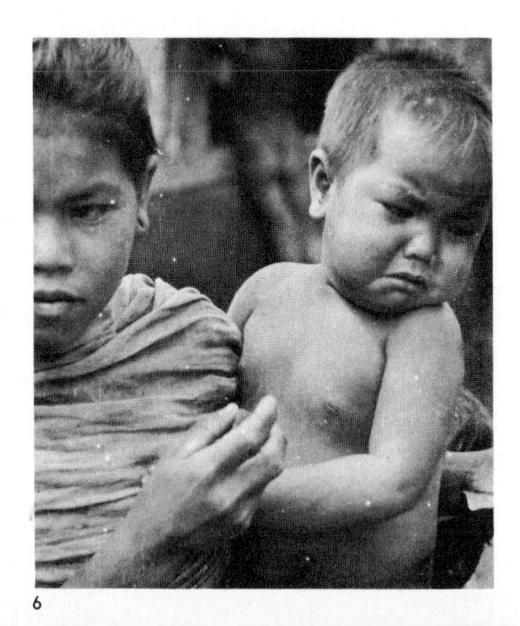

6

7

# PLATE V — I MARTI

I Marti was the eldest daughter of I Karba's father's younger brother, who became known, after Marti was finally named, as Nang Marti. Her mother was an embittered, unsmiling girl, who had had a violent physical struggle with Men Singin (her husband's brother's wife) in memory of which Marti was originally named I Paed (a word indicating pulling and hauling), which was changed after a few months to I Marti. Her mother took very little care of her, and she was almost always in her father's arms, even as a very small baby. As a little baby she was quiet, plastic, and impassive (fig. 1), and although she developed into an episodically lively child (fig. 4), she was always ready to retreat, passive, unsmiling, distrustful, into her father's arms (fig. 2). Her response to new stimuli, in this case a toy bear that I had introduced, was to turn away, giving a low fretful whine.

She had a long series of ear infections, and her father almost always was the one who brought her for treatment. She was stoical, quiet, resigned, as long as he was there. He was a very patient, stolid man—poor, with a few activities, quite content to carry her about with him or sit for hours, holding her.

1. I Marti, 15 weeks, in the arms of her father (Nang Marti), taken after she was dressed for her *neloeboelanin* ceremony (105-day birthday). Own yard.

7/28/36. 2 C 32.

2. I Marti, 11 months, in the arms of her father (Nang Marti), with toy koala. Her father offers bear to Marti, who lies back and doesn't take it. Our yard.

3/21/37. 6 C 31.

3. I Marti, 13 months, in lap of her father (Nang Marti). He is playfully offering her his pipe, just before I medicate her infected ear. Our yard.

5/13/37. 8 U 22.

4. I Marti, 13½ months, and father (Nang Marti) on road in front of our house. Her cousin (I Karsa) in a temper tantrum. Karsa lies on road howling because our assistant (I Made Kaler) had refused him a pencil. Marti makes tentative moves toward him, trying to step on his hands.

5/25/37. 9 H 9.

5. I Marti, 16 months, and I Kenjoen, 17 months. Our yard.

8/20/37. 14 M 26.

6. I Marti, 16 months, lying on her back fussing. In line, Nang Marti, I Nampah, I Kenjoen, 17 months, I Karmi, I Ngembon, I Gati, Men Oera, I Karni. I Karba, 18½ months, standing watching Marti. Our yard.

8/20/37. 14 M 1.

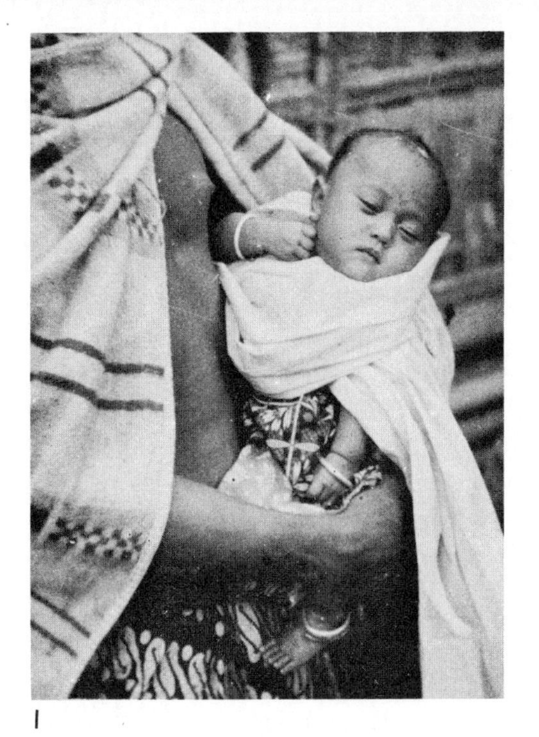

1

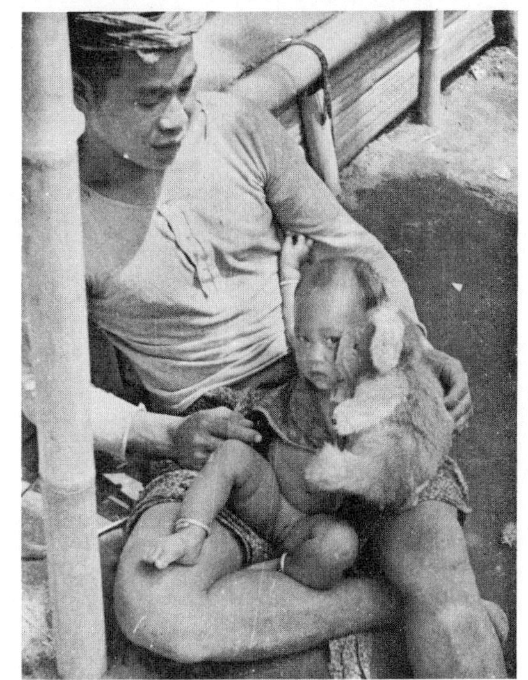

2

3

4

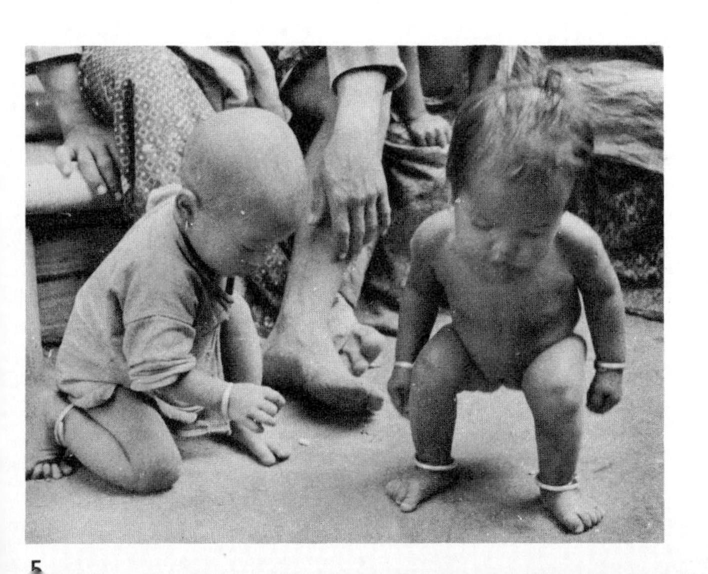

5

6

## PLATE VI – I MARTI (continued)

I Marti was weaned young, at the conception of I Marta, but this made very little change in her life, as her mother took active interest in the new baby, and Marti continued to accompany her father everywhere. After Marta's birth she became somewhat gayer and more responsive (figs. 1, 2, and 4), but her basic sadness and passivity is conspicuous again when she reaches the withdrawn stage in 1939 (figs. 5 and 6). My notes are filled with people's commands to her, to pick something up, to stand, to come, to go, with the accompanying remark that she did not pick it up, refused to stand, or just stood still.

1 and 2. I Marti, 19 months, and I Karsa (her father's brother's son), playing with three puppies in our yard. Karsa has just tied one puppy. Marti (fig. 2) puts her finger into the mouth of her father (Nang Marti). I Malih, a visitor, watches.

11/21/37. 18 Y 35, 18.

3 and 4. I Marti, 22½ months, and her father (Nang Marti) in their yard. I Karsa (her father's brother's son) in the background (fig. 3), and in the foreground (fig. 4). Marti is wearing a new dress bought in the Kintamani market.

3/3/38. 22 C 27, 22 D 29.

5. I Marti, 34 months, trailing a bath towel. Own yard.

2/9/39. 35 O 24.

6. I Marti, 3 days later, in lap of her father (Nang Marti). Nang Oera's yard.

2/12/39. 36 L 4.

1

2

3

4

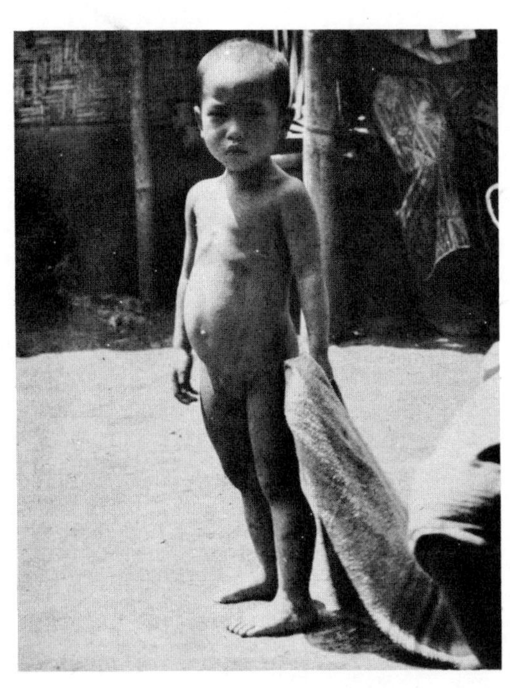

5

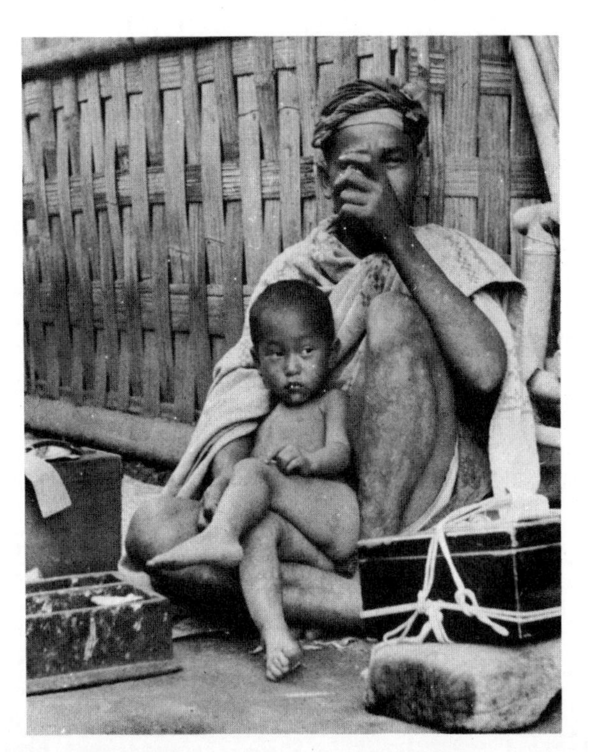

6

## PLATE VII – I MARTA

I Marta, younger sister of I Marti (Pls. V and VI), was born after the period when we were working continuously in Bajoeng Gedé and there are a limited number of photographs of her. She has been selected for intensive presentation, however, because of the contrast that she presents to her older sister, as this is the only sibling pair where we have birth dates for both children. Where Marti is usually found with her father, Marta is habitually with her mother, whose grim expression softens in response to this second, better-loved child (figs. 1 and 4), and Marta's expression is characteristically an intent frown (fig. 5), paralleling the frown on her mother's face (figs. 5 and 6). Where Marti's stance is narrow, Marta's is wide (fig. 3) and she reaches vigorously toward outside objects (fig. 4). At the same time she is extraordinarily graceful, showing the same kind of combined vigor, sturdiness, and grace as does I Karba (her father's brother's son).

The last two pictures on this plate (figs. 5 and 6) and all on the succeeding plate were taken the same day and present a picture of Marta in which her liveliness and variety of responses are the more conspicuous because they were all manifested within one half-hour, and in the presence of people who were strange to her.

1. I Marta, 14 weeks, in arms of her mother (Men Marti). Own yard.
3/3/38. 22 C 17.

2. Same day. Nang Marti holding I Marti, 22½ months, who holds I Marta, 14 weeks. I had asked, "Can Marti hold the baby?" The answer: "Yes, only both have to be held." Own yard.
3/3/38. 22 D 19.

3. I Marta, 14½ months, in foreground. Her father (Nang Marti) squatting. I Marti, 34 months, and I Karsa (her father's brother's son) in background. Nang Marti is taking betel chewing materials from the betel tray. Own yard.
2/9/39. 35 M 38.

4. I Marta, 14½ months, carried by her mother (Men Marti). Same day. She is well able to stand, but is still carried like a small baby. Reaching with left hand. Own yard.
2/9/39. 35 Qa 2.

5 and 6. I Marta, 14½ months, bathed by her mother (Men Marti) in their yard. Marta in her mother's arms after bath (fig. 6). Own yard.
2/11/39. 35 S 1, 12.

1

2

3

4

5

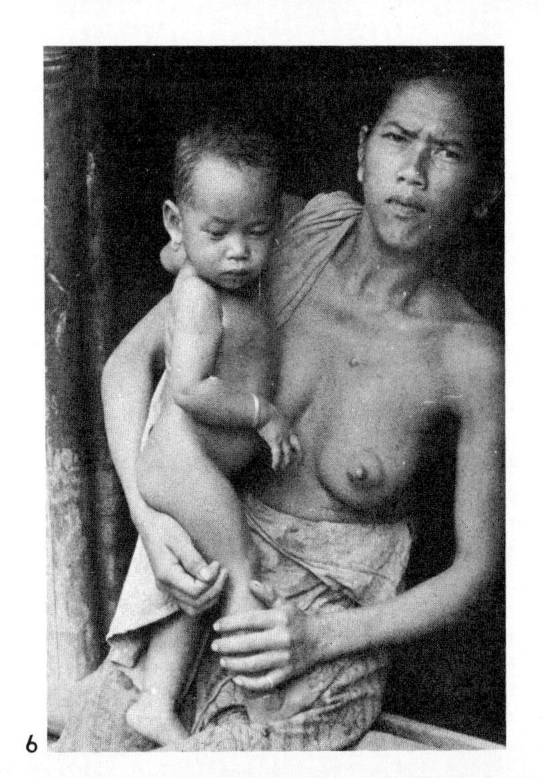

6

# PLATE VIII – I MARTA (continued)

The six pictures on this plate were all taken within the space of about ten minutes, during which Nang Marti engaged his small daughter, I Marta, in play, alternating between giving her a chicken, demanding it back, handing her marbles, which I had brought, and having her hand the marbles to him. Crowing and laughing, Marta ran back and forth, responding first to one command, then another, in marked contrast to her older sister, I Marti, who either stands (fig. 3), reluctant to take part in the game, or sits, statuesque and sad (figs. 4 and 5). In contrast, Marta is physically alert, constantly in motion, all her body parts co-ordinated in a light elasticity.

1 through 6. I Marta, 14½ months. Own yard. Marta (fig. 1) standing with her arm around the neck of her father (Nang Marti). Marta brings small ball to her father (fig. 2), who has called her. Her sister, I Marti, 34 months, stands by father, head covered. Marta running lightly balanced toward Marti (fig. 3). Marta running away from her father (fig. 4). Marti sits looking pained as Marta takes the center of the stage. In fig. 5, Marta turns back toward father as he calls her. Father gives her a small chicken to play with (fig. 6).

2/11/39. 35 T 12, 23, 40; 35 U 5, 17, 27.

1

2

3

4

5

6

## PLATE IX – I TONGOS

I Tongos was the slightest, most graceful of these eight children, and in many ways the child who seems to express best the special lightness of physique that is so conspicuous in Bali.

Tongos was actually the son of the maternal grandfather of I Marti and I Marta, but because the rules of membership in the village structure of Bajoeng Gedé did not permit multiple marriage, a marriage was arranged instead with a little old bachelor who had never married and was so old that the village children had begun to call him grandfather. He took a kind of wry pride in his oddly acquired foster child, but was seldom at home and is not included in any of the pictures. Tongos' mother, Men Tongos, was a slight, frail girl, who depended very heavily for companionship on her next-door neighbors, Nang and Men Goenoeng, so that Tongos and Nang Goenoeng's child, I Raoeh, were almost constant playfellows. Tongos was 10½ months younger than Raoeh, but so much more active that he often took the initiative. His activity was very impersonal. He reached out toward life (fig. 3), but not toward persons, hitching along on his buttocks, in response to little grunting noises that his mother made when she wanted to quicken him into movement for the camera. Most characteristically, he sat, paying attention to very small details, curious, interested, or simply reaching out, delicately, from wherever he was sitting or squatting.

Tongos' movements are harmonious, lack the distortions found in the other children, with a great deal of external rotation and extension of body parts, displaying a sort of wandering asymmetry.

1. I Tongos, 8 weeks, being bathed by his mother (Men Tongos) in their yard, in a tub made of bark used for bathing young infants. His head is placed on a cushion made by rolling up the cloth sling in which his mother has been carrying him.

1/21/37. 4 G 22.

2. I Tongos being bathed by his mother (Men Tongos) on his 210th-day birthday–7 months. He is now bathed in a round earthen tub. Own yard.

6/25/37. 12 B 28.

3 through 6. I Tongos, 8½ months, playing with I Raoeh, 19 months, in Nang Goenoeng's yard. He reaches for betel tray (fig. 3). Men Goenoeng has given long flower toy to Raoeh, her son (fig. 4). Standing with support, Tongos reaches for flower. Tongos plays with a dead hibiscus (fig. 5), a leaf in the other hand. Tongos watching the leaf in his hands (fig. 6). Raoeh's mother (Men Goenoeng) behind him, humming a tune.

8/19/37. 14 E 40, 23; 14 F 14; 14 E 28.

1

2

3

4

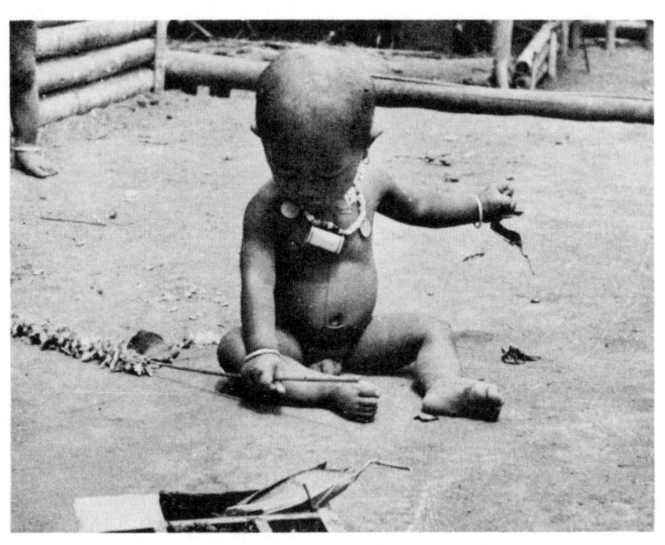

5

6

## PLATE X — I TONGOS (continued)

I Tongos typically sits watching the world (fig. 2), and his mother's relaxed passivity, as she sits beside him (fig. 1) provides a background within which this behavior is emphasized. His playmate, I Raoeh, was too passive to challenge him into activity, and as he got older (fig. 4) his concentration on looking at the world became more pronounced. As he became old enough to encounter the harsher, more provocative touch of adults, which is characteristic of the way in which Balinese children are weaned into impersonality, his reaction is a kind of drawing in, including screwing up his eyes and refusing to look. He remained very light in weight, which meant a longer period of being carried about by his mother (fig. 5).

1 through 3. I Tongos 10½ months, on ground in Nang Goenoeng's yard. He plays with spoon, a stimulus given him by me. His mother (Men Tongos) watches. Note the wide spread of thighs (fig. 2) and the extended arms. Tongos, frogging (fig. 3), with I Karba, 20 months, in background.
10/9/37. 16 Y 33, 27, 28.

4. I Tongos, 15 months, brought by his mother (Men Tongos) to our yard, playfully dressed in adult headdress, sits and fretfully holds ball.
3/1/38. 21 R 36.

5. I Tongos, 26½ months, in arms of his mother (Men Tongos) in the road.
2/12/39. 36 C 4.

6. I Tongos, 26½ months, being bathed by his mother (Men Tongos). Note the harshness of Men Tongos' hand and the tenseness of Tongos' left hand. Own yard.
2/12/39. 36 J 26.

1

2

3

4

5

6

# PLATE XI – I RAOEH

I Raoeh was the son of Nang Goenoeng, a recent immigrant into Bajoeng Gedé, whose courtyard adjoined that of Nang Tongos. The mother of Raoeh, Men Goenoeng, had been adopted into Bajoeng Gedé, had then married away, been divorced, and then married Nang Goenoeng. Nang Goenoeng was a gay ne'er-do-well, talkative, expressive, something of a clown, and Men Goenoeng was a noisy free-moving woman. Neither of them had standing or stake in the village, but they were always to be found wherever there was anything going on, theatricals, vendors, gambling.

Raoeh began life as a wide-awake alert baby, a little heavy, but gay and responsive, the sort of baby whom everybody wanted to hold and carry (fig. 1). But when he was about eight months old he developed a great swelling on the side of his face accompanied by a long fever. When he recovered, the swelling remained (fig. 2), and he had become a fretful, peevish child whom no one wanted to carry. Typically he sat looking at nothing (fig. 5), giving forth wails, occasionally tantrums, and manifestations of possessiveness (fig 6).

Physically, Raoeh is heavy, flaccid, clinging, inactive, pigeon-toed, unattached, sullen.

1. I Raoeh, 23 weeks, in the arms of his mother (Men Goenoeng), a happy, gay, popular baby. Our yard.
   6/30/36. I N 8.

2. I Raoeh, 13½ months, in the arms of his father (Nang Goenoeng) after he acquired the permanent swelling on one side of his face. Our yard.
   3/6/37. 5 H 23.

3. I Raoeh, 17 months, in Men Tongos' yard, at the *otonin* (210th-day birthday ceremony) of I Tongos. Men Goenoeng (Raoeh's mother), is teasing Raoeh by threatening to put Tongos on top of his head, a grave insult to which he is already sensitive. Men Tongos and Dong Dering in foreground.
   6/25/37. 12 B 35. (*B.C.*, Pl. 12, fig. 5.)

4 through 6. Own yard. I Raoeh, 19 months, playing with his foot peevishly as I Tongos, 8½ months, is suckled by his mother (Men Tongos). The head of I Poendoeh, Raoeh's little slavey child nurse, can be seen behind Men Tongos (fig. 4). Men Tongos had just picked up both children, which had started Raoeh's scowling. Later on the same day (fig. 5), Raoeh sits immobile while Tongos holds baby chick and Raoeh holds his penis. Note Raoeh's persistently flexed knees and inward rotation and Tongos' external rotation. Raoeh nursing (fig. 6) holding up in his hand the unusually pendant breast of his mother (Men Goenoeng), imitating the more usual Balinese position of nursing down. (*B.C.* Pl. 47, fig. 4.)
   8/19/37. 14 G 19, 14 E 3, 14 G 28.

1

2

3

4

5

6

# PLATE XII – I RAOEH (continued)

When I Raoeh became heavy and unattractive, his mother brought a little poor relation, I Poendoeh (fig. 1), from another village to live with them. Little girls make ties with one another through the babies whom they carry around, but Raoeh was an unpopular baby, and Poendoeh remained solitary for a long time, dragging Raoeh about from one place to another, or sharing in the casual activities of Men Goenoeng and Men Tongos (figs. 3 and 4). Raoeh's older brother, I Goenoeng, who had been living with relatives in another village, was brought to Bajoeng Gedé and proved to have the same facial distortion that Raoeh had, plus a flattened nose, a dependent disturbed personality, and an appearance of low intelligence. Within this setting, Raoeh remained passive, stolid, peevish, and inactive, and expectably, does not present as marked a picture of alteration of personality at three (fig. 6) as do the other children who had been gayer and more responsive. He is still carried by Poendoeh, has been weaned, and his mother has a four-months-old baby, but the slightly fretful, uninterested expression remains much the same.

1. I Raoeh, 19 months, playing with flower toy while his child nurse, I Poendoeh, sits passively in doorway. Own yard.

   8/19/37. 14 F 17.

2. I Raoeh, 20½ months, blows a bubble sulkily after a visiting woman–in background–had just teased him by putting a necklace on top of his head, which his mother (Men Goenoeng) then removed. Own yard.

   10/12/37. 17 N 2.

3. I Raoeh, 25½ months, in his yard during New Year's festivities. I Poendoeh, Raoeh's child nurse, has just had her hair done by Raoeh's mother (Men Goenoeng). Raoeh, now well, but with a permanent swelling in his face, stands unresponsive to his father's command to go and pick up some marbles. Raoeh's defective older brother, who also has the same facial distortion, is seated on the left.

   3/3/38. 22 E 17.

4. The same day. This is the end of a long sequence in which I Raoeh's brother has been teased by a toy snake by I Sambeh (Nang Ngendon's younger brother), and then Men Goenoeng (Raoeh's mother) started teasing a large chicken with marbles; I Poendoeh took the chicken; Raoeh went to his mother. He got the chicken, his mother stroked the chicken, and then he crawls under her cloth shawl and starts to nurse. Own yard.

   3/3/38. 22 F 16.

5. I Raoeh, 25½ months, spits out marbles which he was carrying in his mouth, and holding a long piece of palm leaf, given him by I Poendoeh, he executes a marching dance. Own yard.

   3/3/38. 22 G 14.

6. I Raoeh, 37 months, in the arms of his child nurse (I Poendoeh). Own yard.

   2/11/39. 35 V 7.

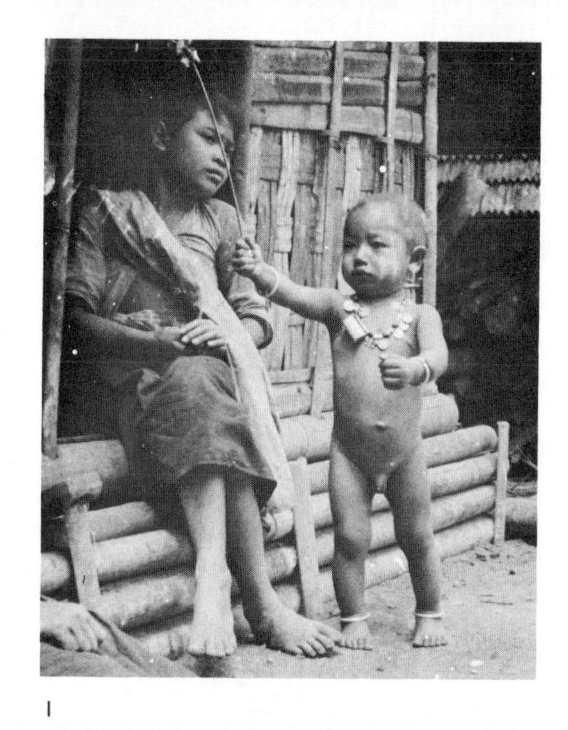

1

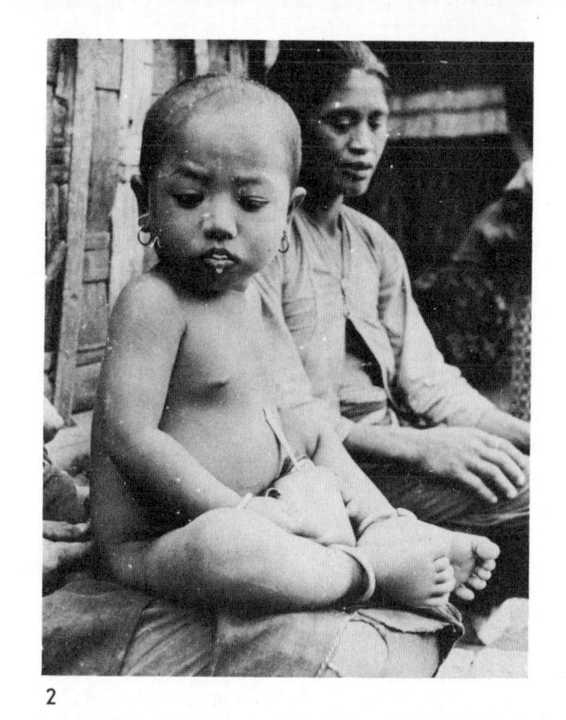

2

3

4

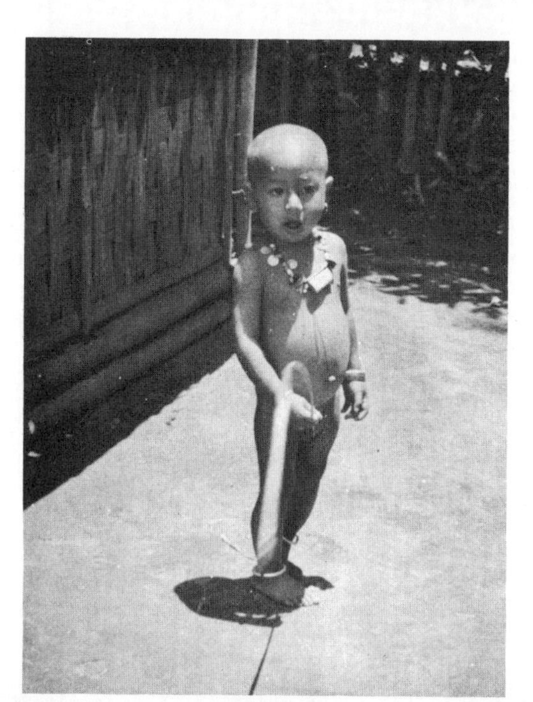

5

6

# PLATE XIII – I NGENDON

In the same block with I Raoeh and I Tongos was a household shared by two sisters both of whom had married strangers.

I Ngendon was the first child of a Bajoeng Gedé mother, I Maring, and an immigrant father, I Sama, who initially shared a house with the family of I Maring's sister, Men Degeng, mother of I Sepek (Pls. XV and XVI). Nang and Men Ngendon were friendly and co-operative. Nang Ngendon's younger brother worked in our household, and they were always ready to bring the baby to be photographed, or to delay a ceremony until we arrived. Ngendon proved, however, to be a remarkably flaccid, dull baby with staring eyes, hard to stimulate into any sort of responsiveness or activity. His flaccidity and low tonus show throughout (figs. 1 and 5), and it was seldom possible to photograph his doing anything except playing with something close to him, which he had been given, or being manipulated by his mother. She was a warm, proud mother (figs. 2 and 6), very stout by Balinese standards. Both Nang Ngendon and Men Ngendon paid a great deal of attention to him, and his low activity seems definitely referable to some physical condition.

1. I Ngendon, 6 weeks, after an illness, held by his father (Nang Ngendon). Own yard.

12/18/36. 3 V 12. (*B.C.* Pl. 21, fig. 8.)

2. I Ngendon, 10 weeks, being suckled by his mother (Men Ngendon). Child is covered with scabies, contracted on a recent visit to his father's village; has been fed prechewed food in his bath, fusses, and refuses to nurse. Mother is trying to work nipple into his mouth. Own yard.

1/19/37. 4 F 16.

3. I Ngendon, earlier in the same scene, being lifted from his bath in an unshaped betel sheath by his mother (Men Ngendon). Own yard.

1/19/37. 4 F 11.

4. I Ngendon, 23 weeks, in a neighbor's yard during the wedding ceremony of I Keneh, plays with his mother's shawl. A neighbor (I Darmi) watches.

4/21/37. 7 C 25.

5 and 6. I Ngendon, 27 weeks, on our veranda. His mother (Men Ngendon) is demonstrating at my request that he can sit with support.

5/13/37. 8 T 23, 25.

1

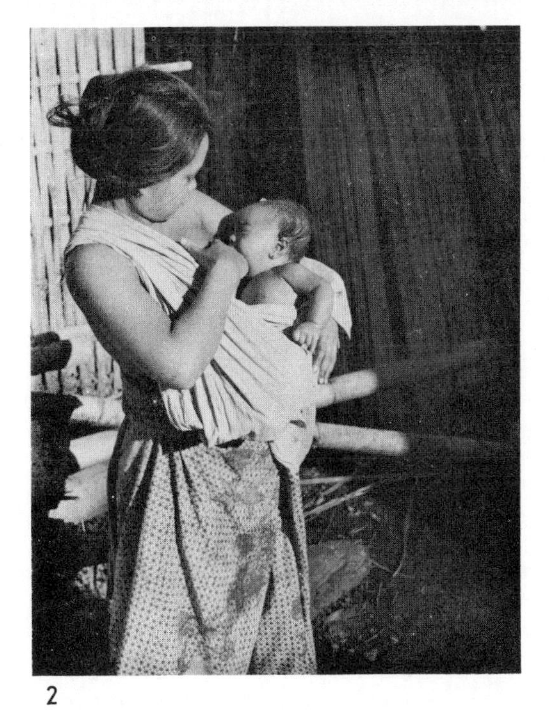

2

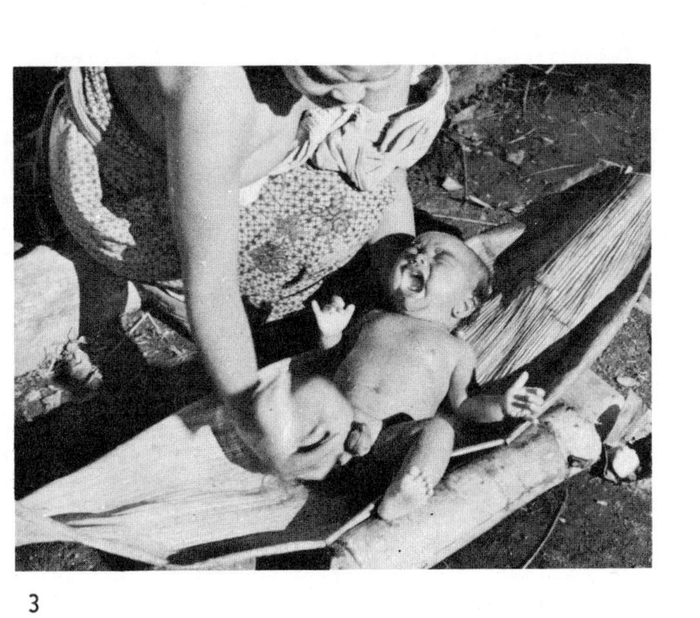

3

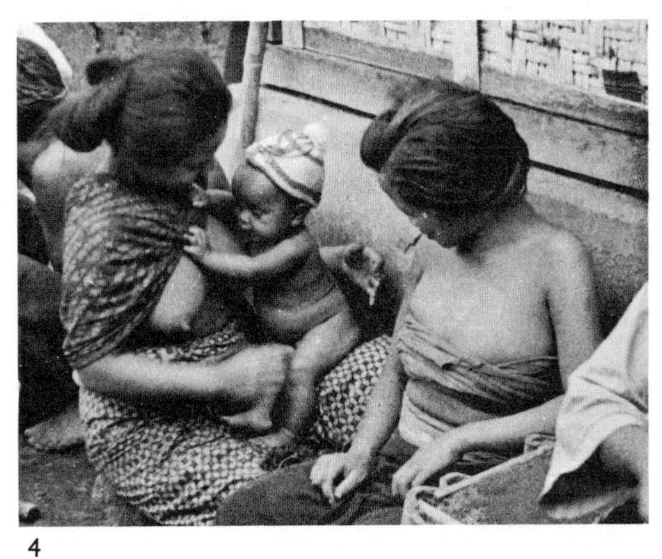

4

5

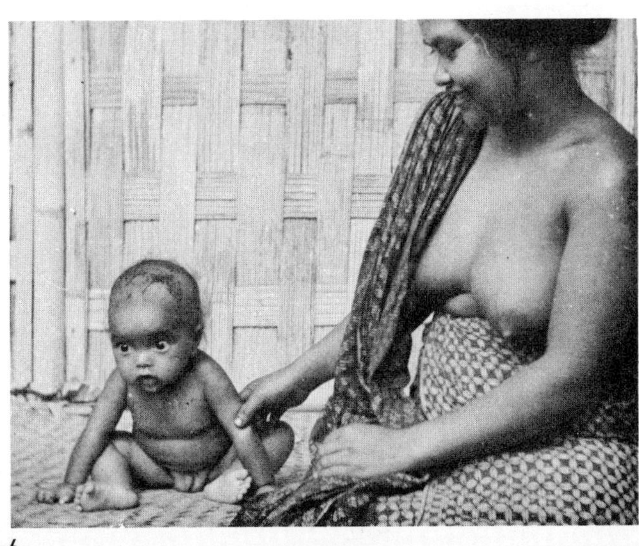

6

# PLATE XIV – I NGENDON (continued)

These six pictures are typical of our relationship with I Ngendon; all were taken in our yard, all in response to some stimulus which I had presented—a mirror, a ball, a spoon, and even the branch of flowers (fig. 6). Ngendon was willing enough to grasp, but then his interest would flag, and he would sit holding onto whatever he happened to have (fig. 4) or sometimes pounding aimlessly with his silver bracelets. He was a very light, weak child, which meant he was carried more, which in turn reinforced his tendency to confine his movements to a very narrow range. His mother and father took most of the care of him, as both were poor and unimportant, with little else to claim their attention. They were away from the village in 1939, so there are no pictures of how he developed.

1 through 3. I Ngendon, 9 months, now able to creep and stand. On our veranda, he creeps after marble, salivating heavily. Puts marble in his mouth. Later, the same day (fig. 2), his mother (Men Ngendon) nurses Ngendon as he lies sprawled across her breast. The twisted body is completely prone, except for the turned-up head, moving with a circular direction. Later, Ngendon on ground creeping (fig. 3). His mother (Men Ngendon) playing with him with mirror that I brought. He began hitting at mirror. He is now on the point of pressing his lips to the surface of the mirror.

4 through 6. I Ngendon, 11 months, playing with I Karba, 20 months, in our
8/18/37. 13 Y 20, 13 Z 2, 14 A 3.
yard (fig. 4), touches spoon to side of cup. Note the way his left leg is drawn up. Ngendon stands on lap of his mother (Men Ngendon) (fig. 5), and after first trying to put spoon in mother's mouth, bites on it. His parents have been too poor to give him a silver teething necklace. Later, his mother has gathered him up to go home. I offered him a spray of blossoms, and he pranced with them (fig. 6).

10/11/37. 17 I 26, 17 J 6, 14.

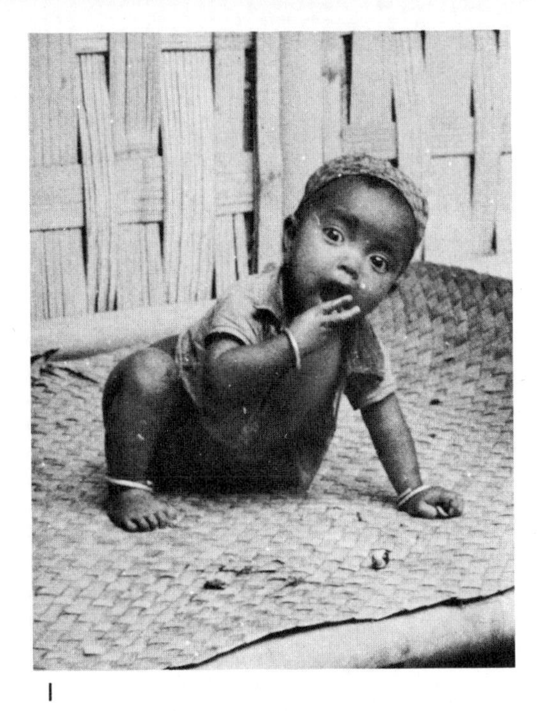

1

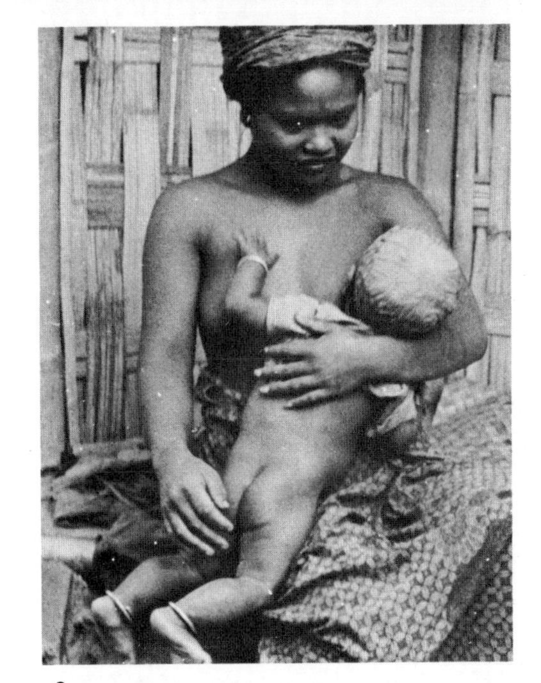

2

3

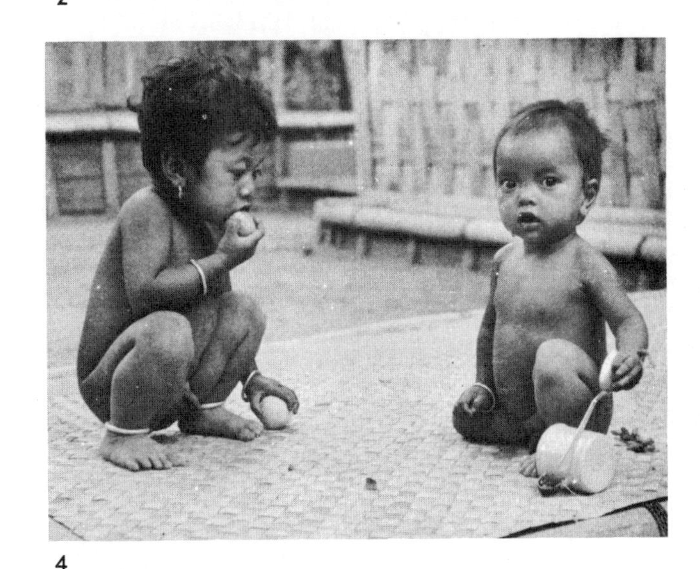

4

5

6

# PLATE XV – I SEPEK

I Sepek was the third son of Nang and Men Degeng, and the first cousin of I Ngendon, whose mother was Men Degeng's sister. Sepek was a fine sturdy healthy baby, symmetrical, active, with superb balance and control, curious, interested, actively oriented toward things about him, independent, and adventurous. His family situation was particularly favorable, a warm friendly father and an unusually permissive and giving mother, and as a child nurse, his eldest brother, I Degeng, who adored him. The particularly good relationship between Degeng and Sepek was facilitated by the fact that I Leket, the knee baby, had been adopted by Nang Degeng's childless brother, now called Nang Leket (fig. 3). Thus the midde child, the source of tension in the typical Balinese family configuration, was removed from the scene. Leket became steadily more miserable (fig. 5; cf. also *B.C.*, Pl. 75, figs. 7 and 8), and his presence at home might have dampened the general gay exuberance in which Degeng responded to his baby brother. Like Karba, but in a very different pattern of relationship, Sepek had ideal conditions to reinforce what appeared to be a natural vigor and outgoingness.

Nang Degeng was an immigrant to Bajoeng Gedé from the village of Salat. They lived most of the time on their farm outside the village, and we only saw them at wide intervals, but Sepek was selected for inclusion as another youngest child, whose age was accurately known, and as a child who in physique and responsiveness was very much like I Karba. It seemed particularly important to include a child with whom I had had little contact, as the fact that I had taken so much care of Karba might be regarded as having altered his personality in a Western direction.

1. I Sepek, 11 weeks, in the arms of his mother (Men Degeng), who carries him high up above her actual breastline, in the position in which most Balinese babies are suckled. Our yard.

9/3/36. 2 K 19.

2 through 6. I Sepek, 10½ months, at his postponed 210th-day birthday ceremony *(otonin)*. On a mat in his yard with his father (Nang Degeng), and father's brother (Nang Leket), his oldest brother (I Degeng, front right), and his brother (I Leket), who had been adopted by the childless Nang Leket. There was a long playful scene while we waited for the officiating priest to arrive. Leket lies on the mat and sings nonsense syllables, and Degeng parallels his behavior. Sepek's father offers him a chain to play with (fig. 3). (*B.C.* Pl. 74, fig. 2). Sepek is just about to stand (fig. 4) and maintains his balance for about a minute. He stands with wide stance, and Leket lies and looks up at his buttocks. Sepek stands, having dropped the large leaf with which he has been playing, then toppled as camera clicked (fig. 5). Earlier, Men Leket lifting Sepek up (fig. 6) and holding him very firmly as he balances on one foot.

4/30/37. 7 S 21, 24, 19; 7 T 28, 19.

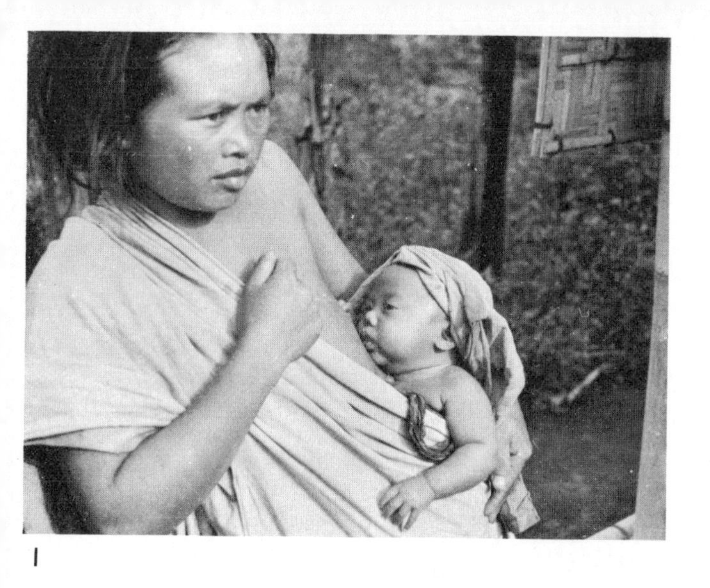
1

2

3

4

5

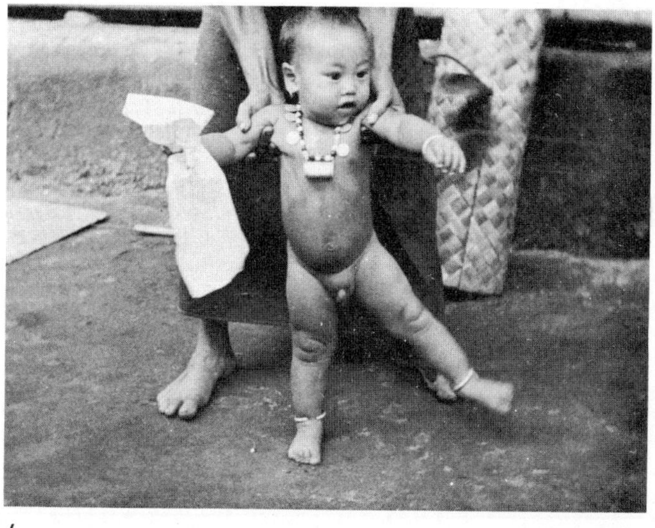
6

# PLATE XVI — I SEPEK (continued)

With two exceptions (fig. 1, Pl. XV, and fig. 5 on this plate) all of these pictures of I Sepek, which have been selected to characterize him, were taken on a single occasion, his delayed 210th-day birthday feast, which was not celebrated until he was ten and a half months old. The religious practitioner whom his father was bringing from his own village was late, the afternoon was perfect, the whole family was gathered together willing to put the children down, and we have a series of about 200 photographs of this occasion.*

Our 1939 notes are filled with an attempt to photograph Sepek, who was being carried hither and yon by devoted little neighbor girls, suggesting that he was still a popular and sought-after child.

1 through 4. I Sepek's postponed 210th-day birthday *(otonin)* ceremony (continued from Pl. XV). Sepek, 10½ months, stands at table and pokes at it with a wooden knife. He is barely able to stand, but with this wide stance can exert pressure with the knife. Earlier (fig. 2) Sepek walking toward our assistant (I Made Kaler), who calls to him, while I Leket pulls at paper beside him. Sepek on all fours (fig. 3) creeps toward his mother (Men Degeng). The ceremony still had not begun. Sepek's mother, after suckling him, goes to the gate (fig. 4), Leket in front left, and I Njawa, daughter of Men Leket's sister, and I Sama, in the background.

4/30/47. 7 U 37, 7 T 10, 7 U 16, 7 V 6.

5. In the road, I Sepek, 12 months, carried by his father (Nang Degeng) in a cloth sling like a woman, and I Leket precariously poised and looking miserable, on his right hip.

6/18/37. 11 R 20.

* See Appendix 1, p. 189 for a transcript of notes made on this occasion.

1

2

3

4

5

# PLATE XVII – SLEEPING

Balinese children learn to sleep in almost any position. Securely fastened in a cloth sling, they sleep while their mothers are pounding rice, while their child nurses are playing running games or having temper tantrums, while their mothers are walking long distances carrying loads on their heads. This relaxed sleep is one aspect of the relaxed fluid adjustment that the Balinese baby learns to make, as one part of the mother rather than as a separate being, a part which can move as safely and relaxedly as a hand or a foot. The same type of dis-association of parts of the body (see also Pls. LIV-LVI) appears in sleep and in waking.

As children and later as adults, Balinese go to sleep in situations that are threatening or dangerous, and sleep so soundly that they have to be shaken awake. A thief falls asleep while his case is being decided (cf. *B.C.* Pl. 68); servants fall asleep if they have broken or lost something; a child at a delivery will sleep soundly on the platform bed on which the birth is taking place. Actors, seated behind the curtains of an outdoor theater, in full view of the audience, take off their headdresses between scenes and sleep sitting, and members of an audience sleep standing up when the dialogue becomes dull. The Balinese have the expression, *takoet poeles,* literally, "afraid sleep," in which sleep is represented as the natural sequence of fear, where the expected American response to fear is wakefulness.

1. I Raoeh, 9 months, asleep in the arms of his mother (Men Goenoeng). Our yard. He had been fretful and ailing.
   10/24/36. 3 A 2.

2. I Karba, 17 months, in the arms of his mother's sister (Men Singin) during a *metoeoen* ceremony, one of the series of ceremonies held for the dead. Notice unsupported head. Courtyard of Widow Sereg.
   7/10/37. 12 Ha 35.

3. I Kenjoen, 26 weeks, asleep in the arms of her father (Nang Karma). Our yard.
   9/20/36. 2 Q 21.

4. I Marti, 15 weeks, asleep in the arms of her mother (Men Marti) after being dressed for her *neloeboelanin* (105th-day birthday) ceremony. Own yard.
   7/28/36. 2 C 35.

5. I Karsa, an unweaned older child, asleep in the arms of his mother (Men Singin) after the *otonin* of his mother's sister's daughter (I Kenjoen), during which he had been violently jealous, had a temper tantrum, and then had fallen asleep. Notice the carrying position with legs wide apart and head in a different plane from the body. Our yard.
   10/13/36. 2 Z 5. (*B.C.* Pl. 68, fig. 2)

6. I Doemoen, age unknown, asleep in the arms of her father (Nang Kesir). Torso forward, head thrust back. Our yard.
   10/7/36. 2 V 26.

1

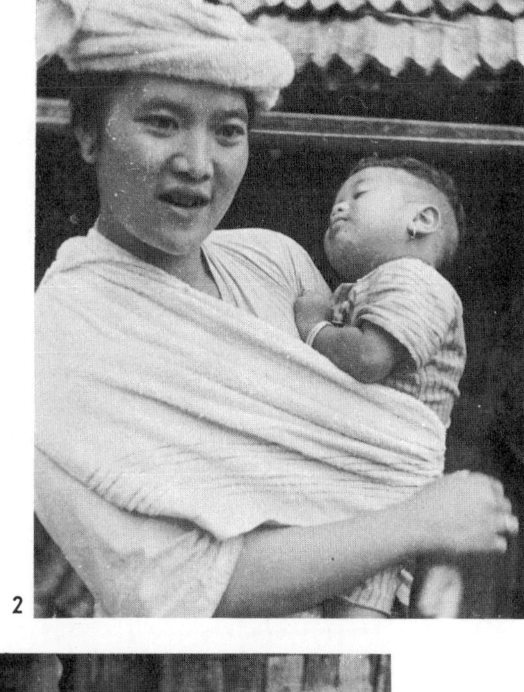

2

3

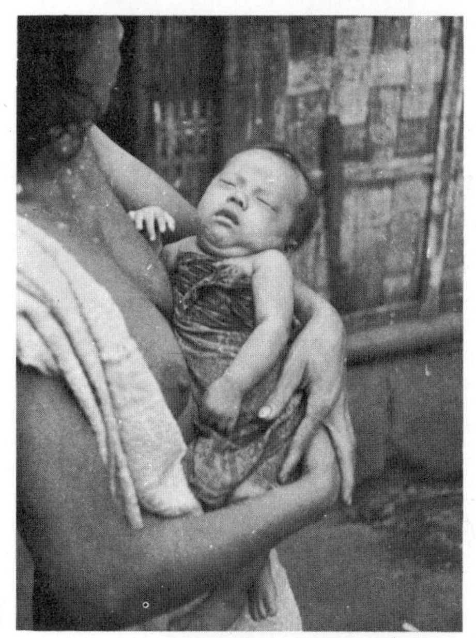

4

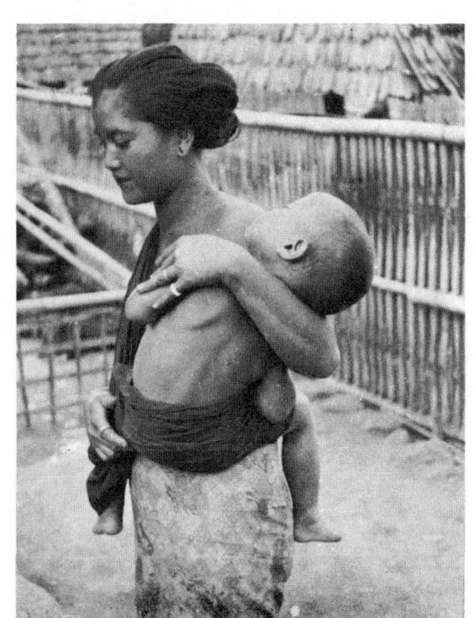

5

6

# PLATE XVIII – SUCKLING

The Balinese style of suckling infants is related to the typical high breast which the Balinese regard as beautiful and which is characteristic of many Balinese women. Even the very young infant is held in a near sitting position against the mother's breast (fig. 7), and the characteristic position (fig. 1) is in a sling high on the mother's hip, its head well above the nipple, to which it has access at its own initiative. When a woman's breasts are more pendulous, the typical carrying position is still followed, and the child learns to turn the nipple up (fig. 3) or to push the fleshy part of the breast up (fig. 4). Men Degeng (fig. 6) nursing I Sepek is unusual in holding him on her lap while she sits on a stool, so that the breast comes down into his mouth. Many children, especially those with older siblings, or those who have been often teased while still suckled (fig. 2), hold onto the other breast much of the time (as in fig. 6).

Infants are suckled by anyone who has milk if their mothers are not around. Child nurses carrying crying babies are told by bystanders, "Take it to its mother," but young girls, old women with dry breasts (*B.C.* Pl. 35, fig. 5), and some fathers, as well as any related or friendly woman with milk, will give a nipple to a crying baby. Children are weaned gradually when possible, often on a dry breast, but sometimes when the mother is pregnant very soon again by putting hot or bitter herbs on the breast.

1. I Kenjoen, 22 weeks, being suckled by her mother (Men Karma). The firm grip on the cloth sling is often replaced by a grip on the other nipple. Although Men Karma has suckled six children, her breasts are still high and firm enough for the customary Balinese position of nursing down. Our yard. 8/23/36. 2 H 25.

2. I Karba, 29 weeks, being suckled by his mother (Men Oera) while she plays with her sister's child, I Kenjoen, 22 weeks. This is the only mother on this plate who is looking at her child and this is part of the play jealousy situation. Nang Karma's yard. 8/26/36. 2 I 38. (*B.C.* Pl. 49, fig. 1)

3. I Marta, 14½ months, nursing in a near dancing posture at the breast of her mother (Men Marti). I Marti (34 months) and Nang Marti in foreground. Own yard. 2/11/39. 35 S 15.

4. I Raoeh, 9 months, suckled by his mother (Men Goenoeng), whose breast, unusually large and pendulous for a Balinese mother, he pushes up with the underside of his left hand. Our yard. 10/24/36. 3 A 6.

5. I Baroek, 11½ months, suckled by her mother (Men Kesir). Compare posture of her elder sibling, I Doemoen (Pl. XVII, fig. 6), taken 28 months before. Own yard. 2/11/39. 35 W 36.

6. I Sepek, 10½ months, being suckled by his mother (Men Degeng). Men Degeng, who has unusually long breasts, seats herself to suckle Sepek, who holds the other nipple with his left hand. Nang Degeng's farmyard. 4/30/37. 7 U 40.

7. I Tongos, 8 weeks, being suckled after his bath by his mother (Men Tongos), who squats down on the ground beside the bark bath basin and offers him the breast. He loses nipple, is given it again, blows out cheeks. Own yard. 1/21/37. 4 Ga 32.

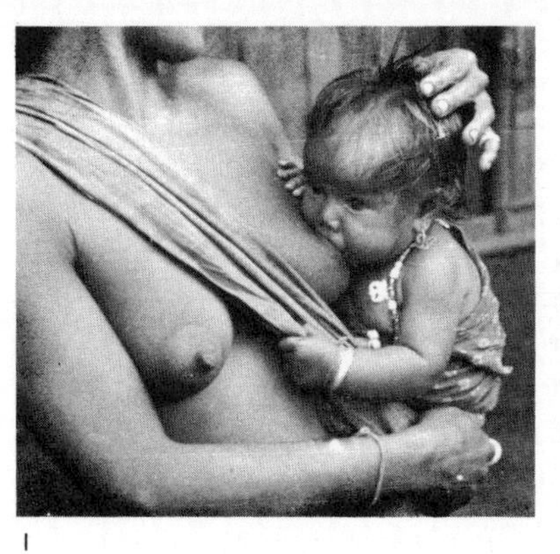
1

2

3

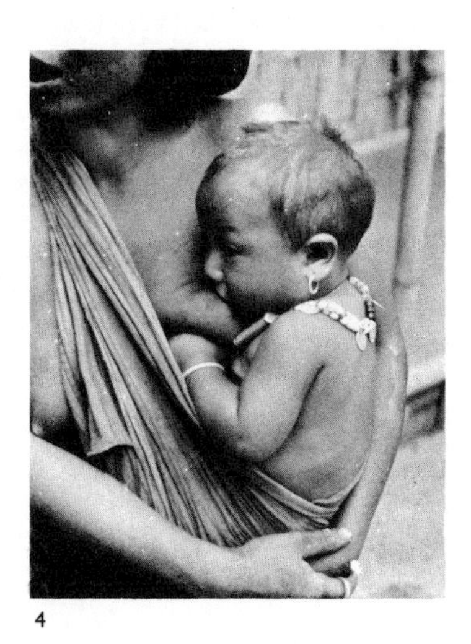
4

5

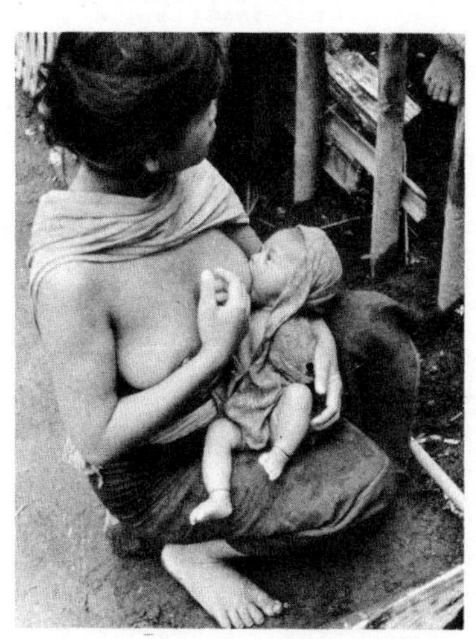
7

6

# PLATE XIX – FEEDING

Where suckling is something that the Balinese baby does, rather than something that is done to it, feeding is a very different matter in that the baby is placed in an extremely passive position. Infants are fed, from a few days after birth, a mixture of rice and banana which the mother prechews and arranges in a mound on the child's mouth. The most usual time for doing this is before or after the baby's bath when it is lying in the bath (fig. 1), although occasionally a mother will hold the baby on her lap. The food is piled up until the infant protests vigorously, and as it cries, the mother pokes a little of the food into the opened mouth. Older children tend to perpetuate this pattern of forcing of food into their mouths (fig. 4), and when given their food in coconut shells, sometimes turn the whole shell upside down on their faces (fig. 5). In adulthood, Balinese drink and eat snacks, which are eaten standing without ceremony, without embarrassment (*B.C.*, Pls. 36 and 37), but continue to display a lack of ease about eating, which is done hurriedly, throwing the food into the mouth from above (cf. *B.C.* Pl. 29). In eating snacks young children continue the pattern of freedom that they had in reaching down for the breast; they are given copper coins and wander off to buy penny drinks from the vendors who frequent the streets of the village, often close relatives. Solid food, however, is something that is cooked for one and given to one. There are strong taboos against interrupting someone who is eating, lest he be provoked to anger.

1. I Ngendon, 10 weeks, being fed prechewed rice and bananas in his bath, from which the water has been drained by his mother. (Men Ngendon). Own yard. (*B.C.* Pl. 26, fig. 1)
1/19/37. 4 F 5.

2. I Sami, 16½ weeks, being fed by his mother (Men Sama), who holds him firmly while she thrusts the food in with her little finger. His body is tensed in resistance. The mother is using the rest of her fingers minimally. Own yard.
1/21/37. 4 H 23.

3. I Karba, 11½ months, being fed by his mother (Men Oera) as she walks about carrying him in a cloth sling. Our yard.
1/26/37. 4 J 22.

4. I Karba, 20 months, seated on the ground in our yard, messily eating a banana given him by a vendor, forcing it into his mouth with both hands after both parents have refused it as a proffered gift.
10/11/37. 17 G 31.

5. I Leket, brother of I Sepek, tipping the coconut shell plate in which small children are given their food right over his face as he eats his rice, while his adopted mother (Men Leket) bathes her sister's new baby. Nang Njawi's yard.
7/13/37. 12 L 12. (*B.C.* Pl. 26, fig. 4)

1

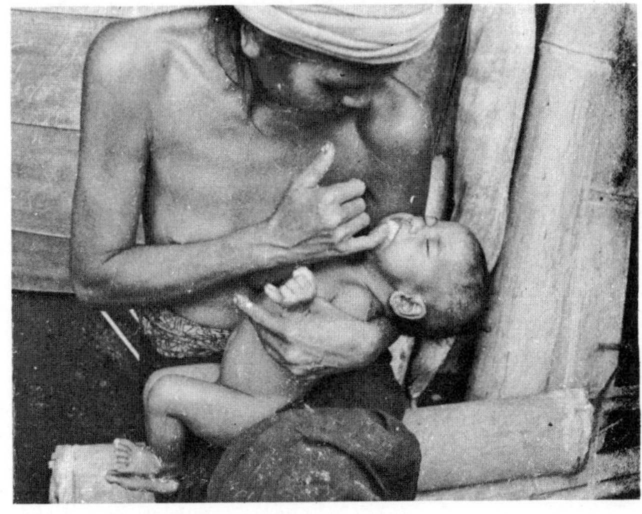

2

3

4

5

# PLATE XX – BATHING

The Balinese enjoy bathing, and bathing is also required for many ceremonial occasions. Pleasure and purification are the main reasons given for bathing, and cleanliness itself is less valued. Infants are bathed night and morning, in a bark container which is sometimes merely a shallow piece of bark supported on pieces of wood or bamboo (figs. 1 and 2), sometimes shaped into a container. The mother often rolls up the cloth sling in which the baby has been carried and puts in under the child's head as a pillow. When children can sit alone they are shifted to a shallow clay container, and the last stage of being bathed in the village comes at two to three years or so, when water is splashed over them from a dipper. After that they accompany their parents to the spring or river where adults bathe and from which water has to be carried daily.

Although the water may be slightly heated, bathing is a chilly business for the little baby, and the forced feeding adds to its discomfort. The mother tries to get it over as quickly as possible. Later, a bath may become a prolonged game between mother and child (fig. 6); neighbor children may be bathed with one's own in total disregard of whether they have just had a bath or not (cf. film *Karba's First Years*).

1 and 2. I Ngendon, 10 weeks, in the arms of his mother (Men Ngendon) as she tries the water in the sheath of betel bark before putting the baby in (fig. 1). Feeding in the bath (fig. 2) after the water has been tipped out. Own yard.

1/19/37. 4 F 1, 7. (*B.C.* Pl. 26, fig. 2)

3. I Tongos, 8 weeks, being bathed by his mother (Men Tongos) in a more elaborate bathtub in which the bark has been shaped into a regular container. Own yard.

1/21/37. 4 Ga 24.

4. I Kenjoen, 15 months, being bathed by her mother (Men Karma) in a clay tub in which she can still sit. Her next older sibling, I Gata, is having a temper tantrum in the background. Own yard.

6/20/37. 11 T 36.

5. I Raoeh, 37 months, too big to sit in the tub, is being given a splash bath by his mother, Men Goenoeng. Visiting boy in the background, I Ngemboet, accompanying us, stands watching. Own yard.

2/12/39. 36 I 39.

6. I Karba, 14½ months, standing in his tub on a high platform balancing himself and playing. Own yard.

4/29/37. 7 M 6.

7. I Tongos, 26½ months, two years later than figure 2, now has water poured over him with a dipper by his mother (Men Tongos)—the last form of bathing in the village. Own yard.

2/12/39. 36 J 33.

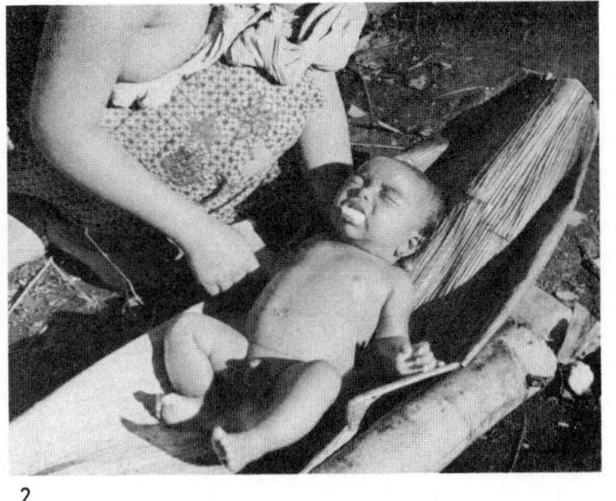

2

1

4

5

6

7

## *Peculiarities of Maturational Path Taken by Balinese Children*

# PLATE XXI – LATE FROGGING

The following eight plates (XXI to XXVIII) illustrate the way in which the Balinese child follows an alternative line of maturation from that which the New Haven children followed. The children on this plate, I Ngendon, I Sepek, and I Tongos, are all shown in pronounced expressions of the position which at an earlier stage the Gesell group have called "frogging" (a position in which arms are either flexed or extended symmetrically and legs are flexed symmetrically *in abduction*). This is maintained long after the period in which it would have been replaced in the New Haven children by positions in which knees were drawn under the abdomen. This frogging accompanied by pronounced knee flexion and external rotation is related in form to the way in which Balinese children squat, and then stand from a squatting position. The way in which Balinese children are carried on the hip of adult or child nurse, legs wide apart, for most of the time during the prewalking period, and for some time afterward, may contribute to the maintenance of this frogging posture.

1. I Ngendon, 9 months, able to creep and stand, here assumes a frogging postion as he reaches for marbles, on a mat on our veranda beside his mother (Men Ngendon).

   8/18/37. 13 Y 10.

2. I Sepek, 10½ months, has been standing, reaching for paper offered him by our assistant (I Made Kaler). He dropped to this wide frogging position. Own yard.

   4/30/37. 7 T 11.

3. I Tongos, 10½ months, on a mat with his mother (Men Tongos) in Nang Goenoeng's yard, has been sitting, then rose to a squatting position and dropped into this frogging posture.

   10/9/37. .16 X 42.

1

2

3

# PLATE XXII – SITTING

When Balinese children are not being carried on the hip, they sit, on laps, on platforms, on mats, placidly, making very little attempt to move from the sitting postion unless directly stimulated to do so. Although sitting positions for adults are stylized, women sitting back on their heels, men sitting with one leg crossed above the other (fig. 2), if the occasion is a ceremonial one, such as a village meeting or a temple ceremony, both sexes, even as adults, have great freedom in the choice of sitting postures, sitting on platforms with feet resting on the ground (figs. 1 and 3), on the ground with knees up (fig. 2 and Plate XXIII, fig. 2), squatting with arms extended (Plate XXIV, fig. 6), etc. Children experience all of these positions as they sit on the laps of adults, on the knee, or resting in the crotch (fig. 7), etc. There is a tendency for mothers to hold their children facing them, oftener than fathers, an orderly accompaniment of the suckling situation, so that seating postures, as experienced in the back, may be said to be more defined by contacts with males, just as postures involving spread thighs, frogging (Plate XXI), and squatting (Plate XXV) are more defined by contacts with females. On ceremonial occasions, such as a birthday celebration, an adult may arrange a child's feet symmetrically (fig. 6), but usually the only regulation of sitting posture is to improve balance. So small children learn two things about sitting; that balance is desirable, and that sitting is one of the body postures which calls for control when etiquette is involved.

1. I Ngendon, 27 weeks, supported by the hand of his mother (Men Ngendon), leaning on his own hands, the left rotated inward. Our veranda.
5/13/37. 8 T 24.

2. I Sepek, 10½ months, sits on hips, legs spread wide to the side and knees hyperflexed and symmetrical, on a mat. His father (Nang Degeng) to the left, his older brother (I Leket) leans back against his adoptive father (Nang Leket). Notice Leket's leg posture. Own yard. 4/30/37. 7 S 30.

3. I Raoeh, 13½ months, on lap of neighbor (Men Singin) in complex sophisticated posture, his father (Nang Goenoeng) in foreground. Our veranda.
3/6/37. 5 H 17.

4. I Raoeh, 19 months, sitting impassively on wooden mortar, hands joined symmetrically. His mother has been trying to divert him into activity for the benefit of the camera. I Tongos, 8½ months, seated with feet cupped, legs apart and outwardly rotated where Raoeh is inwardly rotated. 8/19/37. 14 E 4.

5. I Karba, 12 months, seated on the xylophone using both mallets. His father (Nang Oera) has his hand behind him only to guide his playing. He has the rounded back that would be expected from a younger child. Our veranda.
2/5/37. 4 S 11.

6. I Tongos, 7½ months, seated on a mat at a *metoeoen,* one of the death ceremonies, besides I Mawa, 25 weeks (son of Nang Madera).
7/10/37. 12 G 35.

7. I Marti, 11 months, seated curled exhausted in lap of her father (Nang Marti), expressing rejection of the toy koala. Our yard. 3/21/37 6 C 33.

8. I Kenjoen, 15 months, seated firmly and symmetrically on lap of her mother (Men Karma). Child nurse sister (I Gati) in the background. Nang Karma's yard.
6/20/37. 11 W 17.

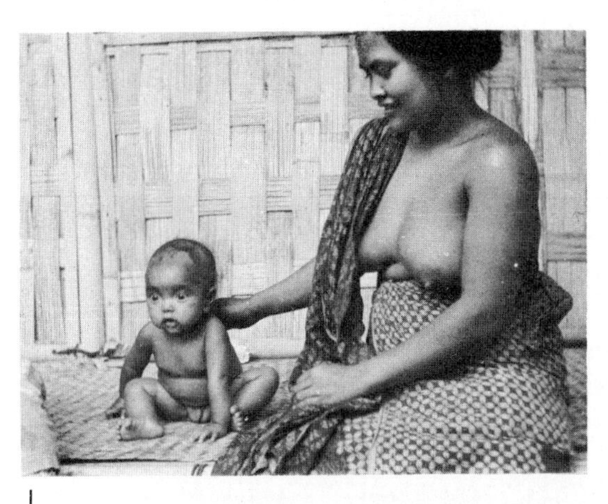
1

2

3

4

5

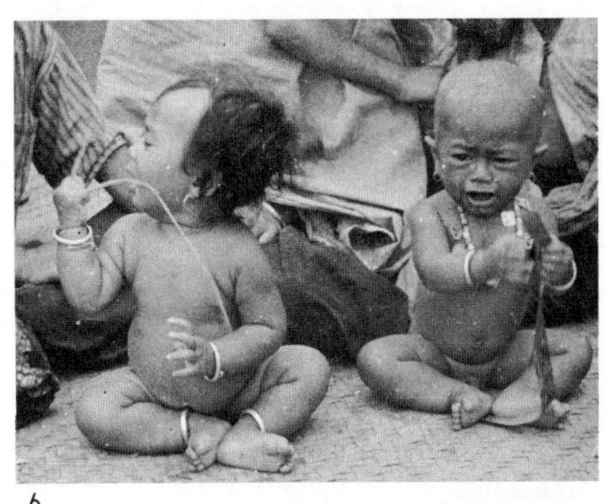
6

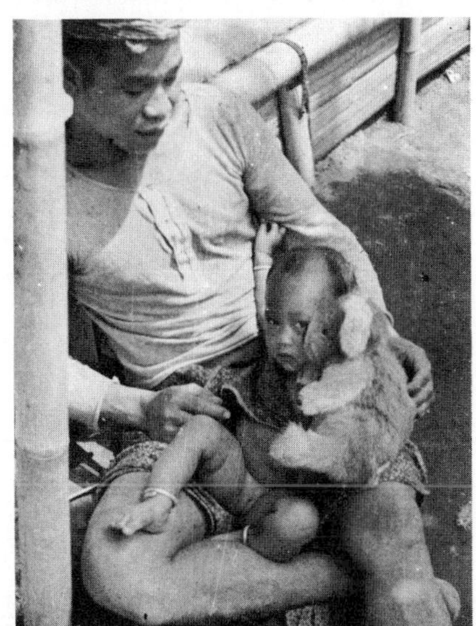
7

8

# PLATE XXIII – CREEPING

Balinese children are heavily discouraged from creeping, which the Balinese feel is demeaning to a human being as it is the form of locomotion used by animals. In situations of great informality and playfulness, when there are no strangers present, a child may be put down on a mat and permitted to creep or hitch itself along on its buttocks, the customary mode of progression of I Tongos (fig. 5). During the earlier stage, crawling, when the infant is about seven to eight months old, the Balinese child is carried continuously, so that opportunities are rare in which the infant could experiment. The circumstance that creeping is so infrequent may account for the extent to which the same child uses all three forms, knee creep, all fours, and hitching along on the buttocks, without any one of the three becoming as specialized as they do in American children. The characteristic outward rotation of the feet also might decrease creeping behavior.

The Balinese feeling against creeping is dramatized in ceremonies that are held in Bajoeng Gedé for those who have broken incest taboos and so behaved like animals. The offending man and woman, wearing wooden pig yokes on their necks, must creep on their hands and knees and eat with their mouths from pig troughs of food, as they say farewell to the gods of life and go to live on the "land of punishment" at the cemetery end of the village. Similar punishments are meted out to low-caste people who have borne twins of opposite sex who are said to have committed incest in the womb.

Occasionally much older children who have been displaced by a new baby will creep, displaying the same shamefacedness about it as such older children do when they try to steal back to the mother's breast. (cf. I Gata in Plate III, fig. 5).

1. I Karba, 7½ months, on our cement veranda floor.
9/23/36. 2 R 7.

2. I Karba, 17½ months, in a half walk, half creek with toes hyperflexed, Men Singin watching. Our yard.
7/15/37. 12 Q 42.

3. I Sepek, 10½ months, half creeping, one knee to ground, as dog follows him after defecation. I Leket (his next elder brother, at right) and his elder brother child nurse (I Dengeng) in background. Nang Degeng's yard, waiting for *otonin* ceremony to begin.
4/30/37. 7 U 12.

4. I Ngendon, 9 months, who is now able to stand with support, in a one-knee, one-foot creep, on mat on our veranda with his mother Men Ngendon.
8/18/37. 13 Y 33.

5. I Tongos, 8½ months, in late frogging position, reaching toward betel tray. I Raoeh, 19 months, in background. Nang Goenoeng's yard.
8/19/37. 14 E 39.

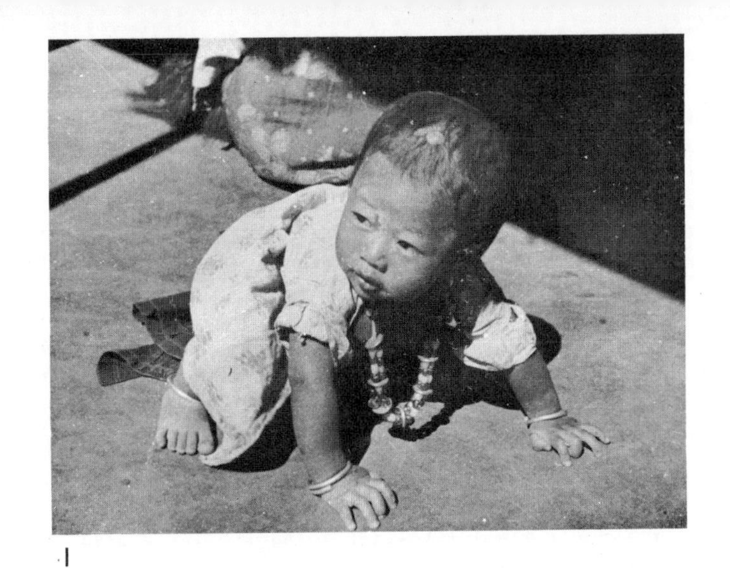

1

2

4

# PLATE XXIV – ALL FOURS

These children, when given an opportunity to creep, and often after they are quite able to stand alone or even walk (figs. 2, 5, and 6), will sometimes sink into the all-fours position. This will alternate in the same child with a knee creep. It might be suggested that the circumstance that Balinese children are given so little opportunity to creep is probably a factor in keeping creeping forms fluid, so that all fours is a possible form for a child who also uses a knee creep. This may reinforce the adults' objection to any type of creeping, as it is the most conspicuously animal form of creeping behavior. This is an example of the way in which cultural forms may become intensified, reinforced, and self-perpetuating as parts of the basic human developmental process become involved.

(As some readers cannot resist doing pseudostatistics, it is necessary to state here that devoting two plates to plantigrade behavior is NOT a measure of its frequency in Bali. In her paper published in 1935* Jane Belo after several years' residence in Bali states that she has never seen a child permitted to creep at all. Our photographs were combed to produce these few examples.)

1. I Sepek, 10½ months, on all fours, to which he has risen from a knee creep. With his father's brother (Nang Leket) at his *otonin* ceremony. Own yard.
   4/30/37. 7 U 22.

2. I Karba, 8 months, on all fours, on our veranda. His father (Nang Oera) has been teaching him to dance (cf. Pl. XLI, fig. 7).
   9/30/36. 2 U 28.

3. I Sami, 7 months, on verge of knee creep, responding to his mother (Men Sama), who holds out her arms to him. Sami already at this early age is in a one-foot creep position. Own yard.
   4/30/37. 7 O 21.

4. Same scene, age, and day. I Sami, on all fours, as I Karba, 15 months, sulks in background. Note parallelism to dog.
   4/30/37. 7 P 29.

5. I Karba, 13½ months, and I Marti, 11 months. Karba on all fours. Our yard.
   3/21/37. 6 C 1.

6. I Karba, 17½ months, long after he can walk, still progresses on all fours as he plays with ball. I Marti, 15 months, sitting against her father (Nang Marti) in background. Our yard.
   7/17/37. 12 Y 19.

* Belo, Jane, "The Balinese Temper."

1

2

3

4

5

6

# PLATE XXV – SQUATTING

In their squatting behavior there is found one of the most marked differences between Balinese and American children. The Balinese squat is much lower, the buttocks often resting on the ground (figs. 1, 4, 7), and the squatting position occupies a different position in the maturational sequence. American children tend to go from frogging to creeping to all fours or to standing, with the squat following later; the Balinese children, with hardly any creeping, go from sitting to squatting to standing, rising from the squat rather than sinking down into it. Here again a number of factors can be mentioned as explanatory: the presence of squatting as a usual form among Balinese adults, the wide spread of the hips that is associated with being carried on the hip for such a long period, the narrow circle within which a Balinese child is usually permitted movement so that movement up may be substituted for movement away from a given position, the extreme fluidity of Balinese movement, and the emphasis that has been placed on balance during the time the child was learning to stand alone.

1. I Karba, 18½ months, and I Marti, 16 months, with a *kapeng* (a copper coin) in our yard. Notice the very low squat, buttocks touching the ground.
8/20/37. 14 L 15.

2. I Karba, 20 months, and I Ngendon, 11 months, playing with ball and spoon. Our yard.
10/11/37. 17 I 27.

3. I Kenjoen, 17 months, and I Marti, 16 months, in our yard. Same scene as in fig. 1. Playing marbles.
8/20/37. 14 M 24.

4. I Marti, 11 months, in wide low squat, playing with I Karba, 13½ months. Our yard.
3/21/37. 6 C 9.

5. I Tongos, 10½ months, pausing in a near squat, after going on all fours, one leg dragging. I Karba, 20 months, standing with ball. In Nang Goenoeng's yard, afternoon of play.
10/9/37. 16 Y 38.

6. I Sepek, 10½ months, squatting and maintaining his balance without his hands touching. In own yard, at his delayed *otonin* ceremony. His father (Nang Degeng) watches, holding the next older child (I Leket) sprawled in front of him.
4/30/37. 7 S 39.

7. I Marta, 14½ months, squatting and looking over her shoulder. Own yard.
2/11/39. 35 T 29.

8. I Raoeh, 25½ months, squatting, arms in balancing position, in front of his older brother (I Goenoeng) while his child nurse (I Poendoeh) does the hair of his mother (Men Goenoeng). Own yard.
3/3/38. 22 E 29.

1

2

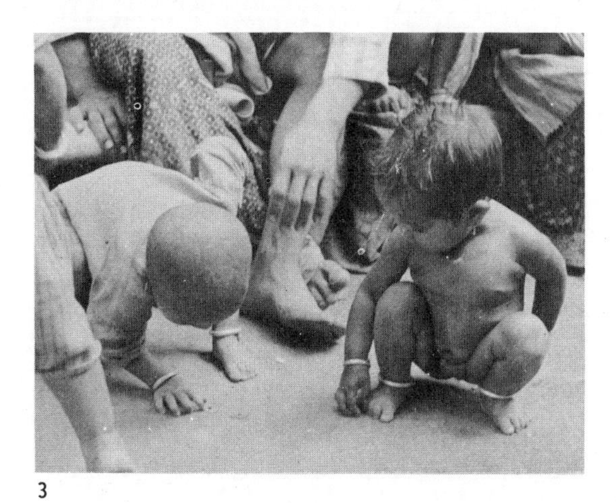

3

4

5

6

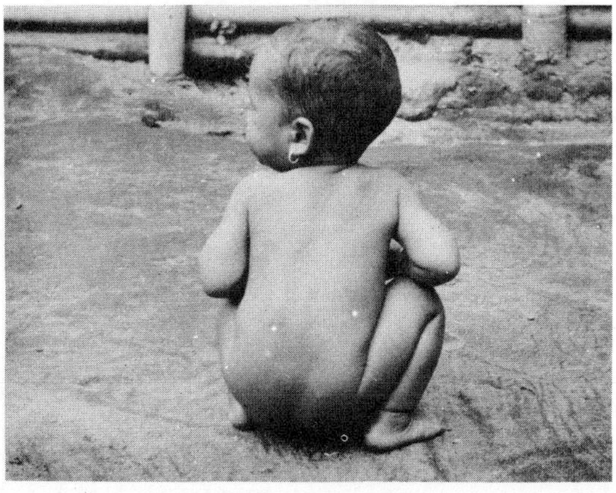

7

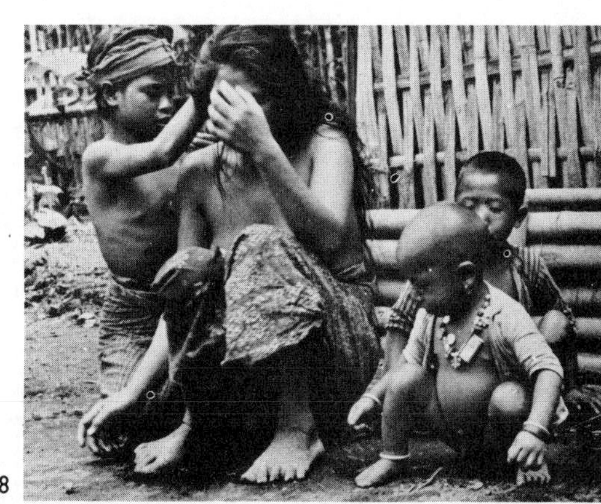

8

# PLATE XXVI – STANDING WITH SUPPORT

Balinese children are helped to stand and taught to walk. For walking itself, there is a special walker that is sometimes made, when a parent is particularly enterprising, to supplement the care that a child nurse will give, of a rail of bamboo (*penegtegan*), as in figure 7. The child who cannot yet walk alone can go round and round such a rail, safe as long as he does not venture away from it, learning how to keep his balance and also that it is safer not to wander into outer undefined space, a lesson that is reinforced later when children wander out into the temple grounds or onto the stage, and are patiently recaptured until they learn not to venture away. Learning to stand has on the whole a static quality, as when I Sepek is stood up by his uncle (fig. 4) or I Raoeh is exhibited by his child nurse (fig. 8), although both of these children can stand alone. Bajoeng Gedé children are both stood up earlier (fig. 1) and held up later, and passive children like Raoeh and I Marti (fig. 6) tend to lean a good deal upon the support of the adults after they have learned to stand alone.

1. I Marta, 14 weeks, stood on the lap of her mother (Men Marti) after she had been held erect in bath, crying. Men Marti says, on behalf of the baby, "Cold am I, cold," using the first person pronoun used to persons born outside the village. Own yard. 3/3/38. 22 C 16.

2. I Tongos, 8½ months, standing holding flower toy under his arm, supported by Men Goenoeng (mother of I Raoeh). Raoeh, 19 months, sits on wooden mortar. Tongos' wide firm stance parallels Men Goenoeng's firm, teaching hands. Nang Goenoeng's yard. 8/19/37. 14 E 21.

3. I Ngendon, 9 months, in standing postion, both hands held by his mother (Men Ngendon), who is showing me that he can stand. Our yard. 8/18/37. 13 Y 24.

4. I Sepek, 10½ months, standing, very wide stance, supported under his arms by his father's brother (Nang Leket) at his *otonin* ceremony, on a mat in his father's yard. 4/30/37. 7 U 23.

5. I Kenjoen, 12 months, supported by our assistant (I Made Kaler), who is trying to make her stand during scene (fig. 7) of her walking around the *penegtegan* (walking rail). Nang Oera's yard. 3/26/37. 6 F 27.

6. I Marti, 15 months, standing with one arm around the neck of her father (Nang Marti) in our yard. 7/17/37. 12 Y 20.

7. Same scene as figure 5. I Karba, 13½ months, supporting himself with one hand on *penegtegan* (bamboo walking rail), which his father (Nang Oera) has built for him in the middle of the yard. I Kenjoen, 12 months, on one knee, can also walk around the walking rail. Karba can walk alone a few steps but then sways and topples down into a sitting position. Nang Oera's yard. 3/26/37. 6 F 18.

8. I Raoeh, 19 months, supported from behind by I Poendoeh (his slavey child nurse). Own yard. Stands on heel with toes up and sideways flexion of ankle. I Tongos, 8½ months, in foreground. 8/19/37. 14 F 15.

1

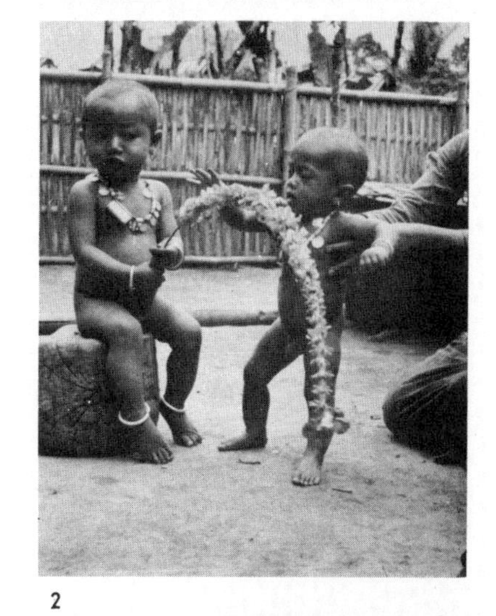

2

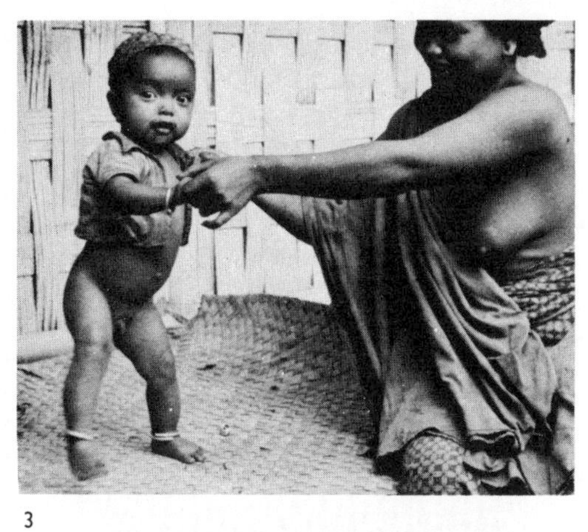

3

4

5

6

7

8

# PLATE XXVII – STANDING ALONE

A conspicuous feature of the behavior of Balinese children just able to stand alone is the excellent balance that they maintain, the ability to pause, poised (fig. 6), to turn and look behind them without falling (fig. 3). When they lose their balance they topple sideways, with a tendency to recompose themselves into a seated or squatting posture rather than to fall on their faces.

1. I Sepek, 10½ months, at his delayed 210th-day birthday, standing with very wide stance, holding piece of paper out of which his brother (I Degeng) has made him a hat. Own yard.

4/30/37. 7 T 20.

2. I Karba, 13½ months, standing alone in front of me, his right hand in a "holding on" position. I Karsa in background. Our yard.

3/21/37. 6 D 27.

3. I Marta, 14½ months, pausing in a run to turn and look at her father (Nang Marti), I Marti, 34 months, sitting at his side. Own yard.

2/11/39. 35 U 2.

4. I Kenjoen, 17 months, urinating in a standing position while I Marti, 16 months, bends over to pick up a marble. Our yard. (Cf. Pl. V, fig. 6, for crowd.)

8/20/37. 14 M 10.

5. I Raoeh, 19 months, standing alone as I Poendoeh (his slavey nurse) adjusts his flower toy. I Tongos, 8½ months, in a reaching squat in the foreground. Nang Goenoeng's yard. On toes as in Pl. XXIII fig. 5.

8/19/37. 14 F 41.

6. I Marti, 19 months, delicately poised on one foot, toes of other foot curled under, finger to lip part of balance. Her father (Nang Marti) in foreground watching her, and her father's brother (Nang Singin) in doorway. Our veranda.

11/21/37. 18 Y 3.

1

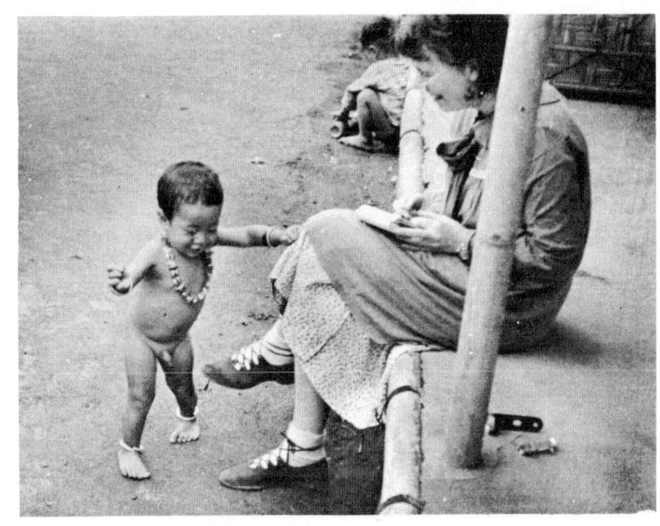

2

3

4

5

6

# PLATE XXVIII – WALKING

The way in which children are taught to walk has been discussed on Plate XXIII. This plate illustrates the freedom of knee action (figs. 5 and 6) and the balance with which children walk. Walking is much more an alternative to being carried than it is in the United States, where walking is rather the alternative to riding in a baby carriage or in some form of walker or velocipede. In Bali, on trips of any length, when tired, watching a ceremony, etc., a child who has long since learned to walk will be picked up and carried. Neither boys nor girls are required to carry practice loads, although little girls begin playfully carrying objects on their heads very early. Walking is something a child is taught to do, is encouraged to do, but is not forced to continue when he is tired.

1. I Ngendon, 9 months, on the verge of walking as his mother (Men Ngendon) holds his hands and I lean toward them. Our yard.
   8/18/37. 13 Z 19.

2. I Marti, 16 months, caught by camera in midst of walking past her father (Nang Marti). I Karba, 18½ months, turning as he walks away. Our yard.
   8/20/37. 14 L 19.

3. I Marta, 14½ months, caught as she walks on a narrower base. Our yard.
   2/11/39. 35 T 32.

4. I Kenjoen, 17 months, walking before a group of women and girls sitting along the edge of our veranda. Toes turned in on both feet.
   8/20/37. 14 M 4.

5 and 6. I Karba, 15½ months, in background running in straight line with small steps, followed by his mother's sister (Men Singin), followed by her son (I Karsa). This kind of knee action happens, if at all, in New Haven children around two years of age. Outside our gate. Note one arm extended in balancing gesture.
   5/25/37. 9 J 2, 3.

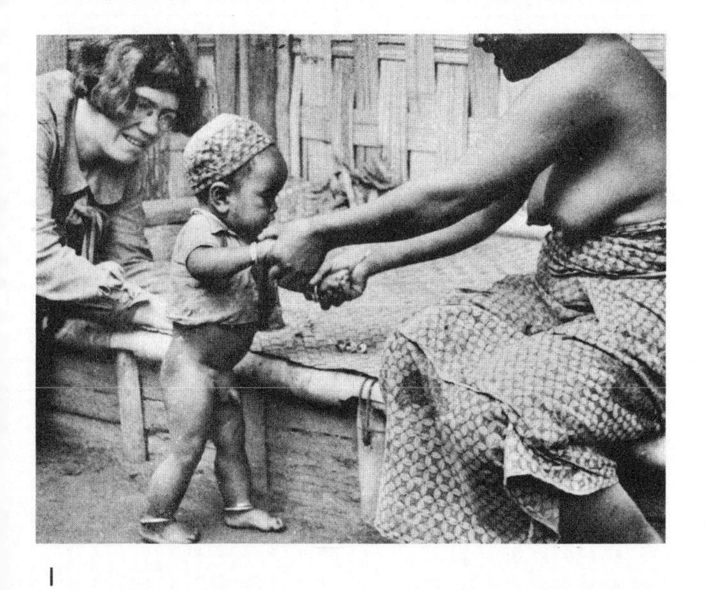

1

2

3

4

5

6

## *Whole-Body Postures*

# PLATE XXIX – BALANCE

The balance of Balinese children is conspicuously good. This must be understood in terms of the general importance of balance in the culture, the way in which infants are carried upright so much of the time that a vertical position is habitual from earliest weeks, the way in which infants are able to relax when the carrier indulges in strenuous movement, the fluidity of gesture that permits movements of a bizarre type (fig. 3). Where American children keep their balance by movement, Balinese children tend instead to rearrange themselves where they are, so that a still balance rather than a moving balance results.

In later life, the preoccupation with balance is found in witchcraft usage and the theatrical presentations of witches and evil spirits who are characterized by dancing, standing on one foot in difficult and discrepant postures (cf. *B.C.* Plate 17). Posturing on one foot is also a component of dances said to be related to war. It is forbidden to put back on the head anything that falls from it, and as women habitually carry on the head, this prohibition is a reinforcement of attention to balance.

1. I Karba, 13½ months, standing alone, his right hand holding his penis, in front of his father (Nang Oera), who has called him to him. Our yard, playing with a group of cousins.
3/21/37. 6 C 20.

2. I Marta, 14½ months. Own yard.
2/11/39. 35 T 30.

3. I Sepek, 10½ months, who is just able to stand without support for about 30 seconds, balancing himself as he squats by extending his arms backward. Own yard, at his *otonin* ceremony.
4/30/37. 7 T 31.

4. I Marti, 19 months, in high squat with a bit of paper which she is offering her father (Nang Marti). I Malih, a village youth, in the background. Our yard.
11/21/37. 18 Y 40.

5 through 8. I Raoeh, 25½ months, holding a long palm frond, dances with marbles in his mouth. He maintains this balance, posturing on one foot through a sequence of pictures. Own yard.
3/3/38. 22 G 10, 11, 12, 13.

1

2

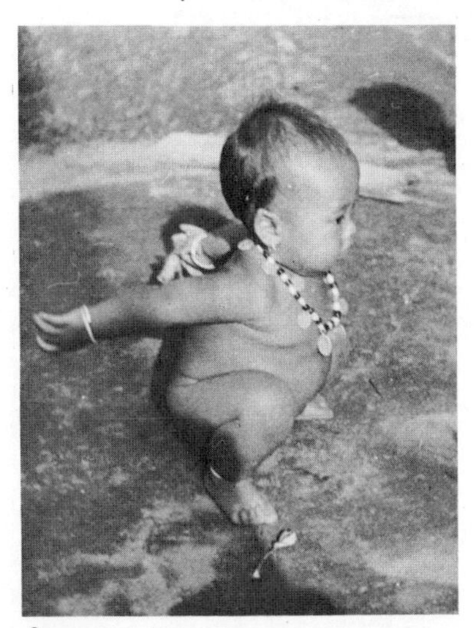

3

4

5

6

7

8

# PLATE XXX – COMPENSATORY BALANCE

In this plate, the ways in which small children keep their balance is further explored. I Karba (fig. 1) uses his left arm almost superfluously, as if to counterbalance his sitting posture. I Marti (fig. 3) reaching for a ball illustrates the same type of compensation. The last four pictures illustrate the device by which Balinese babies tend to maintain their balance while learning to sit by holding onto themselves; this is continued into later walking habits. One of my early images of the Balinese was that they reminded me of tightrope walkers, possibly derived from this tendency to rely on their own body to provide compensations for loss of balance. Walking on stilts is an occasional game, and little girls in trance dance in extreme postions on the shoulders of men who must shift their weight beneath the dancing children to maintain their balance (see *B.C.* Pl. 10, fig. 3).

1. I Karba, 12 months, supported from behind by his father (Nang Oera) as he learns to play the *tjoengklik* (a bamboo xylophone). Father holds one mallet, and Karba parallels this by holding the other in his right hand, left arm widely extended in maintenance of balance. Our veranda.
   2/5/37. 4 S 12.

2. I Raoeh, 19 months, seated very erect, extends one arm in balance holding a marble as if offering it. He alternates this position with both hands on legs (cf. Pl. XXII, fig. 4). I Tongos, 8½ months, in foreground, seated, echoes same pattern of balance, one hand on knee, one extended. Men Goenoeng (mother of Raoeh) at side. Own yard.
   8/19/37. 14 E 19.

3. I Marti, 22½ months, just after being dressed in modern dress bought in the market; picking up ball. Own yard. One arm far out, the other back, illustrates way of keeping balance by putting the new part of the body where it will need to be next.
   3/3/38. 22 D 33.

4. I Marta, 14½ months, picking up marbles at the foot of her mother (Men Marti). Own yard.
   2/11/39. 35 T 36.

5. I Sepek, 10½ months, seated very straight, holding himself erect by putting his hands on his knees. Father (Nang Degeng) behind him, his arm over the knee of the older child (I Leket). Own yard. *Otonin* of Sepek.
   4/30/37. 7 S 4.

6. I Ngendon, 27 weeks, held by his mother (Men Ngendon) firmly by far arm, arms in the position which will appear later as a balancing one. Our veranda.
   5/13/37. 8 T 28.

7. I Kenjoen, 12 months, seated after walking around walking rail, hands on knees. Nang Oera's yard.
   3/26/37. 6 F 26.

8. I Tongos, 10½ months, sitting very straight, balancing with hands on lower legs. I Karba, 20 months, back to camera. Nang Goenoeng's yard.
   10/9/37. 16 Y 9.

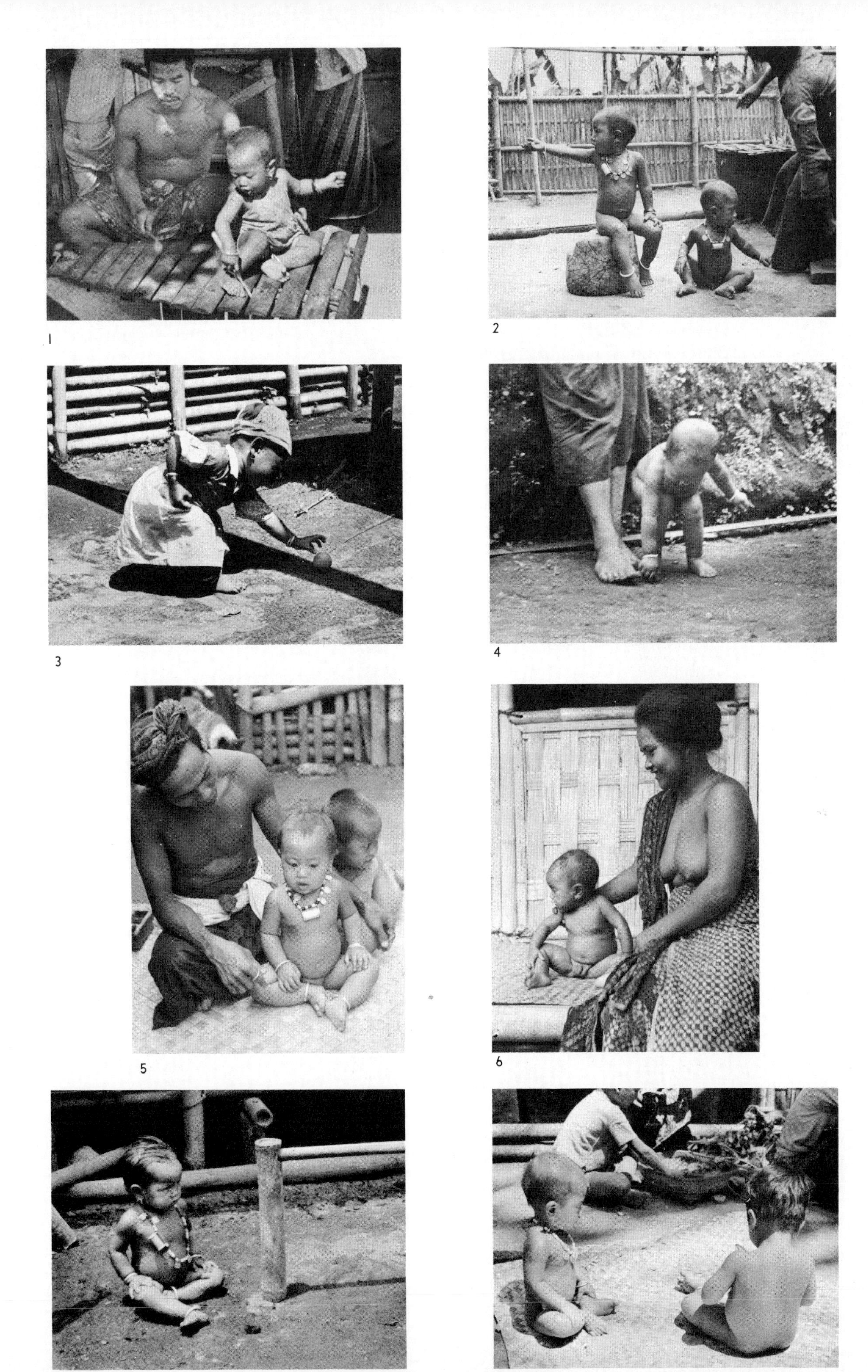

1 2 3 4 5 6 7 8

# PLATE XXXI – POSTURAL FLEXIBILITY

Balinese children are able to assume postures in which the degree of distortion and discrepancy between the position of one limb and another seems to be a function of the extreme degree of flexibility. This aspect was characterized by Louise Ames thus: "Anything which is physically possible is behaviorially possible." Where human beings in most cultures have limitations of style placed upon their behavior so that the older they grow, the narrower the limits within which their posture varies, the Balinese retain the flexibility that is characteristically seen in the human fetus, moving with a fluidity that suggests suspension in amniotic fluid rather than a consistent outer sustained demeanor in an organized world.

1. I Kenjoen, 15 months, sitting on the ground beside her mother (Men Karma), her next older brother (I Gata), eating rice in the background. Own yard. Hand and leg are distorted in relation to each other, while the head is in a still different plane. She has been sitting among the puppies.
6/20/37. 11 W 27.

2. I Doemoen, age unknown, in the lap of her father (Nang Kesir). Our veranda. Fingers and toes included in the extreme flexibility of the whole body.
10/7/36. 2 V 18.

3. I Marti, 34 months, lying on the lap of her father (Nang Marti). Our yard. The upper trunk is hyperflexed to one side and the arms are flexed above the shoulder level.
2/12/39. 36 L 31.

4. I Kenjoen, 34½ months, on the lap of her adolescent sister (I Karmi). Both older girl and Kenjoen are contorted but Kenjoen is both flaccid and discrepant. Own yard.
2/12/39. 36 D 25.

5. I Karba, 20 months, one leg tucked under him in the same posture as I Karmi in figure 4. I Sami, 12½ months, faces him, hands resting on legs and maintaining his symmetrical balance. Nang Goenoeng's yard.
10/9/37. 16 W 29.

6. I Raoeh, 19 months, with I Tongos, 8½ months. Raoeh, seated on wooden mortar, has been scraping his chin with a marble, thrown the marble down, watched it, stood, leaned over to pick up marble, balanced badly, and extended his right hand backward to balance himself. The fingers of the left hand are widespread and flexible, while those of the right hand used in balancing are tensed. Own yard.
8/19/37. 14 E 17.

7. I Tongos, 8½ months, same scene, in Nang Goenoeng's yard. I Raoeh, 19 months, standing with back to camera, child nurse (I Poendoeh) fussing with marble that Raoeh has given her. Tongos' right foot is extremely everted as a balancing device, fingers of left hand resting in cupped position on ground.
8/19/37. 14 F 38.

8. I Marta, 14½ months, seated on the ground after her bath. Own yard. Upright position is maintained here by flexibility of left leg and ankle.
2/11/39. 35 U 23.

1

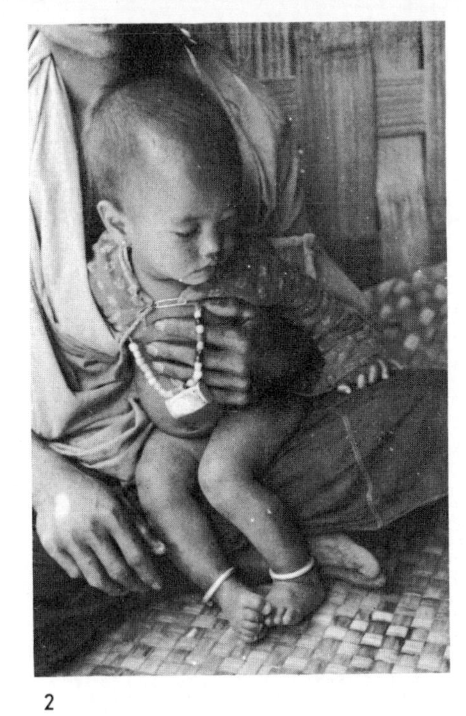
2

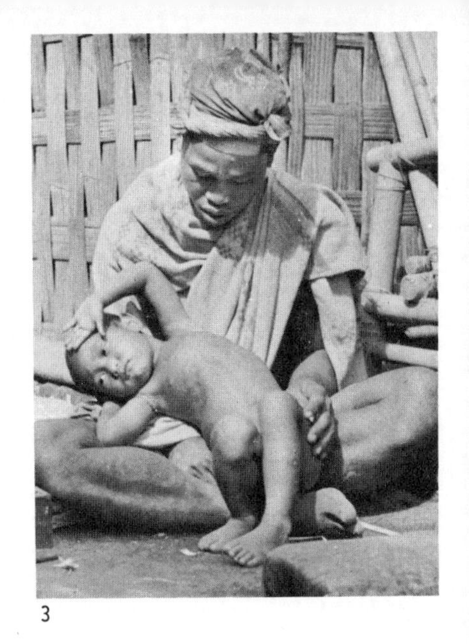
3

4

5

6

7

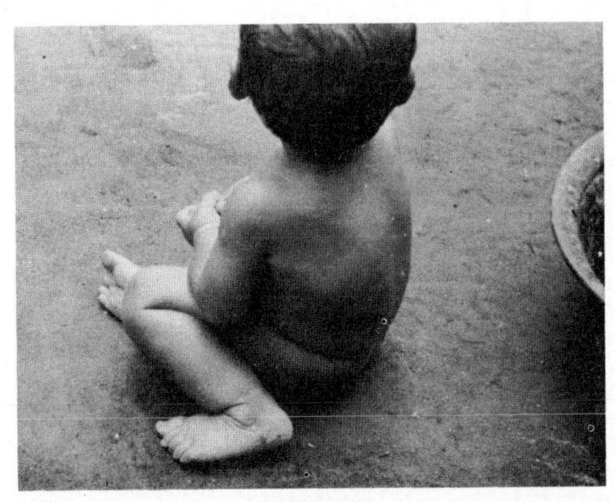
8

# PLATE XXXII – SYMMETRY

Although the Balinese assume so easily such extreme distorted and asymmetrical postures as shown on the preceding plate (XXXI) they are also equally capable of very high degrees of symmetrical behavior, which is occasionally reinforced by a maternal touch. If a child is already seated in a conspicuously symmetrical position (fig. 6), a mother may move one foot a little to make the position more satisfactory, especially if the occasion stresses exhibitionism, as for example, if the ceremony is for the child itself. One aspect of symmetrical sitting behavior is placing the hands on own body, as it were, rounding out the symmetrical picture.

1. I Karba, 20 months, sitting on the ground in our yard, using both hands to force banana into his mouth as he maintains a symmetrical lower trunk position, the sole of one foot fitted against the other.
10/11/37. 17 G 30.

2. I Marta, 14½ months, after bath, hands flexibly interwoven as if each were independent of the other. Wandering tonus in Marta's hand. I Marti, 34 months, in background. Own yard.
2/11/39. 35 U 20.

3. I Raoeh, 25½ months, seated maintaining balance with hands on lower legs. Mother (Men Goenoeng) and child nurse (I Poendoeh) beside him, and brother (I Goenoeng) behind him. Own yard.
3/3/38. 22 E 27.

4. I Sepek, 10½ months, in front of father (Nang Degeng), older brother (I Degeng) behind him. Own yard, on his 210th-day birthday ceremony. Sepek's legs are in flexion where a New Haven child would characteristically put them out in front.
4/30/37. 7 S 5.

5. I Tongos, 10½ months, in Nang Goenoeng's yard, seated with same type of symmetrical flexion as I Sepek (fig. 4 above) at exactly the same age.
10/9/37. 16 X 36.

6. I Baroek, 11½ months, seated on the ground in front of her sister nurse (I Kesir) in same flexed symmetrical sitting position as I Tongos (fig. 5) and I Sepek (fig. 4). Own yard.
2/12/39. 36 D 28.

1

2

3

4

5

6

## PLATE XXXIII – POSTURAL VARIATIONS

In the posture of these children, much of which could be duplicated among American children in general outline, and the specific character of which is typically Balinese, there are also interesting extreme manifestations: the wide web of the hand (fig. 1), the cupped foot (fig. 2), the curious resting on the arms (figs. 3 and 4), and the extraordinary flexible contortions of the toes (fig. 5).

1. I Ngendon, 9½ months, just able to stand, crawling after a mirror that we have given him to play with, in our yard. Notice very wide spread between thumb and first finger.
   8/19/37. 14 A 16.

2. I Karba, 15½ months, in a crowd during the visit of the *barong* (theatrical dragon) from Pengeljangen, while his father (Nang Oera) is teasing him by moving away from him a wooden toy figure with which he has been playing. Notice the cupping of the left foot. In front of the main temple.
   5/18/37. 9 C 5.

3. I Karba, 20 months, on our veranda, has been trapped underneath bamboo blinds that were stacked against the wall. He crawls out, and pauses, poised in low squat, balanced by hands lightly touching the floor.
   10/11/37. 17 G 6.

4. I Marti, 19 months, in similar position to I Karba (fig. 3) on edge of our veranda, watching her cousin (I Karsa) playing with a puppy. Same balancing in deep squat with tips of fingers just touching the floor.
   11/21/37. 18 Y 30.

5. I Sami, 10 weeks, in a neighbor's arms, in the road. Notice the flexibility of the toes forming an arch preparatory to the later cupping as shown in figure 2.
   12/8/36. 3 S 2.

1

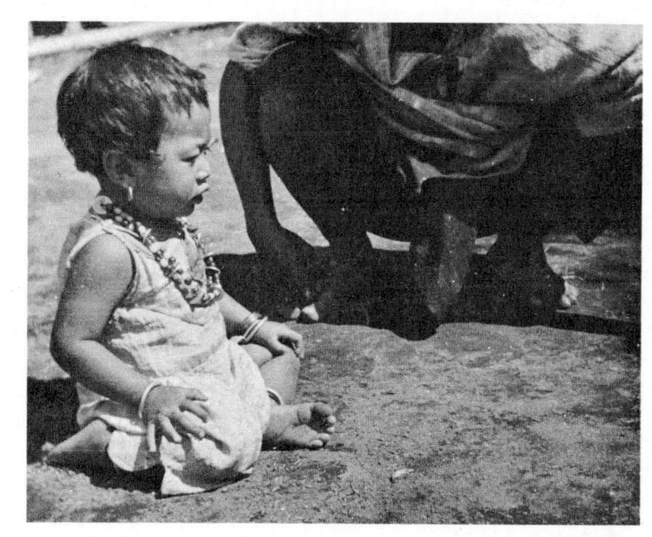

2

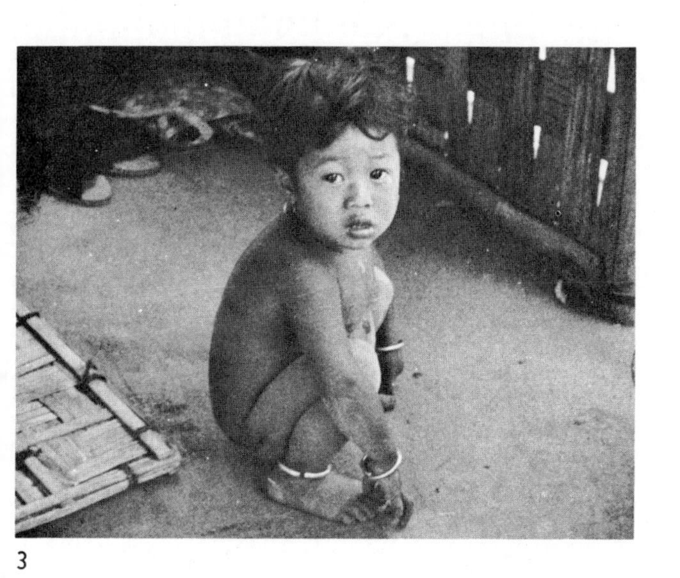

3

4

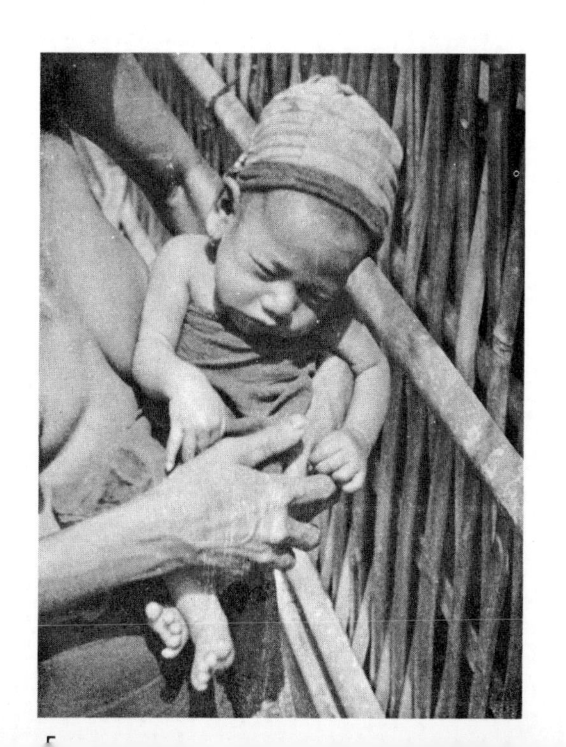

5

# PLATE XXXIV – EXTENSION OF BODY PARTS

Alternation between extension and flexion is a recognized aspect of the growth process, and individual children vary in the extent to which they tend toward one emphasis or the other. The Balinese are distinguished by extremes of extension, as also by the simultaneous occurrence of extreme flexion, as in the extension of Kenjoen's fingers and toes (fig. 3) at the same time that her shoulder is in extreme flexion.

1. I Tongos, 10½ months, seated on mat in Nang Goenoeng's yard. Poised with arms widely extended, fingers flexed, pivoting in seated position.
10/9/37. 16 Y 41.

2. I Tongos, on the same occasion, with I Karba, 20 months, back to camera, one hand extended and the other hanging relaxed.
10/9/37. 16 Y 11.

3. I Kenjoen, 34½ months, with oldest sister (I Karmi) and older brother (I Gata) with a coconut shell cup of rice, on steps of her house. Fingers and toes are in extension, but shoulder is drawn in, presenting such a discrepancy that it looks almost as if two pictures had been taken.
2/12/39. 36 E 6.

4. I Sepek, 10½ months, reaching with fully extended fingers toward paper that is offered him by our assistant (I Made Kaler). Note the openness of the fingers, the lack of any premonitory grasping. Own yard.
4/30/37. 7 T 4.

5. I Sami, 4 weeks, in arms of his mother (Men Sama) after bath as she swings him sideways to dry him. Own yard. His arms are in extreme extension.
10/27/36. 3 B 17.

6. I Marti, 18 months, lying in front of her father (Nang Marti) in attitude of retreat from the doll which she had been offered in the yard of a neighbor (Nang Karma). In spite of her general air of retreat her legs and feet are in extension.
10/10/37. 17 D 25.

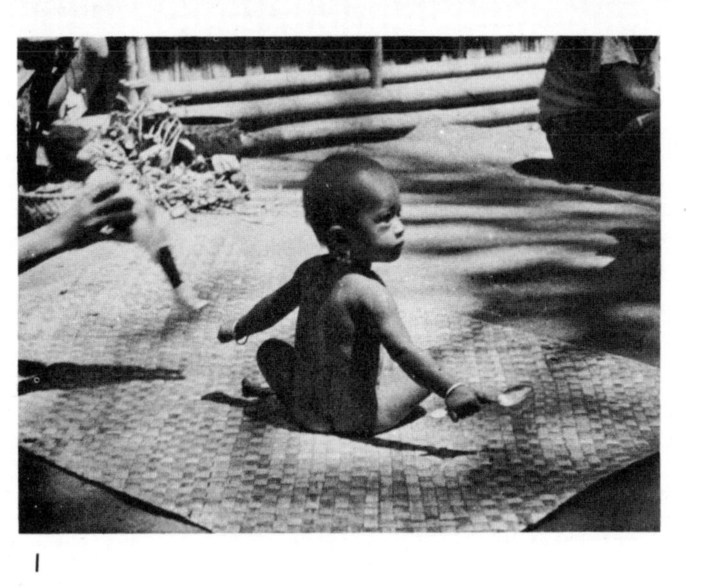

1

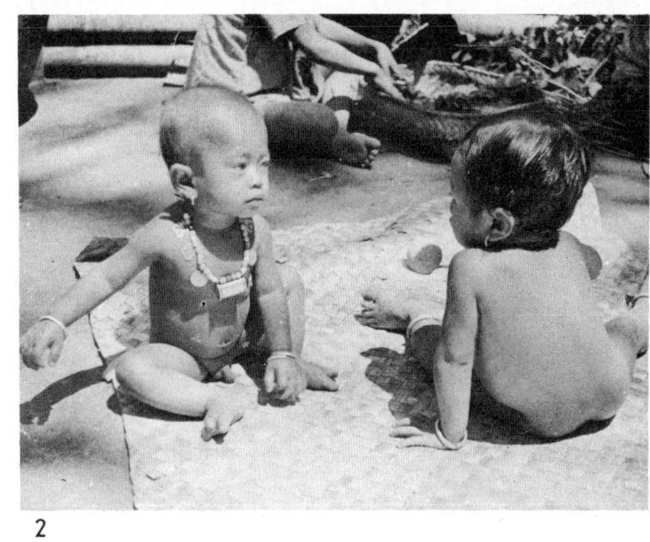

2

3

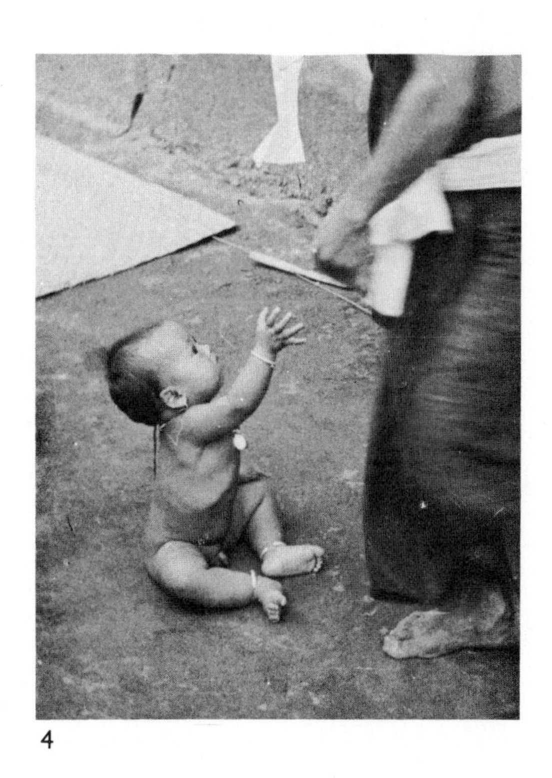

4

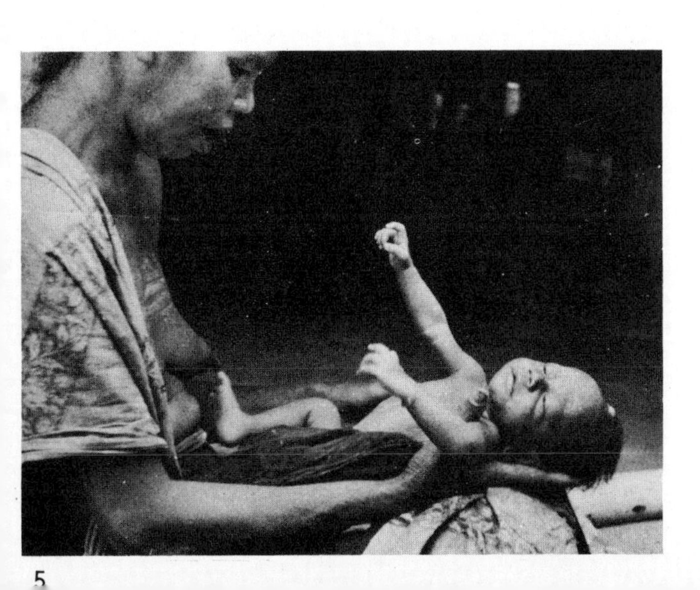

5

6

# PLATE XXXV – FLEXION OF BODY PARTS

Parts of the body of Balinese children remain in extreme flexion that does not parallel the degree of flexion in other parts of the body. So I Ngendon (fig. 1) is in a crying fit, with legs extended, but the little finger of his right hand remains in flexion not paralleling the other body movements. Or the flexion may be carried to an extreme of parallelism as in I Baroek's foot (fig. 2), the sole of which is flexed so as to press against the inner surface of the carrying sling. I Tongos (fig. 3) has both his hands in symmetrical tight flexion while later (fig. 4) his marked flexion of the legs, on which he pivots, is complemented by a hand in extreme extension, which, although reaching, shows no premonitory grasping posture. This same opposition between flexed legs and widely extended hand is shown in I Sepek (fig. 5). I Kenjoen (fig. 6) is in extreme flexion. I Karba (fig. 7) shows a form of flexion that would only be expected of an older, mature New Haven child, as part of a quiet, placid acceptance of the scene around him.

1. I Ngendon, 10 weeks, in the arms of his mother (Men Ngendon), crying furiously just before being put in his bath. Own yard. The little finger of his right hand remains in flexion, not paralleling his other body movements.
   1/19/37. 4 F 3.

2. I Baroek, 11½ months, in the arms of her mother (Men Kesir), the sole of her foot flat inside carrying sling, as part of general flexed position. Own yard.
   2/11/39. 35 W 37.

3. I Tongos, 8 weeks, being bathed in bark bath by his mother (Men Tongos). Nang Ngendon's yard. Both hands in symmetrical tight flexion.
   1/21/37. 4 Ga 23.

4. I Tongos, 8½ months, holding piece of a leaf in one hand and reaching out for another piece. Nang Goenoeng's yard.
   8/19/37. 14 F 25.

5. I Sepek, 10½ months, during the wait for his *otonin* ceremony, in the arms of his mother (Men Degeng), who has also taken Men Njawi's new baby (later named I Kowat) in her arms. As he spreads his hand wide on infant's head, Men Njawi protests, "Won't he be cruel! I Bawa [another baby about the same age] is cruel with it." Own yard.
   4/30/37. 7 V 1′. (*B.C.* Pl. 12, fig. 3)

6. I Kenjoen, 15 months, with her child nurse (I Gati) and her brother (I Gata) standing behind her, both eating rice from coconut shells. Own yard.
   6/20/37. 11 W 37.

7. I Karba, 15 months, with his cousin (I Karsa) behind him and neighbor child (I Lemes) playing in the road during the performance by a visiting theatrical show, the Wajang Wong from Kendoei. Taken in front of the temple.
   5/13/37. 8 U 34.

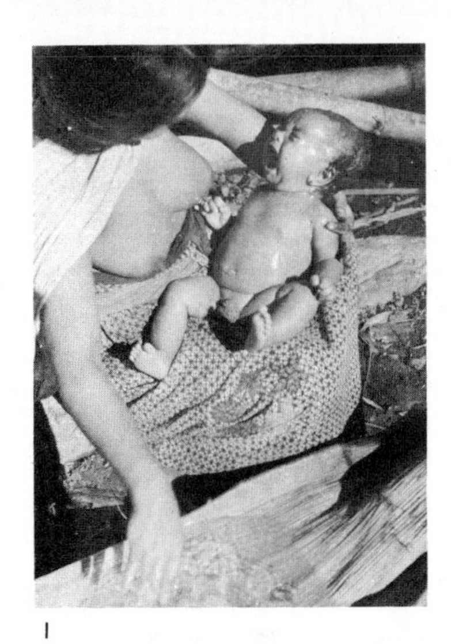

1

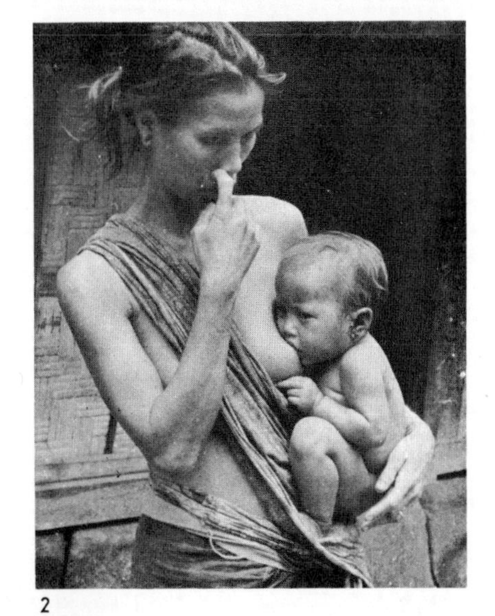

2

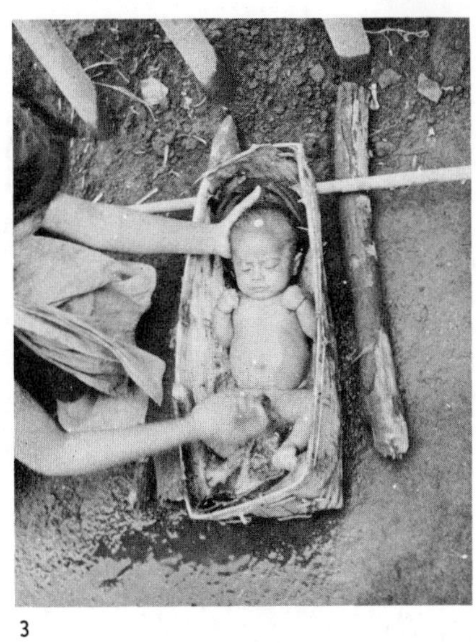

3

4

6

5

7

# PLATE XXXVI – OUTWARD ROTATION

The extreme amount of outward rotation among these Balinese children can be connected with the prevalence of eversion, the emphasis upon the ulnar side of the hand (Pl. XLIV). Culturally it can be related to the dependence upon an external pattern within which activity occurs, as for example the dependence upon the calendar, upon forming clubs that fine their members if they fail to carry out club activities, etc. From the observations of New Haven children, it would also be expected that they would have a need for space orientation—which they do—and a dependence upon other human beings as stimuli. This is a particularly good example in which it is possible to parallel the observations on one type of child—in New Haven—with the culturally regular behavior of the Balinese, as a group.

1. I Sepek, 10½ months, at his delayed *otonin,* stands beside little stool and pounds with wooden knife. Own yard. He pivots his trunk and rotates his knees outward, even to his little toe.

4/30/37. 7 U 38.

2. I Kenjoen, 34½ months, back to camera, entering the door of her father's house. Her brother (I Gata) stands outside holding coconut shell cup of food. Note the modulation of her hip activity, and the forefinger of her left hand, and the left leg of her brother.

2/12/39. 36 E 15.

3. I Karba, 20 months, sits on veranda of our house, rocks on his buttocks, pounding his bracelets on the cement, during a long teasing scene with his parents. Both his legs are rotated outward and he shows good lateral eye movements.

10/11/37. 17 H 28.

4. I Marti, 19½ months, in the arms of her grandmother (Men Bina) at a temple feast, with two visiting women from Biliboe. Marti is scratching her back with her arm outwardly rotated.

11/25/37. 19 I 4.

5. I Tongos, 10½ months, on mat in Nang Goenoeng's yard, playing with spoon, his mother (Men Tongos) watching something else. Note outward rotation of thighs, knees, foot, shoulder, and wrist, ulnar grasp of spoon, and everted feet.

10/9/37. 16 X 38.

6. I Karsa carrying a dipper of water in Nang Karma's yard. His cousin, I Karba, 36 months, stands behind him. Notice the way Karsa carries dipper, with outwardly rotated arm and ulnar grasp of handle.

2/12/39. 36 F 6.

1

2

3

4

5

6

# PLATE XXXVII – INWARD ROTATION

Inward rotation is found in much less extreme forms in Balinese children and is most characteristic of the children who betray the most passivity: I Raoeh (fig. 1), I Ngendon (fig. 2), and I Marti (fig. 3). The less passive children, I Karba (fig. 4 and 5) and I Kenjoen (fig. 6) show much less pronounced inward rotation. I Marta (fig. 4) shows a very slight inward rotation of the right leg and left ankle compared with her sister, Marti (fig. 5). Kenjoen (fig. 6), significantly, is expressing rejection by her inwardly rotated feet (cf. Plate LII, fig. 4). Balinese children go through a period when they withdraw into themselves, and this is least conspicuous in children like Raoeh and Marti (Pl. XII, fig. 6., and Pl. VI, fig. 5), who have shown more inward rotation throughout their earlier childhood and more withdrawn behavior.

1. I Raoeh, 19 months, standing between the legs of his child nurse (I Poendoeh), who is just shifting from carrying and holding him to care for another baby. His right knee is rotated inward, feet and toes turned inward, weak stance from waist down. Own yard.
   8/19/37. 14 G 31.

2. I Ngendon, 9 months, standing with the help of his mother (Men Ngendon) on our veranda. His ankles and feet are rotated inward.
   8/18/37. 13 Y 25.

3. I Marti, 19 months, in our yard with her cousin (I Karsa). Her right leg is rotated inward, her right arm rotated outward.
   11/21/37. 18 Y 21.

4. I Marta, 14½ months, in Nang Ngendon's yard. Note the very slight inward rotation of the right leg and left ankle compared with her sister, I Marti (fig. 3, above).
   2/11/39. 35 T 9.

5. I Karba, 18½ months, playing with marbles with his cousin, I Marti, 16 months, who stands in front of her father (Nang Marti). Our yard. Karba, on the point of picking up another marble, stands with very slight inward rotation of feet.
   8/20/37. 14 L 28.

6. I Kenjoen, 18½ months, to whom her mother (Men Karma) is offering a doll while her child nurse (I Gati) also attempts to get her to take it. Kenjoen is rejecting the doll, feet and toes inward rotated. Own yard.
   10/10/37. 17 C 38.

1

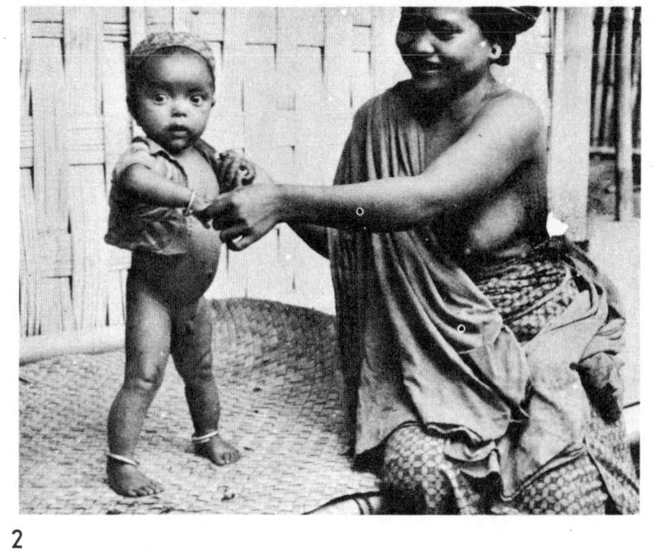

2

3

4

5

6

## PLATE XXXVIII – LOW TONAL ORGANIZATION

This plate illustrates an aspect of Balinese physique that appears to be a key to their entire development—the persistence of a tonus that is so low and meandering that it is reminiscent of fetal tonus, and is seldom seen in a well New Haven baby after a few weeks of age. On this plate the same type of very low tonus is displayed by I Sami, aged 10 weeks (fig. 1), who developed into a lively, wirily active child, and I Kenjoen, at 35½ months (fig. 4), who was one of the most vigorous and well-organized children in Bajoeng Gedé, and I Ngendon, at 6 weeks (fig. 5), who was a passive, low tonus child, and the unnamed baby of Men Reta (fig. 6), who was practically dying when this picture was taken. Although children differ among themselves as markedly as they do here, and differ when they are sick from when they are well, any one of these children is able to sink, suddenly, into this state of low tonus, which suggests an explanation of their flexibility, dependence upon external stimuli, and ability to maintain such discrepant postures, partly in flexion and partly in extension.

1. I Sami, 10 weeks, in arms of his mother (Men Sama), shows extreme lack of tonus; his arm is so flaccid that the breast has pressed way into it, his little toe of right foot is wrapped around the second toe, fingers extended without integration with the rest of the body. Own yard.
12/8/36. 3 S 3.

2. I Ngendon, 9 months, on mat on our veranda, held in sitting position by his mother (Men Ngendon). Her hand digs into his flaccid upper arm, his whole body is limp.
8/18/37. 13 Y 16.

3. I Baroek, 11½ months, in the arms of her sister nurse (I Kesir). Own yard. The child's back is relaxed and rounded.
2/12/39. 36 C 38.

4. I Kenjoen, 34½ months, in the arms of her father (Nang Karma). Kenjoen's older sister, I Ridjek, in foreground, carries her special charge, I Riboet. Kenjoen shows the same rounded back as the much younger I Baroek in figure 3 above. Own yard.
2/12/39. 36 C 37.

5. I Ngendon, 6 weeks, in arms of his father (Nang Ngendon), shows the same type of flaccidity, especially in small of back, which remains characteristic of him much later (cf. fig. 2 above). Own yard.
12/18/36. 3 V 10.

6. Unnamed baby of Men Reta, who died a week later, showing marked flexion and flaccidity. Our yard.
6/22/36. 1 N 4.

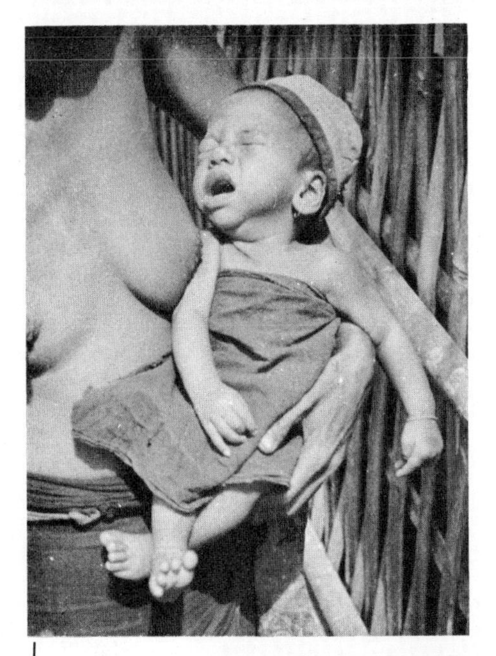

1

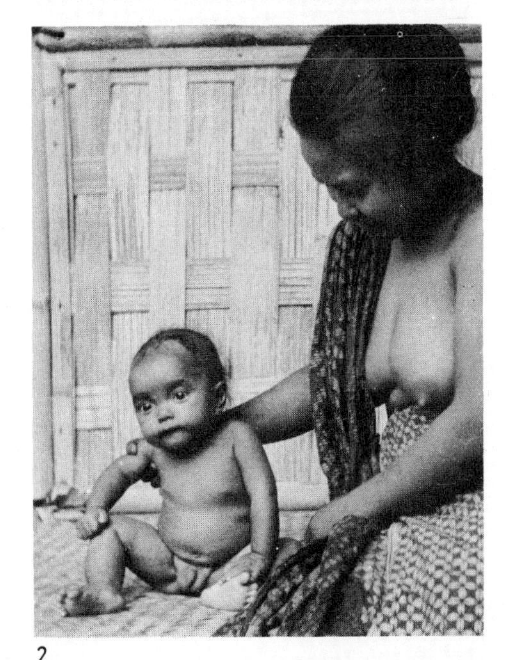

2

3

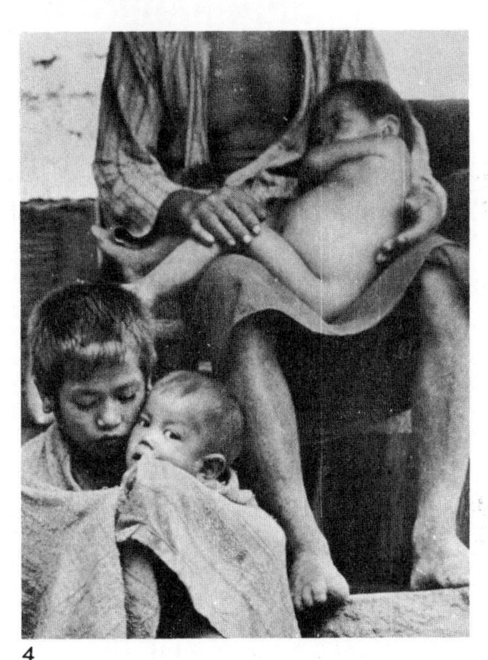

4

5

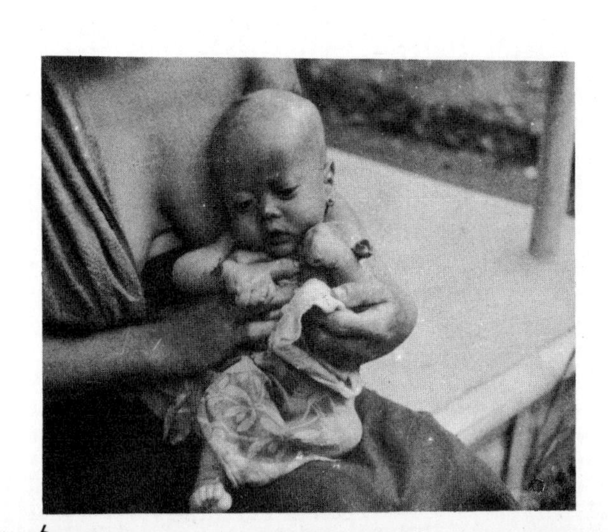

6

# PLATE XXXIX – FIRM HANDS

These three plates (XXXIX to XLI) show the range in the way Balinese adults and older children handle infants. To firm impersonal hands the child responds either with total passivity and limpness (fig. 4), by flexion (fig. 3), by resistance to the intent of the adult (fig. 7), or by oblique inattention. In all of the pictures on this plate, the child is having something done to it, and the firmness in the handling is not designed to set up any interaction with the child, but simply to support it, lower it, lift it, as impersonally as if it were a banana stalk or a bundle of rice sheaves (cf. *B.C.* Pls. 21, 22, 23, for hand postures).

1. I Ngendon, 6 weeks, in his own yard, at his 42-day-old ceremony, the *toetoeg kamboehan,* held for first children, in the arms of his father (I Sama), who will later be called Nang Ngendon. The father's hands form a firm encompassing support, thumbs under the armpits, from which the child is suspended. 12/18/36. 3 V 12. (*B.C.* Pl. 21, fig. 8)

2. I Ngendon, 4 weeks later, in the hands of his mother, I Maring, who will later be called Men Ngendon, held firmly but with the head unsupported and the feet resting against her protruded abdomen, giving him double support at sides of thorax and soles of feet. Own yard. 1/19/37. 4 F 12.

3. I Sami, 10 weeks, being lifted out of the bark sheath bath in his own yard, by his mother (Men Sama). Her left thumb presses on the top of his arm, and his head is given no support, her fingers widespread and firm. 12/8/36. 3 S 20.

4. I Sami, 7 months, in the hands of I Sambeh, younger brother of Nang Ngendon. Sami is now about 5 months older than in figure 3, but in this picture, when he is relaxed after a period of active creeping (see above Pl. XXIV, figs. 3, 4), he looks like a much younger child, completely supported by the older boy's firm hands. My notes read: "Climbs on I Sambeth, then collapses." Own yard. 4/30/37. 7 P 8.

5. I Djantoek (born in 1938 while we were away from Bali) stood on the lap of her mother (Men Singin), showing the reverse type of support, from behind, mother's hands firm, one of the child's feet on her lap. Own yard. 2/12/39. 36 I 29.

6. I Sepek, 10½ months, in the arms of his mother (Men Degeng), as she goes to put him down, at gate of Nang Degeng's house, at the *otonin* ceremony. Sepek, tensed instead of limp, supports himself also with left foot on mother's knee. I Leket (his brother) in foreground, I Njawi (mother's sister's daughter) in background. 4/30/37. 7 V 12.

7. I Kenjoen, 18½ months, being set down suddenly against her will to pick up marbles by her mother (Men Karma), whose hands are very firm. Nang Karma (her father) points to marble. Kenjoen responds with tense spread of thighs. Own yard. 10/10/37. 17 B 30.

8. I Ngendon, 27 weeks, on lap of his mother (Men Ngendon). Our veranda. Here his feet are firmly planted on mother's lap, but she grips him with such firmness that her fingers dig into his flaccid body. Compare the firmness of I Djantoek's body (fig. 5, above). 5/13/37. 8 T 32.

1

2

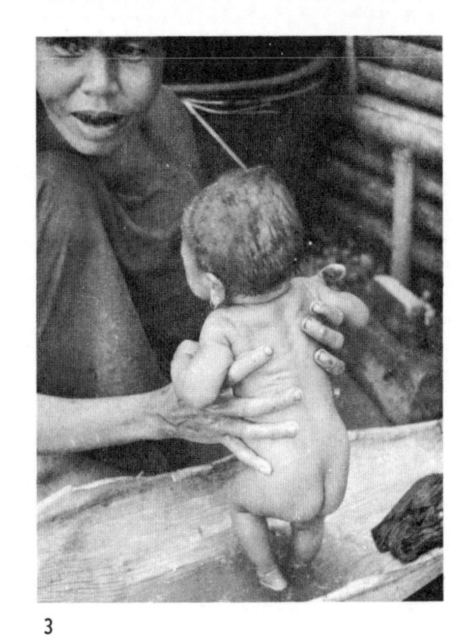

3

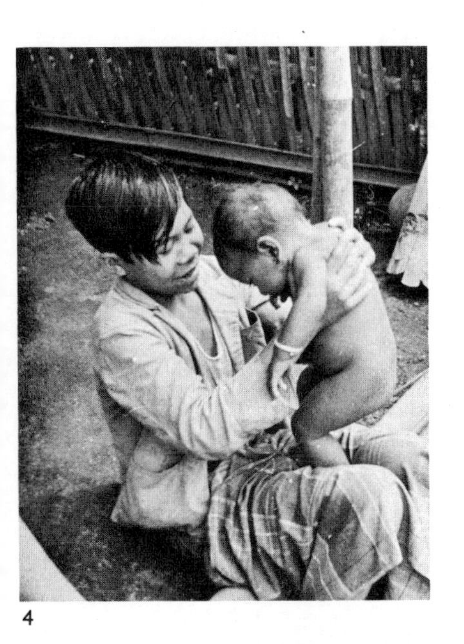

4

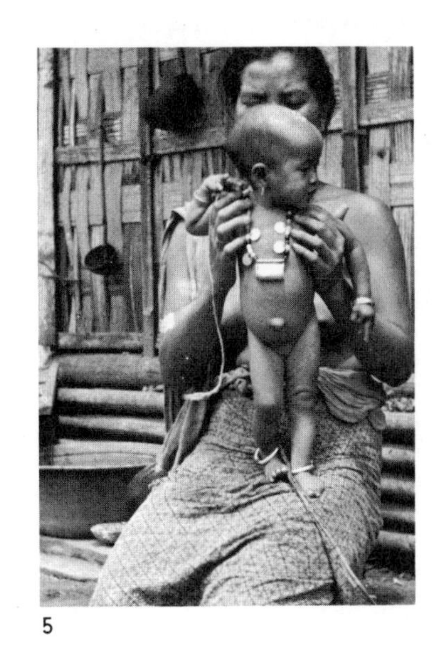

5

6

7

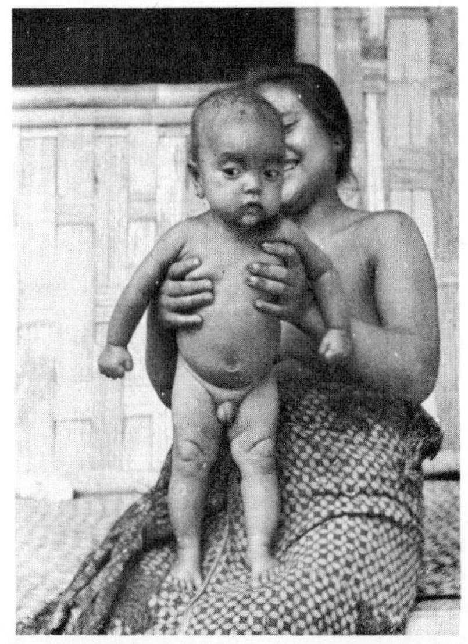

8

# PLATE XL – INATTENTIVE HANDS

The way in which Balinese children are carried, either in a cloth sling or in an arm which uses the sling as a model, sets a style in which the child can be treated safely attached to the body of the adult, like one of the adult's own limbs, and needing no continuous attention. The child is habitually relaxed in the sling, the spread position of the thighs provides a fit rather than a hold on the body of the carrier, so that ordinarily there is no holding on, or grasping or tensing behavior in the child to which the attention of the carrier needs to respond. Under these circumstances, the adult gives minimal attention, a light contact with the wrist (figs. 3 and 5), treating the carried baby as a convenient arm rest (figs. 2 and 7), or the hands may hang completely flaccid, permitting the sling to do all the work (fig. 9), or the child to lean against the seated body (figs. 6 and 8).

1. I Baroek, 11½ months, in arms of her mother (Men Kesir). Own yard. Baroek rests in sling and on mother's knee, mother looks away, and the right hand, although lying along Baroek's side, makes no contact with the child. 2/11/39. 35 W 38.

2. I Doemoen (age unknown) in the arms of her mother (Men Kesir). Our yard. This is the same mother (fig. 1)–more than two years earlier–carrying the child who died sometime after I Baroek was born, late 1938. Here, although Men Kesir is smiling at Doemoen, her left hand is inattentive. 10/10/36. 2 W 6.

3. I Tongos, 8 weeks, being suckled by his mother (Men Tongos) in his own yard. Again her hand is unrelated to child. 1/21/37. 4 Ga 29.

4. I Marta, 14½ months, her head resting against her father (Nang Marti). Own yard. Her head rests against his shoulder, but his hands are unrelated to her. 2/11/39. 35 T 14.

5. I Karba, 24½ months, being suckled by his mother (Men Oera). Our veranda. Karba is held at such a precarious angle that his mother's firm hold on his left knee is necessary; nevertheless, her left hand hangs loose, although his head rests against the forearm. 3/1/38. 21 R 30.

6. I Raoeh, 25½ months, being suckled by his mother (Men Goenoeng). Own yard. Her hands are lightly cupped and unrelated to him. She has just been stroking the chicken that is now being held by I Poendoeh (the child nurse). 3/3/38. 22 F 15.

7. I Tabeng (age unknown) in arms of child nurse (I Ngembon), beside father (Nang Lintar) and older sister (I Meres). Own yard. Ngembon's hand hangs limp from wrist while Tabeng, firmly held in sling, rests foot against her lap. 2/12/39. 36 M 27.

8. I Sami, 7 months, after a period of very active play, falling into a momentary sleep in arms of I Sambeh (younger brother of Nang Ngendon). Own yard. This picture is two frames later than Pl. XXXIX, fig. 4. Sambeh's hands, a moment ago firm, while Sami relaxed upon them, now lie completely lax and inattentive. 4/30/37. 7 P 10.

9. I Baroek, 11½ months, in arms of her sister child nurse (I Kesir). Own yard. Kesir's hands are inattentive, her left finger just touches Baroek's ankle. 2/12/39. 36 C 12.

1

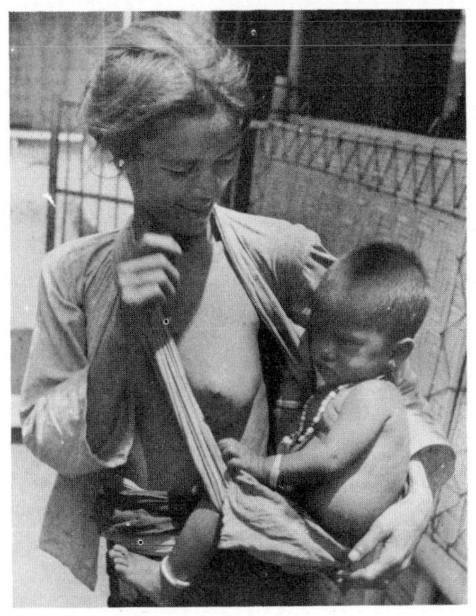

2

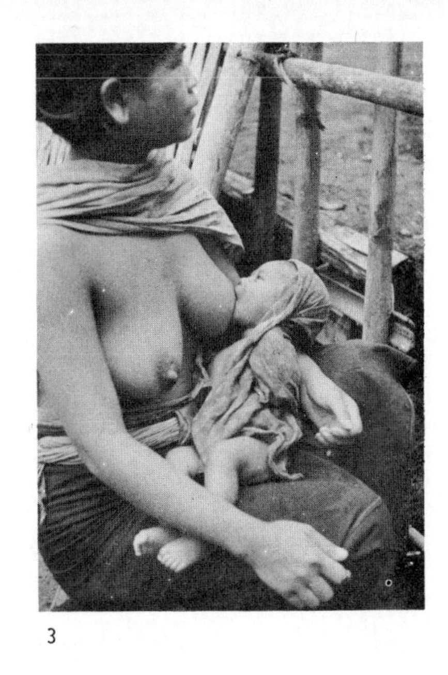

3

4

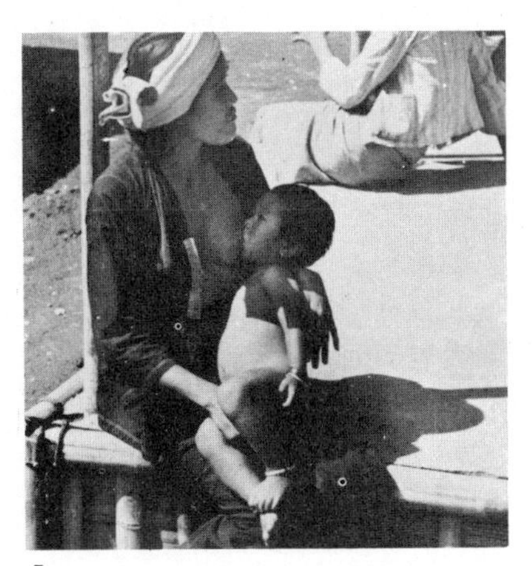

5

6

7

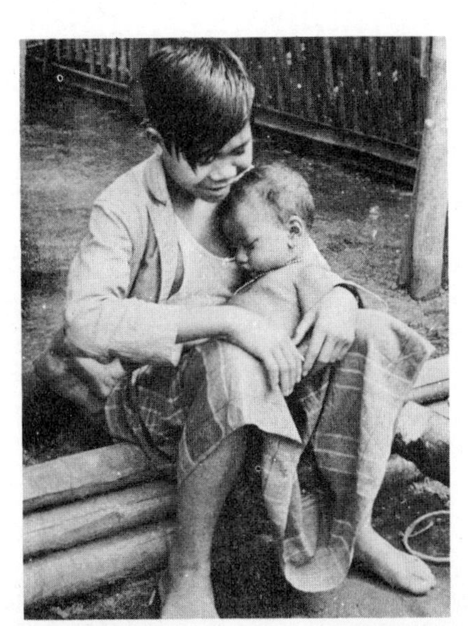

8

9

# PLATE XLI – ATTENTIVE HANDS

In strong contrast to the handling of children as objects or ignoring them as if they were parts of the own body to which one is temporarily not attending are all of those activities in which the older person is profoundly aware of the child's response, so that the situation becomes one of kinesthetic communication. Beginning with bathing and feeding situations and continuing through learning to balance and walk, to play musical instruments and to dance, there is learning by an active submission to the manipulating hands of another. The adult's hands are purposeful and attentive, the child's body becomes involved in response, so that the teaching situation develops from the original contrast between types of handling in which the child's response is allowed for and types of handling in which it is not. Men Sama feeding I Sami is a borderline case; she is holding his other hand attentively aware of its separateness, but expecting no other response except that of movement, while in the dancing lesson I Mario's whole body and the whole body of his pupil are involved.

1. I Djantoek (born in 1938 while we were away from Bali) being bathed by her mother (Men Singin). Own yard. Mother's thumb curves with accuracy under baby's head, fingers of her right hand move with precision over the surface of the baby's head.

2/12/39. 36 H 26.

2. Diasih, 13 months, being bathed by Men Diasih (I Wadi). Own yard. Mother's hands grasp the child firmly, and child's body is actively responsive.

2/11/39. 35 X 34.

3. I Karba, 11½ months, carried by his mother (Men Oera), whose hands guide his as he eats. Our yard.

1/26/37. 4 J 15.

4. I Sami, 17 weeks, fed by his mother (Men Sama). Own yard. Her little finger pushes the food expertly into his mouth, but the rest of her hand is not involved, although the thumb is extended. Her left hand holds baby's left hand firmly out of the way. Baby's body is actively tensed in response, little toe of left foot extended.

1/21/37. 4 H 24.

5. I Karba, 12 months, being taught to play the *tjoengklik,* a bamboo xylophone, by his father (Nang Oera). Our veranda. Father's shoulder muscles and arms and attentive hands are related to the grasp the child has on the handles of the mallets.

2/5/37. 4 S 3.

6. Dancing lesson in the village of Tabanan, given by I Mario, the Balinese *kebiar* dancer. Here the pupil must combine responsiveness and tensity and every muscle of the teacher's body is attentive and involved.

12/1/36. 3 N 35.

7. I Karba, 8 months, given a dancing lesson by his father (Nang Oera). Our yard. Father's left hand holds Karba's buttocks firmly, each finger and wrist involved, as his right hand demonstrates a dancing posture. Karba responds with his whole body to his father's teaching gesture and the dance tune which his father is humming.

9/30/36. 2 U 31. (*B.C.* Pl. 15, fig. 5)

1

2

3

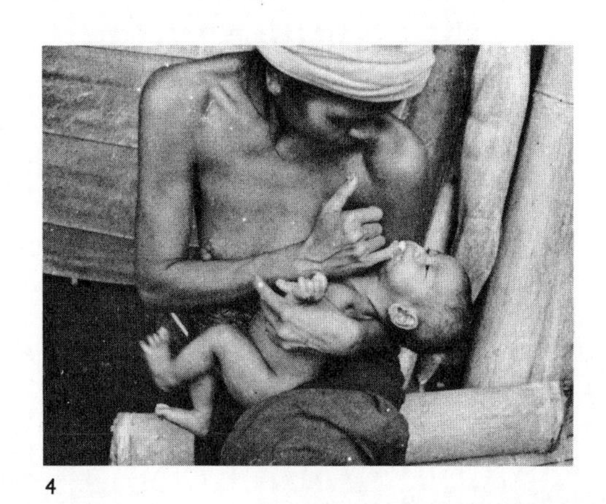
4

5

6

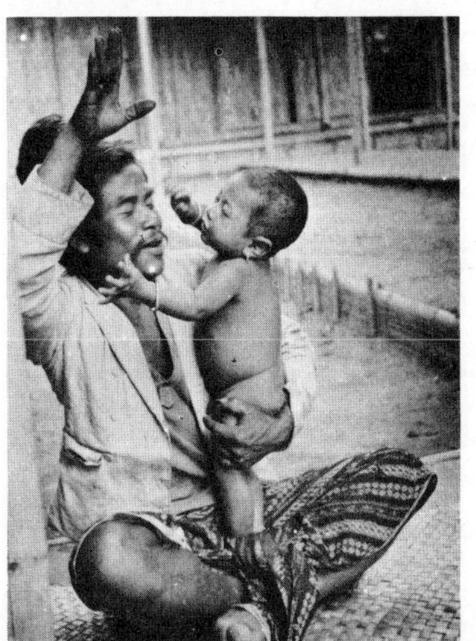
7

## PLATE XLII – PREHENSION

Balinese children's prehension is of a different character from the precise prehension found in the New Haven children at forty-four to fifty-two weeks. The impulse seems to come more from the upper arm, which is held loose and relaxed, the relaxation and lack of goal orientation extending into the fingers (fig. 3), leaving them in extension, or with a strong ulnar emphasis (cf. Pls. XLIV and XLV). The reaching hand does form in an appropriate premonitory posture (fig. 2).

1. I Sepek, 10½ months, grasping wooden knife by handle, walks with it. His father's brother (Nang Leket) in background. Own yard, delayed *otonin* ceremony. The thumb is used almost as a finger, the handle of the knife grasped with the ulnar side of the hand.
   4/30/37. 7 U 20.

2. I Tongos, 8½ months, reaching for escaping chick with which he has been playing. I Raoeh, 19 months, sits. Nang Goenoeng's yard. Tongos' hand is hyperextended and shows no premonitory grasping (cf. Pl. XXXV, fig. 4).
   8/19/37. 14 E 9.

3. I Karba, 20 months, supporting end of spoon handle against palm of his hand, as bowl of spoon is used to pry ball out of cup. Nang Goenoeng's yard. The cup, ball, and spoon had been presented as standard stimuli. Here there is poor thumb opposition and the hand shows the same type of lack of premonitory grasping as seen in figure 2 above.
   10/9/37. 16 X 2.

4. I Karba, 12 months, playing the *tjoengklik,* bamboo xylophone. Our veranda. Karba is crossing his mallets in a highly professional manner. The mallet handles are grasped with the ulnar side of the hand, poor thumb opposition, strong little finger.
   2/5/37. 4 R 29.

5. I Karba, 13½ months, reaching for the handle of the camera case. Our yard. He is using the thumb and volar surface of the left hand, with two middle fingers uninvolved.
   3/21/37. 6 D 35.

6. I Kenjoen, 18½ months, holding handle of spoon with ulnar grasp. Men Karma in background. Own yard.
   10/10/37. 17 A 27.

7. I Karba, 14½ months, exploring with great delicacy and hyperextended fingers the head of the younger child, I Sami, 7 months. Men Sama's yard. Note also the double twist in Karba's right large toe.
   4/29/37. 7 N 39.

8. I Karba, 17½ months, handing a ball to I Marti, 15 months, using total hand. Our yard. In the background, Nang Marti's hand, rippling, undulating, flaccid, parallels Karba's.
   7/17/37. 12 Y 10.

1

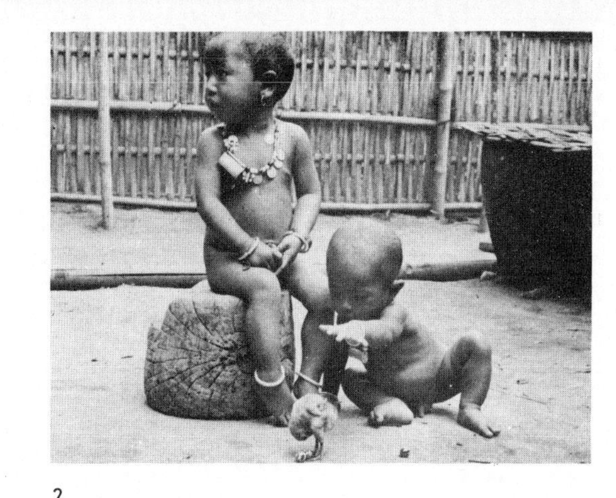

2

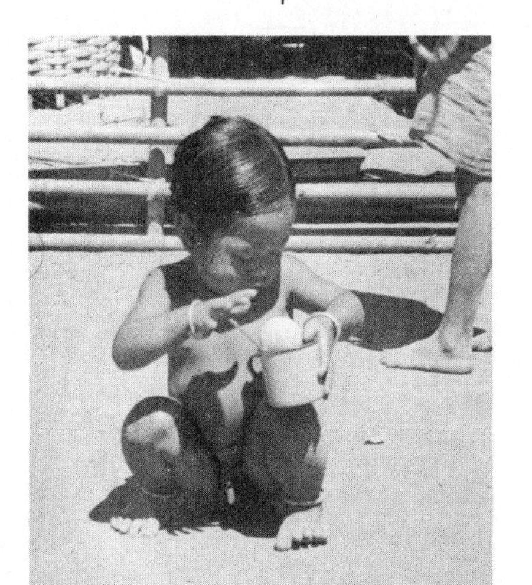

3

4

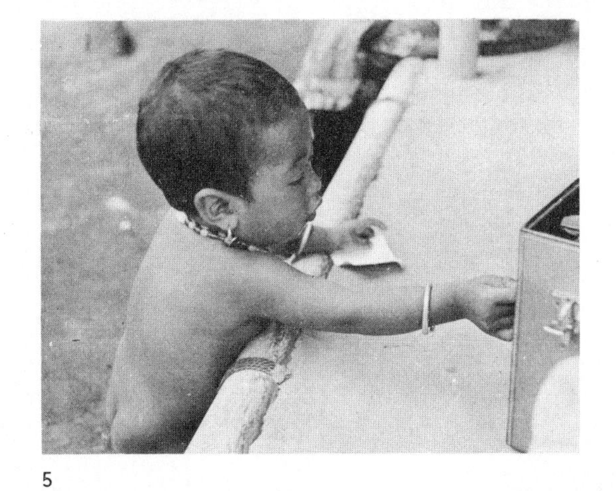

5

6

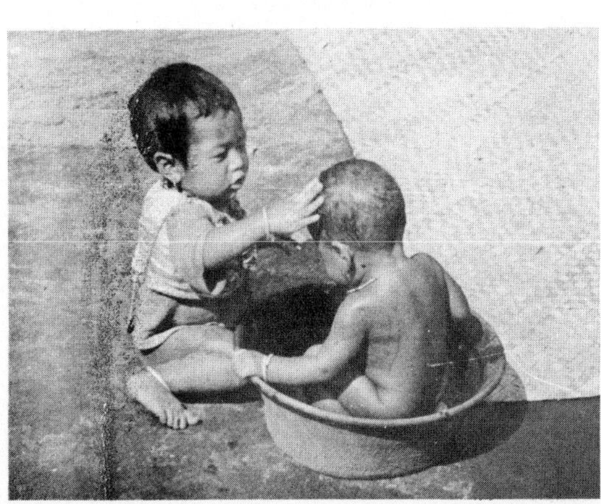

7

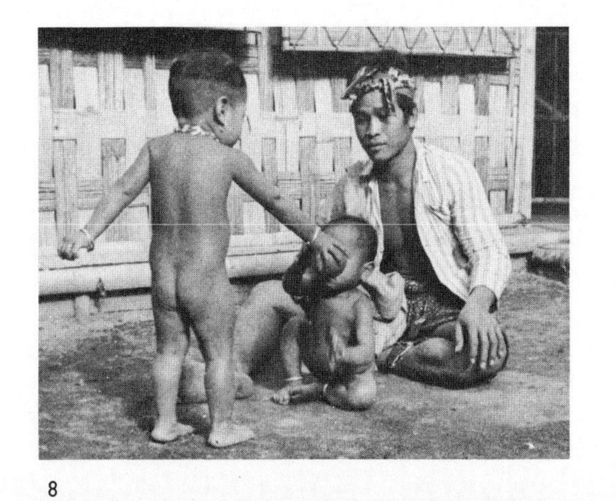

8

## PLATE XLIII – PREHENSION (continued)

This plate shows situations in which the children were offered or given objects by me so that photographs could be made of their treatment of objects. The marble, cup, ball, and spoon were all used systematically with a large group of children, but because of the openness of the play situations that resulted, it has been found more meaningful to select here pictures that show the peculiarities of Balinese prehension, especially the lack of use of the thumb (fig. 4), the use of the third and fourth fingers in place of the forefinger (fig. 2), and the prevalence of the ulnar grasp (figs. 1, 4, 7, 8).

1. I Raoeh, 9 months, reaching for metal betel mortar offered him as toy. Nang Oera's yard. Grasp emphasizes ulnar digits.
   10/24/36. 3 A 8.

2. I Ngendon, 9 months, on mat on our veranda, grasping a marble. His thumb is opposed to the second joint of his fourth finger instead of to tip of forefinger, which would be characteristic of New Haven babies at the same age.
   8/18/37. 13 Y 18.

3. I Ngendon, 11 months, in arms of his mother (Men Ngendon), playing with flowers. Ngendon's hands are delicately attentive to his task and his mother's hands are firmly clasped, providing a firm base for his activities. Our yard.
   10/11/37. 17 J 16.

4. I Karba, 20 months, and I Tongos, 10½ months, grasping the same spoon. Different ages but the same ulnar grasp. Nang Goenoeng's yard.
   10/9/37. 16 Y 8.

5. I Karba, 20 months, and I Sami, 12½ months, playing with cup, ball, and spoon. Karba is lifting out ball between thumb and middle finger; his forefinger is nonfunctional, little finger extended. Nang Goenoeng's yard.
   10/9/37. 16 W 25.

6. I Marta, 14½ months, reaching to pick up a marble, own yard. There is a delicate precision of grasping in the fingers but no premonitory tensing or radial deviations as seen in the New Haven children.
   2/11/39. 35 U 15.

7. I Marti, 16 months, beside our veranda, on the point of picking up a marble. Nang Marti, I Karba, 18½ months (back of Marti), I Karmi, and I Kesir in background. Ulnar fingers are flexed.
   8/20/37. 14 M 16.

8. I Raoeh, 19 months, facing Men Tongos, holds the flower toy in both hands. Right thumb is nonfunctional; ulnar grasp of wand. I Tongos, 8½ months, off left. Own yard.
   8/19/37. 14 F 4.

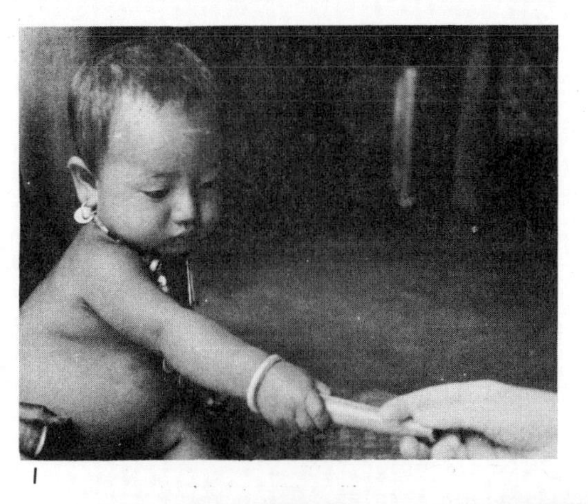
1

2

3

4

5

6

7

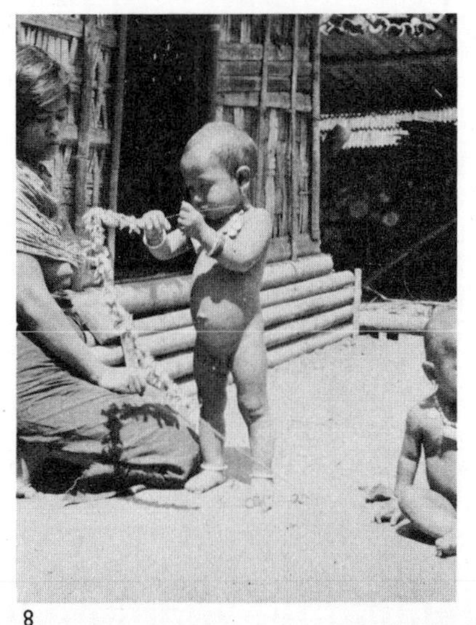
8

# PLATE XLIV – ULNAR GRASP

This plate further illustrates the importance of the ulnar grasp, often even to the point of positions of the hand that appear distorted, with a marked rotation of the wrist (fig. 4), or in a more extreme form in I Ngendon's position as he puts the spoon into his mouth (fig. 8). I Raoeh in his father's arm (fig. 3) illustrates well the way in which this use of the ulnar side of the hand fits into a form of learning in which the teacher manipulates from behind, rather than with a direct attack on an object or situation. The oblique empathic approach of the Balinese, the lack of focus and goal orientation, are all congruent with this emphasis on the ulnar rather than a radial grasp. In motor demeanor the strong little finger and ulnar emphasis go with the large amount of eversion and of outward rotation.

1. I Kenjoen, 26 weeks, in arms of her father (Nang Karma). Our yard. Ulnar grasp of his shirt by her left hand.

9/20/36. 2 Q 6. (*B.C.* Pl. 73, fig. 6)

2. I Karba, 24½ months, standing with handle of pinwheel, *tjakra,* in our yard, where a large crowd was gathered. My notes say, "Karba with *tjakra* turns it, hand gropes for position to give the turning wing a clip." Here there is a perfect ulnar grasp, both hands.

3/1/38. 21 Q 30.

3. I Raoeh, 9 months, on lap of his father (Nang Goenoeng). Nang Oera's yard. Playing with metal betel mortar, which he was shown taking in Pl. XLIII, fig. 1. Ulnar grasp with good wrist rotation.

10/24/36. 3 A 11.

4. I Raoeh, 13½ months, on lap of his father (Nang Goenoeng). Our veranda. Men Singin watching him idly. He grasps his father's cloth shawl, with three ulnar digits flexed, wrist rotated outward, working as a unit, while his left hand parallels his father's left hand, except that the father's hand is more segmented.

3/6/37. 5 H 22.

5. I Marta, 14½ months, leaning against her father (Nang Marti), as I Marti, 34 months, stands in front. Men Marti in background. Own yard. Marti is holding a marble, grasping with forefinger, thumb inactive.

2/11/39. 35 S 26.

6. I Tongos, 8½ months, grasping one end of flower toy, while I Raoeh, 19 months, just being lifted by Men Tongos, holds the other. Nang Goenoeng's yard. Tongos is grasping the toy with a complete ulnar grasp, flexed distal phalanges, thumb extended and nonfunctional.

8/19/37. 14 F 11.

7. I Raoeh, 25½ months, squatting next to his brother (I Goenoeng), beside his mother (Men Goenoeng), whose hair is being done by his child nurse (I Poendoeh). He is reaching for a marble, right hand holds another marble in an ulnar grasp, and left reaches out with a suggestive premonitory grasp. Own yard.

3/3/38. 22 E 31.

8. I Ngendon, 9 months, playing with spoon, held by his mother (Men Ngendon). Our yard. His left hand holds spoon in ulnar grasp, inwardly rotated.

8/19/37. 13 Z 21.

1

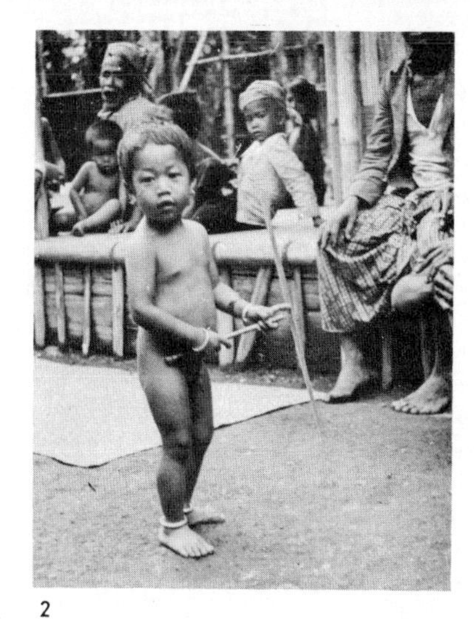

2

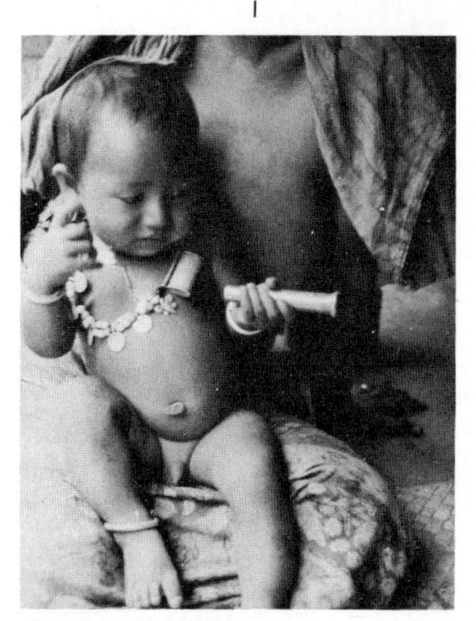

3

4

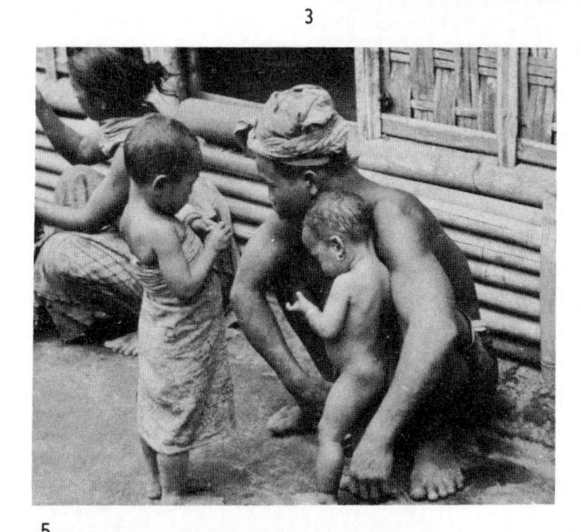

5

6

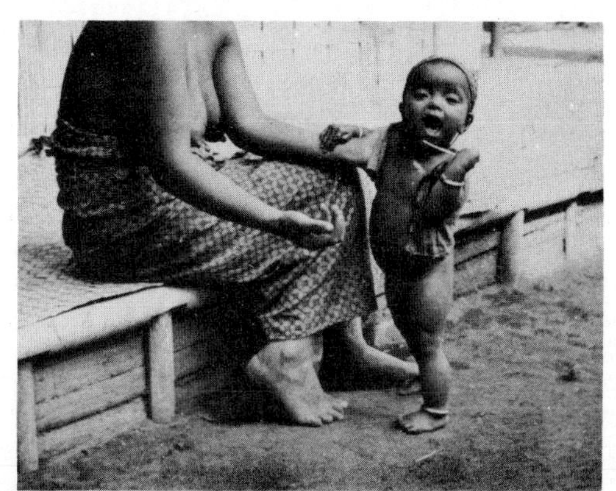

7

# PLATE XLV – THUMB OPPOSITION

Thumb opposition, grasping between thumb and forefinger, is very much less developed in the Balinese children than in the New Haven children. In the Balinese children there is a tendency to bring the finger to the thumb, rather than the thumb to the finger (fig. 7), to oppose the thumb to the inner surfaces of other fingers instead of to the tip of the forefinger (figs. 3, 5, and 8), and to use the mesial side of the thumb (fig. 7). The predominance of the thumb opposition to the third and fourth fingers supports the lack of premonitory posturing and the lack of radial deviation.

1. I Karba, 10 months, carried by his mother (Men Oera). Our yard. He grasps his mother's jacket between thumb and middle fingers.
8/12/36. 3 T 30.

2. I Marti, 19 months, holding a small piece of paper between thumb and middle finger. Our yard.
11/21/37. 18 Y 29.

3 through 5. In figure 3 I Kenjoen, 17 months, and I Marti, 16 months, playing with marbles in our yard, a crowd seated along veranda edge. In figures 4 and 5, I Karba, 18½ months, and Marti play with marbles, thumb opposing middle phalanx of middle fingers.
8/20/37. 14 M 25, 14 L 12, 14.

6 and 7. I Karba, 20 months, and I Ngendon, 11 months, playing with cup, ball, and spoon. Our veranda. Karba is holding a banana in the other hand, with mesial surface of thumb against the banana. In figure 7, Karba picks up a copper coin, drawing forefinger toward the thumb.
10/11/37. 17 I 28, 17 H 22.

8. I Tongos, 15 months, wearing man's headdress, holding marble in right hand, between thumb and fourth finger, where it has been placed by his mother, ball in his left hand. On mat on ramp in road. Photograph taken during a quick check-up visit to Bajoeng Gedé and Tongos was brought to be photographed at our request. Passive throughout.
3/1/38. 21 S 1.

1

2

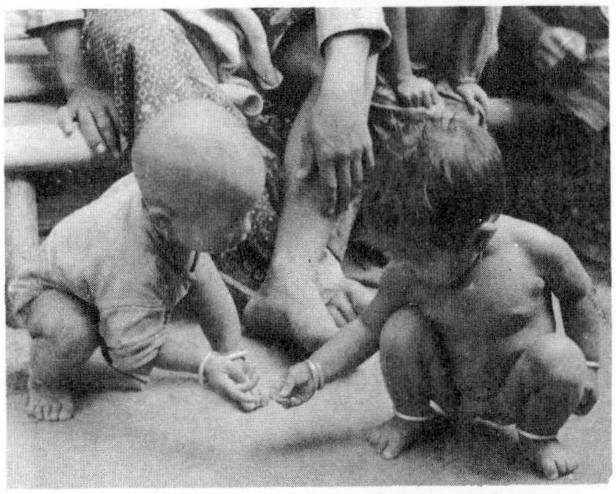

3

4

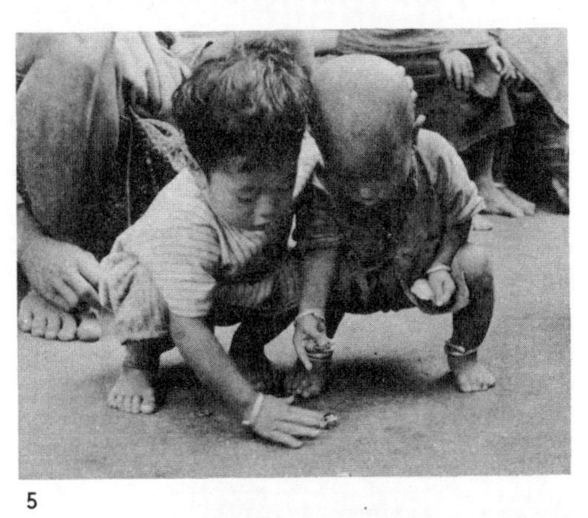
5

6

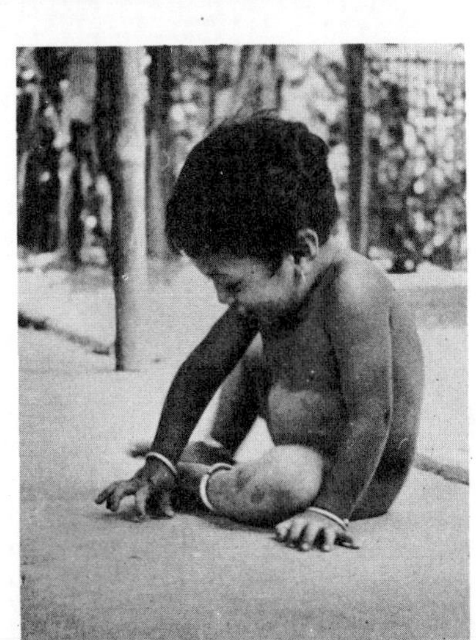
7

8

# PLATE XLVI — INDIVIDUATION OF FINGERS

The fingers of Balinese children, especially when not holding something, fall into the most complicated and seemingly discrepant, though often graceful, attitudes. The little finger appears to wander off (fig. 6), or the forefinger alone may be in extreme abduction (fig. 4, right hand). The inner surfaces of the second and third fingers may be used for grasping (fig. 2). The hand may be differentiated in a different plane, as well as the individual fingers (figs. 3 and 7). There is a frequent contrast between the way the forefinger and the little finger are used, and the two middle fingers (cf. Pl. XLIV). The middle finger is usually flexed or is used in grasping (figs. 6 and 7). These finger postures, highly stylized, are used extensively in the dance.

1. I Ngendon, 9 months, putting marble in mouth. Our veranda. Grasps marble between thumb and lunar digits. Forefinger and middle fingers are extended.

8/19/37. 13 Y 8.

2. I Raoeh, 37 months, carried by his father (Nang Goenoeng). Own yard. Grasps father's shirt between forefinger and middle finger.

2/12/29. 36 J 1.

3. I Sepek, 10½ months, being taken by his father (Nang Degeng) from his brother (I Degeng), who has carried him out. *Otonin.* Own yard. Degeng's left hand is flexed with thumb and fourth finger opposed.

4/30/37. 7 S 3.

4 and 5. I Karba, 24½ months, playing with pinwheel toy. Our yard. Nang Banera in background. Forefinger of left hand is hyperextended and abducted in figure 4; fingers of right hand are hyperextended in figure 5.

3/1/38. 21 Q 36, 32.

6. I Sami, 4 weeks, in lap of his mother (Men Sama). Own yard. Hand is open with middle finger flexed and little finger extended and abducted.

10/27/36. 3 B 14.

7. I Karba, 13½ months, our yard, during a morning of play with his cousins. Middle finger of left hand flexed.

3/21/37. 6 C 13.

1

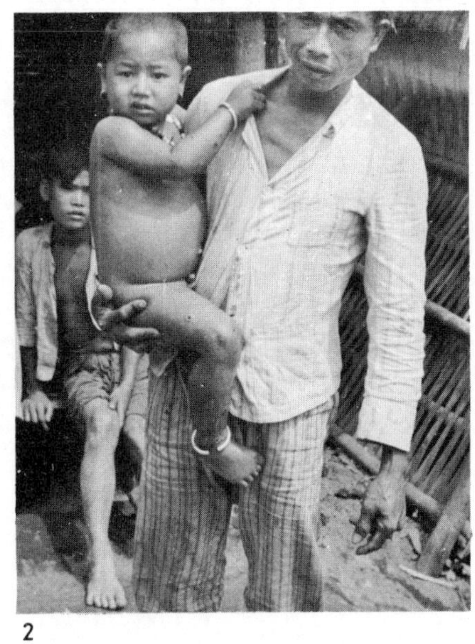

2

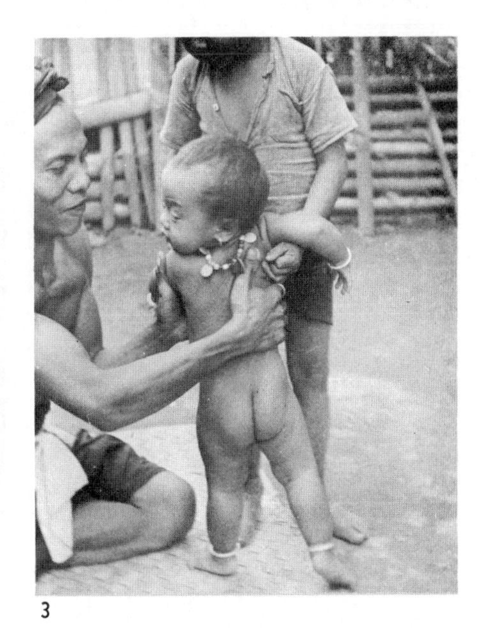

3

4

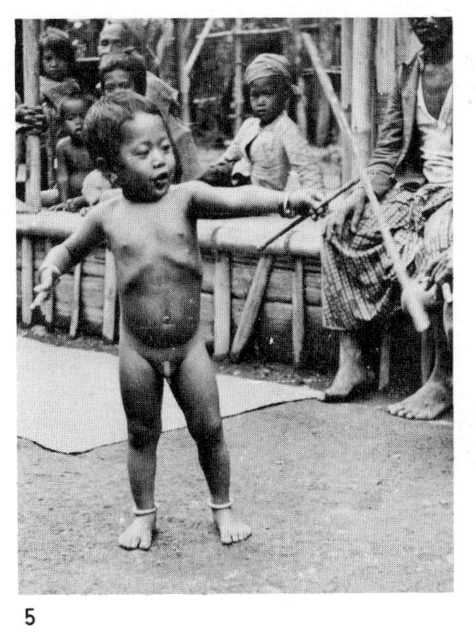

5

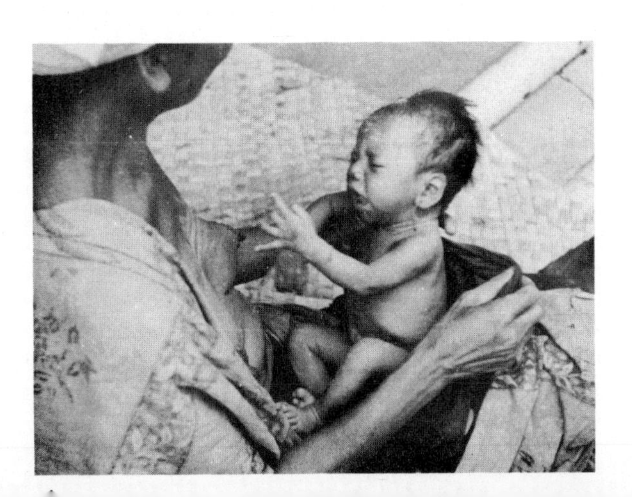

6

7

# PLATE XLVII – INDIVIDUATION OF FINGERS (cont.)

Types of individuation of fingers that would be classified in the Gesell series as hyperdifferentiation and disproportion can be seen, in context with pictures on earlier plates (especially Pl. XLVI), to be just a functional trait in the Balinese children. I Ngendon's hands (fig. 1) look as if they were living a life of their own, in complexity of flexion, and I Raoeh's bent-back fingers (fig. 2) show the same extreme flexibility, as does I Tongos' thumb, which is both flexed and extended (fig. 2), and I Kenjoen's right hand (fig. 3) against I Gati's shoulder.

1. I Ngendon, 9½ months, playing with mirror given to him by us as a stimulus. Our veranda. Though fingers are extended, they are flexed at distal joints.
   8/19/37. 14 A 6.

2. I Raoeh, 19 months, and I Tongos, 8½ months, playing with marbles. Raoeh's right hand is hyperflexed as he presses against it. Marked evidence of poor tonicity. Own yard.
   8/19/37. 14 E 13.

3. I Kenjoen, 17 months, in the arms of her sister nurse (I Gati). Gati is refastening the sling that carries Kenjoen (cf. *B.C.* Pl. 79, fig. 4). Our veranda. Ulnar fingers are curled in flexion.
   8/19/37. 14 B 4.

4. I Raoeh, 25½ months, in the lap of his child nurse (I Poendoeh). His brother (I Goenoeng) in right foreground. Left hand shows forefinger extension and ulnar flexion. Own yard.
   3/3/38. 22 F 4.

5. I Karba, 16 months, playing with a gamelang mallet in the road in front of our house, during a pause in the performance of the *djoget* orchestra. I Ngemboet, one of our staff, in background.
   6/9/37. 11 M 31.

1

2

3

4

5

## PLATE XLVIII – LITTLE FINGER ABDUCTION

The unusual strength of the little finger is illustrated by the role played by the ulnar side of the hand, where the length of the little finger in proportion to the fourth finger may possibly also be a factor, as in the adults' hands (figs. 2 and 3). The little finger is also found in this extreme abduction of a type only found in the New Haven children in very young infants. Mothers use the little finger to poke food into infants' mouths.

Another way of looking at the emphasis on the little finger is to recognize that the Balinese use the whole hand, which seen from our styles of hand use, looks like a disproportionate emphasis on the ulnar digits.

1. I. Kenjoen, 22 weeks, being suckled by her mother (Men Karma). Our yard.
8/23/36. 2 H 25. (*B.C.* Pl. 35, fig. 1)

2. I Kenjoen, 15 months, playing with a bit of cooked rice, in the lap of her mother (Men Karma). Her child nurse (I Gati) and her brother (I Gata) eating. Own yard.
6/20/37. 11 W 20.

3. I Ngendon, 22 weeks, carried by his mother (Men Ngendon) at a wedding ceremony during the offering in the *Poerah Deboene* (a temple where offerings were made for a marriage).
4/14/37. 6 U 31.

4. I Sami, 7 months, being suckled by his mother (Men Sama) as she squats. Our yard.
4/30/37. 7 O 33.

5. I Karba, 12 months, playing at playing the *tjoengklik,* bamboo xylophone. Our veranda.
2/5/37. 4 R 27.

6. I Karba, 36 months, leaning on his father (Nang Oera). Own yard.
2/9/39. 35 Q 28.

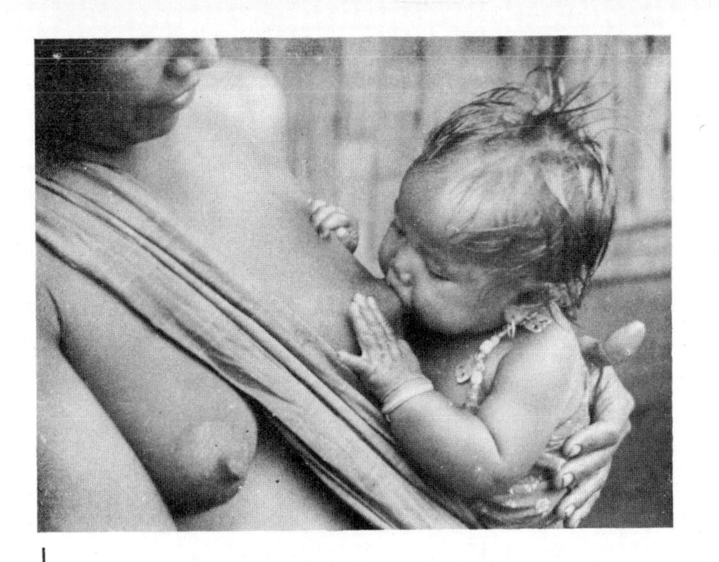

1

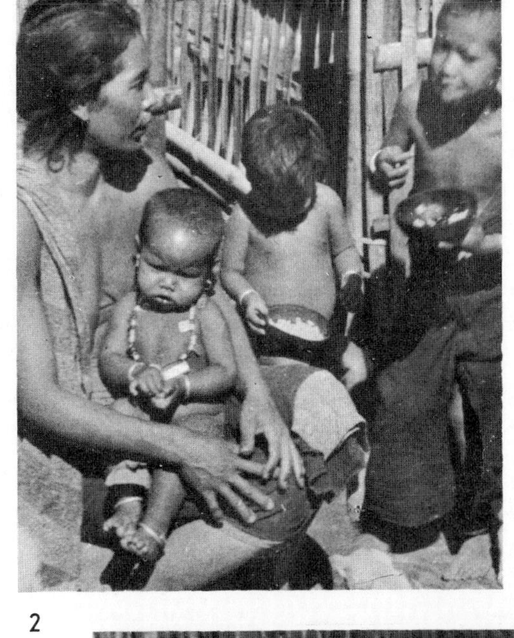

2

3

4

5

6

# PLATE XLIX – FOREFINGER EXTENSION AND ABDUCTION

This plate presents a series of extreme examples of forefinger extension and abduction. The recurrence of this behavior in small childrn is interesting in the light of the very strong taboo against ever using the forefinger for pointing. Instead, it is correct to use the thumb with an outward rotation of the wrist, so that there is a progression within the child's behavior from the disapproved to the approved kind of pointing, with the outward rotation of the wrist as a possible bridge. I Karba (fig. 3) shows mobile hyperextension of forefinger, rotated outwardly.

1. I Kenjoen, 26 weeks, on lap of her father (Nang Karma), her older brother (I Gata) standing beside them. Our yard. Kenjoen's forefinger is abducted, as is Gata's little finger.
   9/20/36. 2 P 13.

2. I Karba, 14½ months, standing alone in tub on high stand, mother (Men Oera) nearby. Own yard.
   4/29/37. 7 M 15.

3. I Karba, 16 months, with his father (Nang Oera), in the road during visit of the *djoget* from Malat.
   6/9/37. 11 M 32.

4. I Marti, 22½ months, dressed in store clothes, picking up a marble. Own yard.
   3/3/38. 22 D 12.

5. I Kenjoen, 15 months, in arms of her mother (Men Karma). I Gata, the knee baby, sitting on his mother's knee. Own yard. Kenjoen's two forefingers abducted meet in a fleeting version of a stylized prayer postion.
   6/20/37. 11 V 25.

6. I Raoeh, 13½ months, in his father's arms, our kitchen veranda. In the foreground, I Tjoengkoeh, a harmless psychotic artist who frequented our kitchen, is ornamenting a bamboo.
   3/6/37. 5 H 3.

7. I Marti, 16 months, and I Karba, 18½ months, playing with marbles, watching crowd in background, Nang Marti, I Ngembon, I Gati, I Karni, and behind them I Kenjoen, 17 months, and I Karmi. Our yard.
   8/20/37. 14 L 10.

8. I Marti, 34 months, on the lap of her father (Nang Marti) as he reaches into the betel tray for betel materials. Later, after this picture, Marti also picked on a piece of areca nut from the tray. This may be regarded as a special form of premonitory reaching. Own yard.
   2/12/39. 36 L 8.

1

2

3

4

5

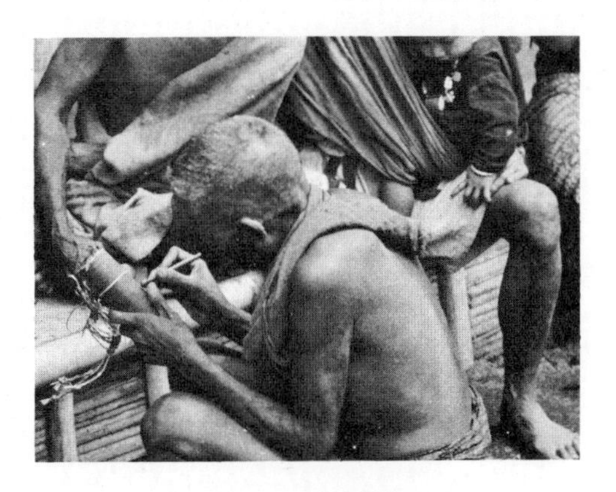

7

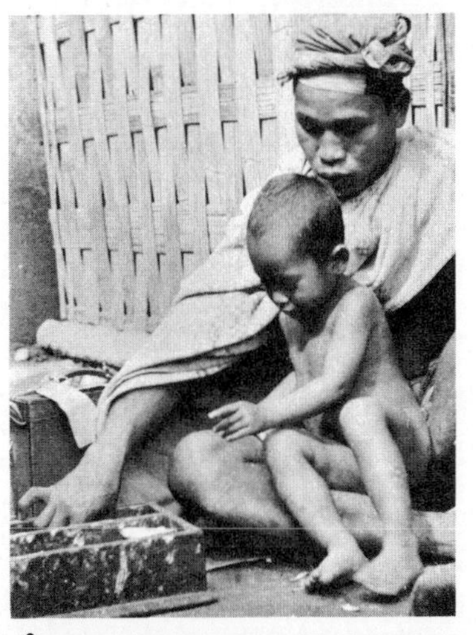

8

# PLATE L — CUPPED HANDS

Balinese children's hands are found in cupped and flowerlike positions with proximal extension and distal flexion. The fingers may be overlapped, so that the fourth and fifth finger are wound about the third and forefinger (fig. 1), or like a petaled flower (fig. 2), which I Raoeh shows at 13½ months. This is an example of the type of posture which very young American babies show and which persists in the Balinese. The fingers may be handled as a flexible cluster (fig. 4) with the distal phalanges flexed. I Karba's cupped hand (fig. 5), as a response to his father's hyperextended demonstrating hand, illustrates the relationship between these flexible cupped hands in childhood and the capacity for the adult hyperextended dance postures. I Tongos (fig. 6) has one hand flexed in a cluster and the other opening, illustrating the two complementary cupping positions. I Kenjoen in a temper (fig. 7) has her hand tensed in a clawlike position, which parallels in flexion the discrepantly extended hand of her child nurse.

1. I Raoeh, 7 months, at his *otonin,* on lap of his mother (Men Goenoeng). Nang Goenoeng's *sanggah* (family temple). Notice in cupping of left hand that all fingers including thumb are flexed toward a central point.
   8/14/36. 2 G 1.

2. I Raoeh, 13½ months, on the lap of his father (Nang Goenoeng), our veranda, as his father reties his headcloth, during a group conversation on our kitchen veranda.
   6/3/37. 5 H 32.

3. I Marta, 14½ months, standing, as her father (Nang Marti) offers her a young chick. Own yard.
   2/11/39. 35 U 26.

4. I Marti, 19½ months, in the arms of her grandmother (Men Bina) at a ceremony, *Saba Jeh,* in Peloedoe, hamlet near Bajoeng Gedé.
   11/25/37. 19 I 8.

5. I Karba, 8 months, being given a dancing lesson by his father (Nang Oera), who hums a dance tune as he demonstrates for Karba to imitate. Our yard. Notice father's hyperextended fingers.
   9/30/36. 2 U 29. (*B.C.* Pl. 15, fig. 4)

6. I Tongos, 10½ months, on the ground, reaching up toward the strange visiting woman against whom I Raoeh, 20½ months, is leaning. Nang Goenoeng's yard.
   10/12/37. 17 M 14.

7. I Kenjoen, 17 months, in a temper tantrum, carried by her sister nurse (I Gati). Our veranda. Notice ulnar action of Gati's left hand with middle finger hyperflexed.
   8/19/37. 14 B 1.

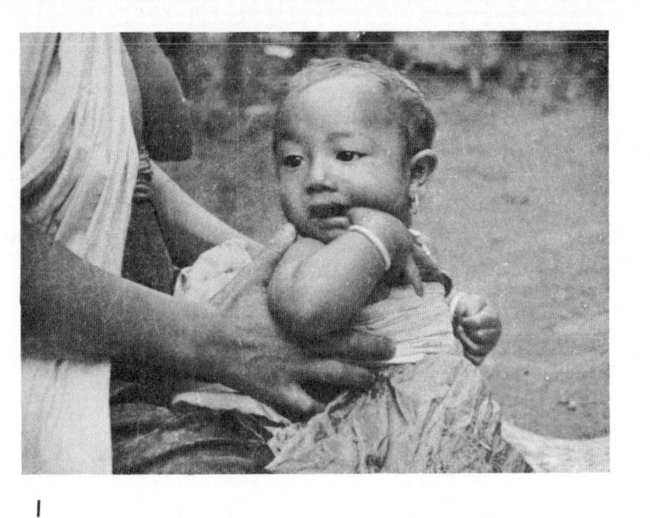

1

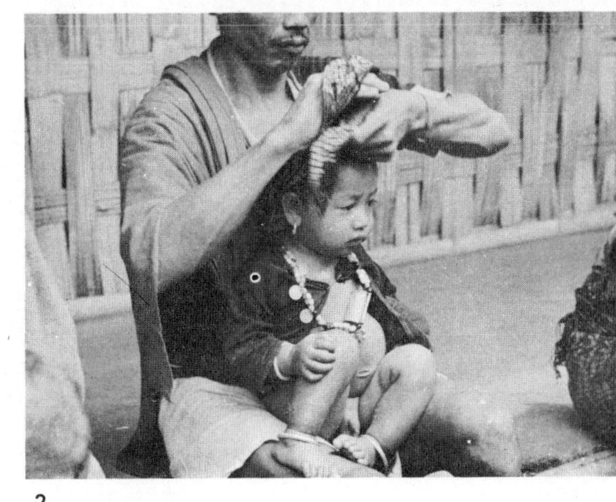

2

3

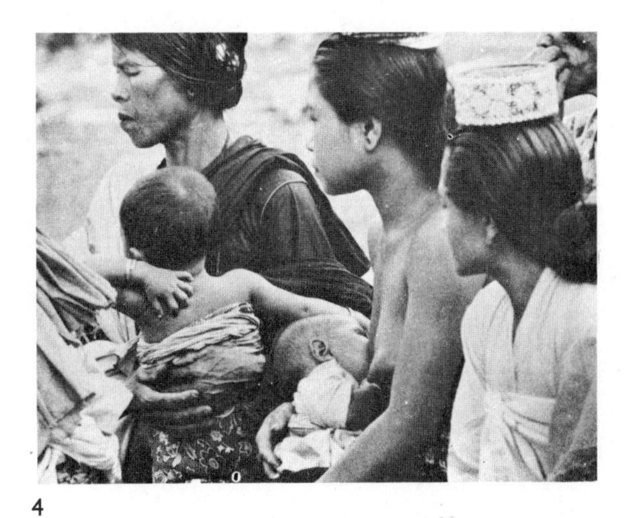

4

5

6

7

# PLATE LI – FANNING HANDS

Widely fanning hands are the complementary hand posture to the cupped hands shown on Plate L, sometimes in full hyperextension, as both of I Baroek's hands (fig. 3), or I Raoeh's left hand (fig. 2), sometimes in contrast, one hand drawn in and tightly flexed and the other hyperextended and fanned (fig. 5). Raoeh's hands (fig. 1), partly flexed, partly extended, show extreme lateral extension of both index and little finger. Note the great width of the web between the fingers. This wide web shows in Raoeh's hand at 25½ months (fig. 2). This wide spread shows between I Karba's little and fourth finger (fig. 4) and I Tongos' thumb and forefinger (fig. 5).

1. I Roaeh, 7 months, on the lap of his mother (Men Goenoeng) at his *otonin,* in family *sanggah* (house temple).
8/14/36. 2 G 4. (*B.C.* Pl. 100, fig. 2)

2. I Raoeh, 25½ months, in the lap of I Poendoeh (his child nurse). His elder brother (I Goenoeng) in foreground. Raoeh has been holding marbles which have just been taken from him by I Wara, a young man of the village. Own yard.
3/3/38. 22 F 2.

3. I Baroek, 11½ months, in the arms of her mother (Men Kesir). Own yard.
2/9/39. 35 Qa 8.

4. I Karba, 10 months, carried by his mother (Men Oera). Our yard.
12/8/36. 3 T 33.

5. I Tongos, 26½ months, ready to pick up ball (cf. Pl. XXXV, fig. 4, and Pl. XLII, fig. 2). Own yard.
2/12/39. 36 J 40.

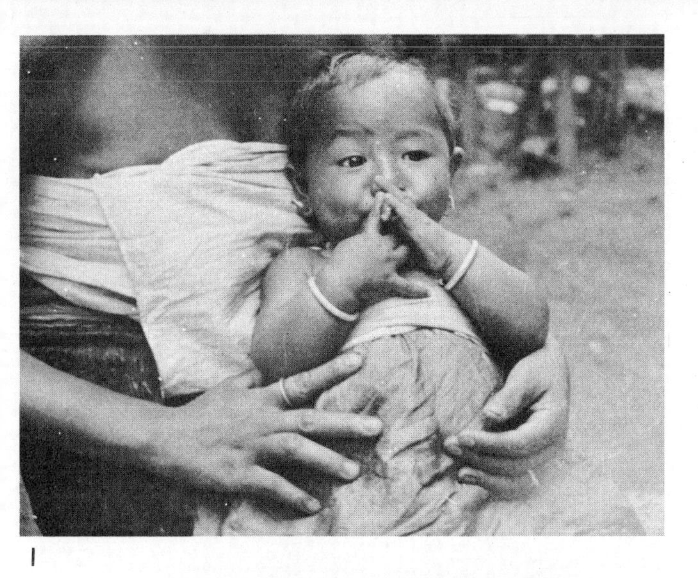

1

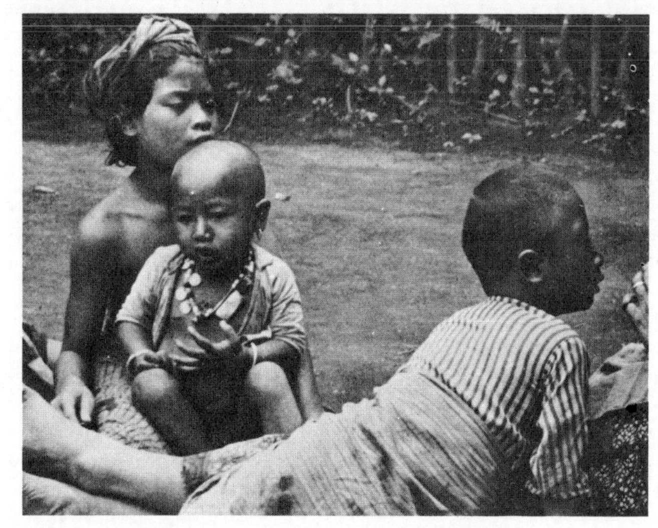

2

3

4

5

## PLATE LII – TOTAL FOOT POSTURES

Balinese adults use their feet to pick things up from the ground, so that the foot behavior with which a Balinese child comes in contact is more active than that of shoe-wearing adults. This plate is chiefly concerned with the way in which Balinese children's feet support their weight, which may be related to their lack of tonus. In figure 1, I Karba is balancing on his heel, as is I Marta (fig. 2). In figure 3, where Karba is learning to walk, his toes are off the ground, while I Kenjoen (fig. 4) and I Marti (fig. 5) also have their toes well off the ground. I Ngendon (fig. 6) and I Sepek (fig. 7) sit, heels together in perfect symmetry, but one big toe flexed, the other extended.

1. I Karba, 16 months, as his father (Nang Oera) is taking the mallet that belongs to the Malat *djoget* orchestra away from him. One of the Malat musicians in the background. Road in front of our house.
6/9/37. 11 M 25.

2. I Marta, 14½ months, standing, holding a fruit, her father (Nang Marti) squatting beside her. Nang Oera's yard.
2/9/39. 35 M 39.

3. I Karba, 13½ months, walking with the help of his bamboo rail walker, while his neighbor child nurse (I Djeben) sits on the rail. Own yard.
3/26/39. 6 F 14.

4. I Kenjoen, 18½ months, standing between the legs of her father (Nang Karma). Kenjoen has been gingerly and hostilely exploring a doll that I had introduced as a stimulus. Men Karma said, "Give it to your father." Kenjoen does not take doll but runs to her father and stands against his knee, rejecting the doll situation. I Gelis (a neighbor boy) in the background. Own yard.
10/10/37. 17 D 27.

5. I Marti, 16 months, eating a piece of Chinese cake, while the marble that I have rolled on the ground lies at her feet. Nang Marti (her father) behind her. I Karba, 18½ months, approaching. I Ngembon in background. Own yard.
8/20/37. 14 L 1.

6. I Ngendon, 26 weeks, seated beside his mother (Men Ngendon). Our veranda.
5/13/37. 8 T 22.

7. I Sepek, 10½ months, seated on mat between his father (Nang Degeng), elder brother (I Degeng), and his uncle (Nang Leket). His *otonin*. Own yard.
4/30/37. 7 S 30.

1

2

3

4

5

6

7

## PLATE LIII – TOE POSTURES

Throughout life, Balinese toes are more highly differentiated than the toes of Americans, accustomed to wear shoes. They have the flexibility that most barefooted people have, and in addition their toes show the same type of individuation as their fingers and the same type of multiple capacity to intertwine made possible by the low tonal organization. Balinese children's toes overlap (figs. 1 and 2) and curl up in the same type of postures found in the fingers (Pls. XLVI and XLVII), or cup like the cupped hands (Pl. L). The fingers of I Karba's left hand (fig. 7) parallel the position of the toes of his left foot, and each of I Kenjoen's toe positions (fig. 2) is paralleled by the fingers of the same hand, while a different kind of parallelism is shown between I Marti's right foot (fig. 4) and her father's right hand.

1. Legs of I Kenjoen, 27 weeks. On the lap of her father (Nang Karma), our veranda. I Gata's hand and head show in background.
9/29/36. 2 T 14.

2. I Kenjoen, 18½ months, sitting near her mother (Men Karma), holding marbles. Own yard.
10/10/37. 17 B 11.

3. I Djantoek (born in 1938 while we were away from Bali) in arms of her mother (Men Singin). Own yard.
2/12/39. 36 I 24.

4. I Marti, 34 months, lying against her father (Nang Marti). Camera box in foreground. Nang Oera's yard.
2/12/39. 36 L 3.

5. I Raoeh, 19 months, clinging to Men Tongos, next-door neighbor, who has been playing with Raoeh, and I Tongos with the flower toy. Own yard.
8/19/37. 14 F 1.

6. I Marti, 22½ months, being dressed by her father (Nang Marti) in dress which has been bought in the market. Own yard.
3/3/38. 22 C 8.

7. I Karba, 15½ months, playing with wooden carving in a crowd during a visit from the *barong* of Pengelijan in front of main temple.
5/17/37. 9 C 14.

1 2 3 4 5 6 7

## PLATE LIV – DISASSOCIATED BODY PARTS

One part of the body, a little finger, as with I Ngendon's right hand (fig. 1), a hand, as with I Marti's right hand lying on her father's shoulder (fig. 2), an arm, as Men Oera's (fig. 3) and Men Singin's (fig. 5), may appear almost as if disconnected from the body, a bodily expression of the type of disassociation seen on the face of Men Madera (fig. 4). This capacity to disassociate a part of the body is sometimes institutionalized in trance behavior. There are special trance performances near Salat in which only the hand is put in trance, and sometimes a trancer will come out of a trance, but the hands will remain "in trance." (*B.C.*, Pl. 23, figs. 7 and 8)

1. I Ngendon, 10 weeks, being bathed in bark sheath by his mother (Men Ngendon). Own yard.
1/19/37. 4 F 8.

2. I Marti, 34 months, standing beside her father (Nang Marti). Own yard.
2/11/39. 35 T 20.

3. Men Oera, mother of I Karba, 36 months, sitting on own door step. Karba peeking out. I Renoe (neighbor) is carrying I Diasih (her father's sister's daughter's first child).
2/11/39. 35 Z 8.

4. Men Kesir, holding I Doemoen, age unknown. Men Madera, her children, I Madera behind her, and I Mawa, 11 months, climbing up the bank. Men Singin, extreme left, has been doing the hair of her sister (Men Kesir) as they all sit waiting for carriers to come to take our boxes out to the main road. A casual desultory group. Our yard.
10/28/37. 18 E 15.

5. Men Singin, pregnant, sitting on stone beside the opening in Nang Karma's fence, which leads into the next yard. Her sister (Men Karma) with I Kenjoen, 23 months, on her lap and I Ngembon (her sister's daughter) beside her during a scene in which each of her four sisters teased their children with Men Kesir's new baby, later named I Baroek.
3/3/38. 21 Y 36.

1

2

3

4

# PLATE LV — A DISASSOCIATED HAND

This is a single sequence of behavior in which the camera was focused on the bath that I Ridjek was giving I Riboet, and the other children were merely included because of the general composition of the group and a general practice of getting group scenes whenever possible. I Karba's attention shifted and wandered; he moved his head, moved his eyes, shifted his feet, changed his whole posture radically in figure 4, but during the entire four to five minutes, his left hand remained in the identical position, as if forgotten against the wall.

1 through 8. I Marti, 34 months, I Karsa, I Karba, 36 months, I Ridjek (elder sister of I Kenjoen), and I Riboet (age unknown), Ridjek's mother's sister's daughter, Marti, walking about eating, holding her sarong. Karba leaves his hand against the wall. Nang Karma's yard. Ridjek is bathing Riboet from a dipper of water which Karsa brings. During the entire scene, about four minutes, Karba's hand remained in the same disassociated position while he himself shifted about.

2/12/39. 36 F 4, 6, 7, 8, 9, 11, 12, 13.

1

2

3

4

5

6

7

8

# PLATE LVI – DISASSOCIATED EYES

Eyes look in one direction while action is directed elsewhere. Infant's eyes looking away from the breast parallel the disassociation in the eyes of the suckling mothers (cf. Pl. XVIII, where only one of the mothers is looking toward her child). These wide lateral glances, loose and poorly co-ordinated in the young children, are counterpointed in the highly skilled side glance which is used in the dance called a *ngeledet* in which the eyes are snapped in and out of an extreme sidelong position, in opposition to a sharp lateral head jerk. This is a characteristic type of interplay between everyday life and the theater, where counterpoint is very frequent, as when grief and strong sibling rivalry, the expression of which is forbidden in real-life situations, are heavily dramatized on the stage.

1. I Kenjoen, 26 weeks, being suckled by her mother (Men Karma) after a scene in which her older brother (I Gata) has been flirting with his mother, and Kenjoen had put her hand out on him. Gata put his hand on her, and then Kenjoen has gone straight to the breast. Our yard.
   9/20/36. 2 Q 2. (*BC*. Pl. 73, fig. 6)

2. I Kenjoen, 17 months, playing with spoon and cup. Own yard.
   10/10/37. 17 A 26.

3. I Sepek, 10½ months, after laughing and jabbering in the arms of his mother (Men Degeng), goes for the far breast—for just an instant. Own gate. I Njawi (his father's brother's wife's sister's daughter) in background.
   4/30/37. 7 V 18.

4. I Sepek, 10½ months, stands holding a flower. *Otonin* ceremony. Own yard.
   4/30/37. 7 T 30.

5. I Raoeh, 9 months, being suckled by his mother (Men Goenoeng), both looking away. Our yard.
   10/24/36. 3 A 5.

6. I Raoeh, 19 months, being suckled from one breast by his mother (Men Goenoeng) while he plays with her other nipple. Own yard.
   8/19/37. 14 G 33. (*B.C.* Pl. 47, fig. 8)

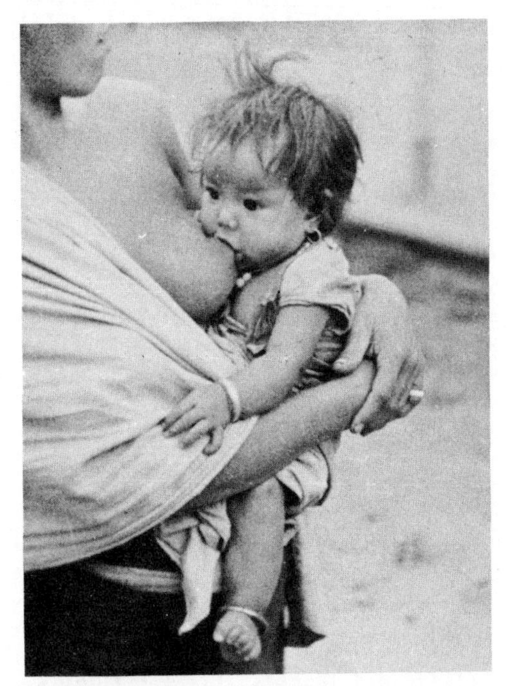

1

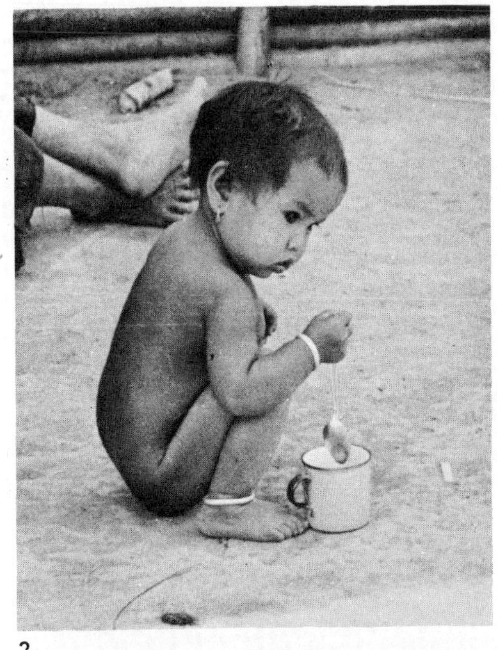

2

3

4

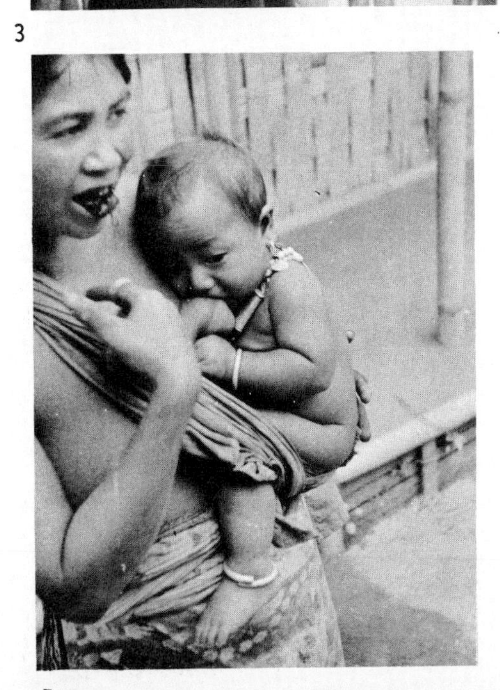

5

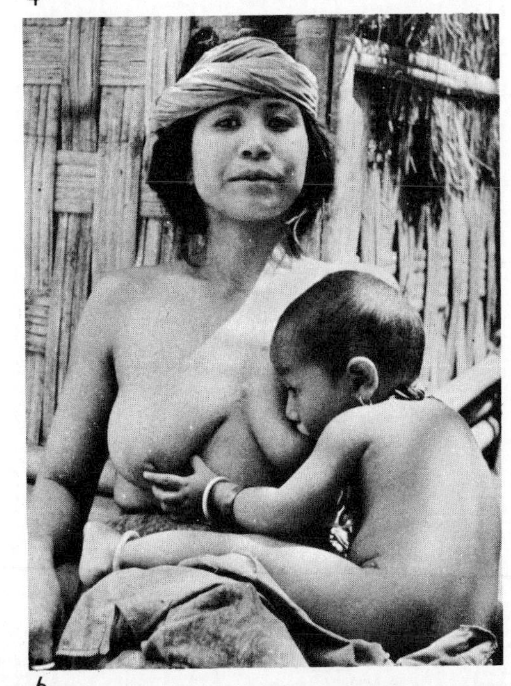

6

# PLATE LVII – TANTRUMS

The experience of screaming and writhing in a temper, often provoked by the teasing of an adult, is a familiar one to Balinese children. This plate shows I Kenjoen in the arms of her grandmother (fig. 1), her child nurse (fig. 3), and her older sister (fig. 2), who was taking over her care as she became heavier, all three ignoring her anger. Children show temper-tantrum behavior around two years of age, and this often changes into sulking (fig. 4), which may again be followed by violent tantrums before the child withdraws into a period of sullen nonresponsiveness. The child nurse (fig. 3) still had temper tantrums herself during the first year in which she cared for Kenjoen. I Nampah, the little girl in the right foreground (fig. 1), a neighbor, has just recently stopped having tantrums, and quite visibly withdraws from this situation, while the grandmother simply looks away and the older sister can laugh. Notice the consistency with which one arm is flexed in each of these tantrums.

1 and 2. I Kenjoen, 34½ months, held by her father's mother (Men Gangsar), screaming with rage (fig. 1). I Karmi (her older sister) is laughing. I Nampah, a neighbor child, stands gravely by. Kenjoen (fig. 2), screaming, in the arms of Karmi, her older sister, who has begun to care for her since she has become so heavy. Own yard. I Karba, 36 months, looking out of doorway, and Kenjoen's brother (I Gata) looking into doorway.

2/9/39. 35 P 5, 11.

3. I Kenjoen, 17 months, screaming, in the arms of I Gati, her sister child nurse who is her constant attendant, but who is not yet very skilled at arranging the cloth sling (cf. Pl. XLVII, fig. 3). Kenjoen had started to cry, got furious as the sling was rearranged, fell asleep long enough to take two frames (cf. *B.C.* Pl. 79, figs. 7 and 8), and is now crying again, while Gati pays no attention, looking fixedly away from her. Our yard.

8/19/37. 14 B 9.

4. I Karba, 15 months, sulking over the attention that has been paid by everyone present, Men Sama, I Sambeh, ourselves, to I Sami, 7 months, whose bath has just been photographed (cf. Pl. I, fig. 4). Sami squats in front of Karba trying to attract his attention. Nang Sama's yard.

4/30/37. 7 P 35.

5. I Marti, 34 months, sitting in the middle of the road, outside Nang Sama's house, refusing to accompany her father home, crying.

2/12/39. 36 E 28.

6. I Karsa, screaming with jealous anger. His mother (Men Singin) has been carrying I Karba, 29 weeks, who looks away while Men Singin picks up the screaming Karsa, who has been striking at her. Nang Karma's yard.

8/26/36. 2 I 36. (See *B.C.* Pl. 49, figs. 6 – 8)

7. I Raoeh, 20½ months, bent into a reverse arc, screaming in the arms of his mother (Men Goenoeng) while she and a visitor from another village laugh. Raoeh has been playing with cups and marbles, given him as a stimulus. He gets the marbles out of the cup, drops them in his lap. Men Goenoeng says, "Lost, with your penis." Raoeh screams with rage. Nang Goenoeng's yard.

10/12/37. 17 N 37. (*B.C.* Pl. 57, fig. 8)

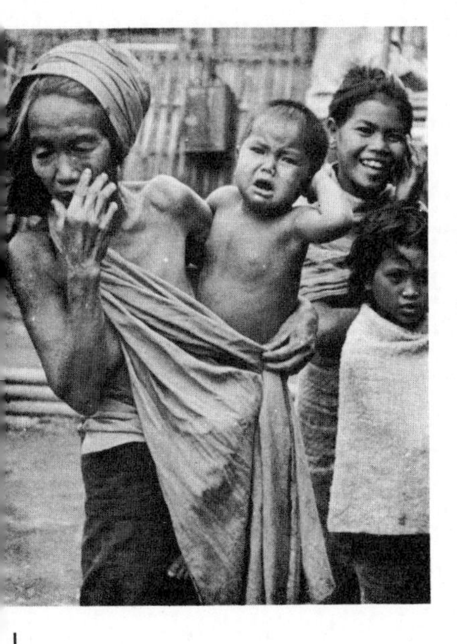

1

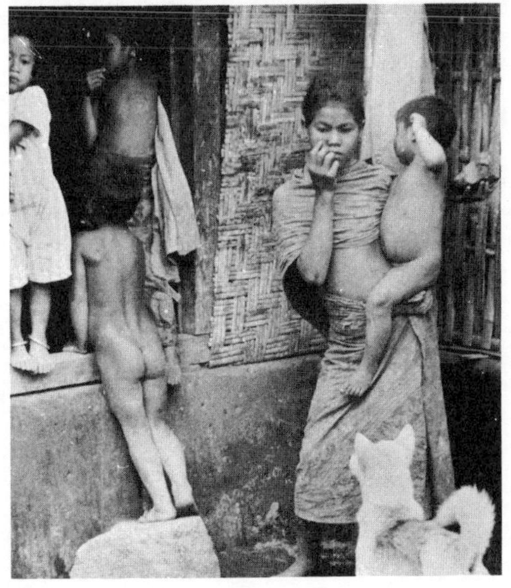

2

3

4

5

6

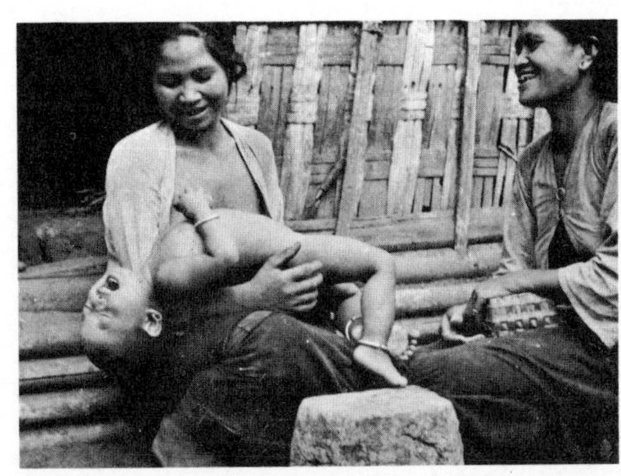

7

## PLATE LVIII – FINGER TO MOUTH

Balinese behavior, in spite of the amount of hyperextension, outward rotation, and relaxed response to outer stimuli, continually returns to the own body, as children sit, hands on knees, or people stand in crowds, fingering the surfaces of their own faces. When Balinese put their fingers into their mouths the pattern is to keep lips slightly parted, not sucking, finger exploring deep in the mouth (cf. *B.C.* Pl. 28).

In this plate it is the hand to mouth that intensifies the sense of a closed circle, each individual enacting a plot of withdrawal into the theater of his own body, so flexibly capable of living out any form.

1. I Raoeh, 13½ months, on the lap of a neighbor (Men Singin), beside his father (Nang Goenoeng). Our veranda.
3/6/37. 5 H 18.

2. I Karba, 24½ months, standing in front of his father (Nang Oera). Our veranda. Karba had not seen us since January 9, and was shy and frightened. He had hurt his fingernail, and now stands, sore finger in mouth, while his father eggs him on to be more responsive. "You said yesterday that you wanted to see the *Toean.* This is the *Toean's* house. Beautiful!"
3/1/38. 21 N 18.

3. I Meres, age unknown, with her father (Nang Lintar), shy, on our last visit. Own yard.
2/12/39. 36 M 18.

4. I Doemoen, age unknown, pressing on gum, but smiling delightedly in arms of Men Kesir. Our yard.
10/10/36. 2 W 8.

5. I Karsa watching us, knuckles to mouth, on the first day of our 1939 visit, and shy after not seeing us for a year. Own yard.
2/9/39. 35 O 4.

6. I Kenjoen, 23 months, hand to mouth, in the arms of her mother (Men Karma) while her brother (I Gata) has a tantrum beside her. Her sister (I Karmi) watches the camera, while a neighbor child (I Nandoer) grins at I Gata. Own yard.
3/3/38. 22 B 22.

7. I Marti, 34 months, standing behind her father (Nang Marti), shy at seeing us after a year. Note that mouth is open, finger exploring it (cf. *B.C.* Pl. 28). Own yard.
2/11/39. 35 T 21.

8. I Marta, 14½ months, running knuckles to mouth. Own yard.
2/11/39. 35 T 19.

1

2

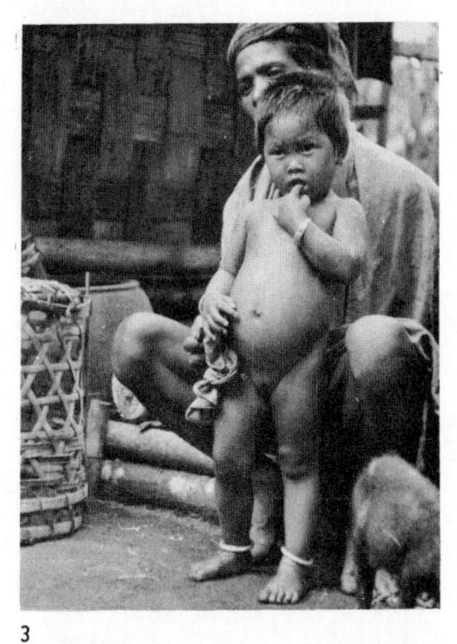

3

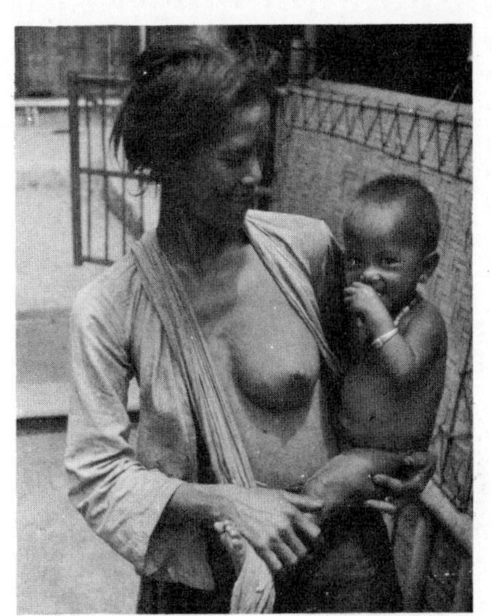

4

5

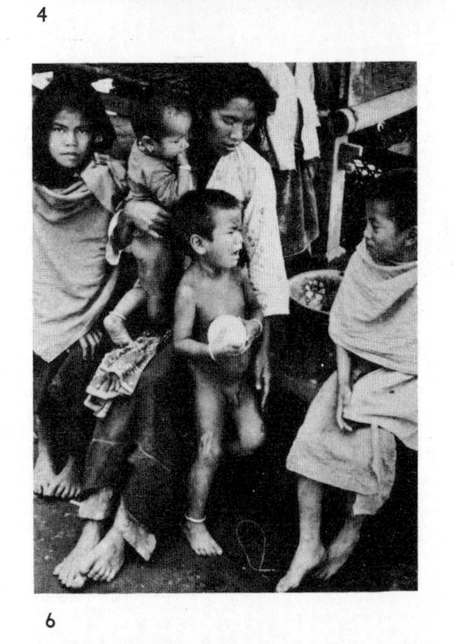

6

7

8

# *Conclusions*

THIS RESEARCH SET out to answer a variety of questions of different theoretical levels. We have brought to bear a battery of insights and analyses and invoked large bodies of research materials in the hope of illuminating, through a particular study of eight children in a Balinese cultural setting, our knowledge of growth in culture.

On the basis of this analysis, our general findings are:

1. Balinese Bajoeng Gedé children seem to go through the same general stages of behavior as American New Haven children, but significant and consistent differences can be identified in one sequence on which there was adequate material, the sequence from creeping to walking. Where the American children go from frogging to creeping on all fours, then to standing and walking, with squatting coming after standing, the Balinese children, who do much less creeping (and spend most of the period when American children are moving actively about either sitting or being carried) combine frogging, creeping, and all-fours behavior simultaneously in a flexible, interchangeable state, from which they go from sitting to squatting to standing. The distinctive elements here are: (a) the much greater activity of the American child, for whom creeping and all-fours behavior is a stage that is prepared for by the earlier stages of crawling, a stage that is precluded in the Bajoeng Gedé children because of the way they are handled; (b) the greater prolongation of the frogging posture, which may be at least partly attributable to the many hours spent each day astride a human hip; and (c) the way in which the Balinese child can rise to a squat and from a squat to standing, combined with the great amount of hyperextension. Seen in terms of the spiral analysis of development, the Balinese neglect the possibilities of the crawling stage and give very partial play to the creeping stage as contrasted with our pattern of cultural facilitation of crawling and creeping, but they reinforce the frogging-squatting sequence that we neglect by their methods of carrying the child on the hip and by the postures of the parents.

2. A second area of contrast is found in the Balinese emphasis upon extension and outward rotation, greater eversion, and use of the ulnar

side of the hand, as opposed to the greater inward rotation, inversion, and use of the thumb, with good volar opposition between thumb and forefinger, of American children. This is associated in Balinese culture with flexible and partial adjustment to peripheral stimuli, and dependence upon supporting forms, calendrical, spatial, and so on, to give orientation and continuity to the personality.

3. An area of contrast is found in the persistence in the Balinese children of a type of meandering tonus, characteristic of the fetal infant, with an accompanying very high degree of flexibility, and a capacity for the maintenance of positions of greater discrepancy, in which parts of the whole body or of the hand or the foot are simultaneously partly in flexion and partly in extension (Plate XXXI). The same children are able to assume, in the space of a few moments, postures of highly integrated or tense motor attention and of complete flaccidity (cf. I Sami, Plate I, Fig. 4; Plate XL, Fig. 8; and Plate XXXIX, Fig. 4).

With these three major findings in the analysis of the development of motor activity, we then attempted to find the specific ways in which the low tonal organization of the Balinese child was maintained, as this appeared to be central to the compliant sitting as contrasted to the great motor activity of American children, to the lower development of volar opposition and of the thumb in general, so that a more plastic, relaxed type of grasping obtained in Balinese children, and to the extraordinary flexibility and ability to maintain postures of toes and fingers, arms, legs, and head, that are found in fetal and very young infants but seldom persist beyond a few weeks here, such as the cupped and fanning hands in Plates L and LI. Balinese adult postures have been illustrated in this book only as adults in association with children have manifested them, but they are illustrated in variety in *Balinese Character* (Plates 21 and 22).

This low tonal organization, which Dr. Gesell describes as "meandering tonus," seems, then, to be a crucial feature of the behavior of these Balinese children. If it is looked at strictly in terms of the physique of the individual children, it might be attributed to physical stock and so be regarded as a genetic characteristic peculiar to some proportion of the people of Bali, or as a nutritional effect, which would have to be explored much further with special attention to the variations in diet in different parts of Bali, because this demeanor is common to the babies whom we have observed in other parts of Bali also.

When we add a cultural analysis, we can say that if the low tonus of the Balinese infant, which seems to resemble closely the tonus of the newborn, is taken as given, our task is to analyze the conditions under which it persists and becomes an important component in motor organization in later life. If we refuse the facile and unsatisfactory type of interpretation which is content with saying that children learn from parents and flexible parents will product flexible children, and seek for the specific nexus between adult and infant behavior, the way in which Balinese adults carry and handle children seems to be crucial. The sling permits the child to be attached to the mother or the child nurse without either person's making any active effort whatsoever once the sling is fastened, and when the sling is absent, the Balinese arm imitates it in relaxed inattention. This very light tie between child and carrier, tactily close, but without grasping by either one, seems to establish a kind of communication in which peripheral responsiveness predominates over grasping behavior or purposeful holding on.[1] Furthermore, the child is carried on the left hip, leaving its left hand free to grasp, but since receiving anything in the left hand is bad manners, the child's efforts to grasp are continually frustrated as the mother or the carrier pulls back the reaching left hand and pulls out the hitherto passive right hand that was lying relaxed against her body. It is furthermore possible to suggest that the persistence in the child of its low tonal organization is a continuing stimulus to the adult for the maintenance of the type of handling of the child that perpetuates this low tonus, so that while the habitual method of handling a child is passive and involves minimal interaction (Plate XL), even when the child is held firmly it is with a firmness that evokes passivity rather than co-operative activity (Plate XXXIX), and is transformed in learning situations into a functional interrelation in which the low tonus becomes high flexibility, capable of absorbing the pattern of activity that the teacher is imparting (Plate XLI, Fig. 6). This interpretation brings together the discussions of kinesthetic learning in *Balinese Character* (Plates 15 and 16), my original hypothesis that whole-body learning and total skin contact would be found to be of great significance in Balinese character formation, Frances Macgregor's original focus when, without any background information, she responded spontaneously to the photographs, and a recognition by the Gesell group that the relaxed, inattentive behavior of the mothers was of unusual interest.

This combined analysis highlights the importance of dealing with the living members of a society, young and old together, as an ongoing system, seeing the behavior of the infants evoked by and evoking the handling they receive as an integral part of the culturally regular behavior of the adults.[2] Whether the origination of this type of low tonal organization is to be placed hundreds of years ago in some change in child care, some change in nutrition, some shift in temperamental model for the whole population, or is to be regarded as reconstituted in each new generation of infants by some genetic predisposition or biochemical prenatal environment, if it is to persist and be translated into the particular patterns of motor-activity characteristic of the Balinese, the interaction between the infant with initial infantile flexibility and the adult in whom this flexibility is highly patterned is essential. We hypothesize that Balinese babies taken away soon after birth and reared by adults who lacked this flexibility would lose it also, and that Balinese adults presented with six-month-old New Haven infants, in attempting to handle them would themselves be modified, although not as drastically, as hands that expected limpness were met with tension and hands that attempted to teach through sensitive light tactile communication, and an expectation of co-operative bodily surrender to a movement pattern, would meet instead with wriggling, struggling intractability.

We know that when individuals migrate from one culture to another, their children to some degree, their grandchildren to a greater degree, their great-grandchildren even more, approximate to the new posture and gesture patterns of the new culture. Only by identifying which particular systems of communication, between adult and infant and between child and child, are operative in which changes can we begin to plan responsibly to rear children who do not merely repeat the behavior of previous generations but can initiate new behaviors that will in turn alter the behavior even of their grandparents. The focus of planned cultural change lies in learning, and the learning of the infant and the child and the response-evoking aspect of the child constitute one exceedingly important point where disciplined human intelligence can intervene constructively in the process of molding a culture closer to the needs and the capacities of all those who live within it.

Within our own existing culture, the extreme isolation of each individual home, while in many ways a handicap and a liability for the child's development, also makes it possible for individual pairs of parents to study the developmental pattern of each of their few highly cherished children. Instead of fitting each child to the procrustean bed of cultural expectations—modeled in Bali on a child that will have low tonal organization and be hyperextended, outwardly rotated, and ulnarly emphasized, with a high development of kinesthetic and kinesthetically modeled visual learning ability, modeled in the United States on a child who will be extremely active, focused, able to learn mostly by doing—the modern parent can begin to fit the way the child is handled to the particular sequences of growth, the particular readiness, the particular innate sensitivities and innate insensitivities, of a given child. It is probable that for every gifted individual whose innate potentialities have been fortunately elaborated, either because these potentialities fitted the cultural expectations or because those individuals who cared for him were specially congenial or skillful in evoking his abilities at the crucial moment, hundreds of equally gifted individuals remain mediocre or are deeply hurt by the lack of fit between a culturally stylized handling of developmental phases and the child's own rhythms.

We can attempt to alter our whole culture, and especially our child-rearing patterns, so as to incorporate within them a greater freedom for and expectation of variations. This is done, for instance, in the idea of reading readiness—that reading should not be taught until the child is ready to read and that for each child there is such a time. If the concept of spiral development as set forth by the Gesell group is added to this, it should be possible to chart out for each child when the next moment of readiness will come if something has miscarried at the first moment when a child could have learned most felicitously. A missed opportunity becomes the guide to the next opportunity as the child's individual rhythm of growth is interpreted within the human growth pattern as stylized by our cultural requirements and expectations.

Such a study as this both sets limits and points to new possibilities. To the extent to which Balinese peculiarities can be attributed to using as a model a particular physical type—as may perhaps be the case in the apparent greater proportional length of the little finger as contributory to the emphasis on the ulnar side of the hand (Plates XLVI,

XLVII, and XLVIII), or in the use of the high-breasted woman as the model for carrying-suckling behavior (Plate XVIII)—we can see the way in which a society can institutionalize for all those within it the special potentialities of some particular type. To the extent that individual children, however, continue to respond with such a high degree of individuality, even in the homogeneous, static culture of Bajoeng Gedé in 1936, we can see the enormous role that is played by the particular constitutional and temperamental endowment with which the child is born. We can develop our culture to allow play for each specific human gift, and provide elaboration for each generalized human potentiality, if we take into account both the special gift and the general gift, letting each inform and supplement the other.

M. M.

# *Appendixes*

# APPENDIX 1

# *Practical and Theoretical Steps Involved in This Research*

## BY MARGARET MEAD

IT IS THE CONTENTION of this book that research on human behavior is viable only when there is a climate of opinion within which its methods and implications are known. I therefore propose to outline here, in some detail, the assumptions and the procedures on which this work was based, the assumptions I was making at each stage and the procedures that were used.

Anthropological field work is based upon the assumption that human behavior is systematic, that it is one of the properties of human organism to systematize experience in ways that can be learned and taught and used in human interrelationships. It is further assumed that there is a basic psychic unity of mankind, which makes a human being, himself a member of a culture, a suitable instrument for the exploration of other cultures. In such research the principal tool is consciousness of pattern, so that the grammar of a new language is learned through the persistent search for regularities comparable to, although extremely different from, the regularities in one's own language. Training in anthropology is primarily a training through systematic exposure to records of the traditionally patterned behavior—the culture—of members of other societies, in an increasing consciousness of the varieties of pattern that may be found in kinship terminology, in house form, in religious ritual, and so on. The field work itself is necessarily highly selective, as one or two observers cannot possibly get full records of everything that happens in a native community. The fieldworker proceeds by making a large number of observations that he can refer to categories which have shown cross-cultural usefulness in previous anthropolgical work, such as language, social organization, technology. Some of these categories will be those that are traditionally recognized in our own culture, such as "language" and "the family"; others will be technical categories that are used only in scientific work, such as "ritual idiom" or "kinship system," and are not part of the general apperceptive mass of members of our own culture. To the task of filling in observations under headings that are already known to be useful, the anthropologist also brings a training in the expectation of form; that is, he will note whether or not the people live in "villages," and he will expect that villages will have formal elements, such as ritual arrangements of space, orientation to one or more ceremonial or public places, possibly status relations between more or less desirable areas, and so on. All these systematic observations are part of the regular professional obligation of any trained anthropologist. Hence in the Balinese field work upon which this Balinese study draws as a background for the choice of a village in which to settle, a preliminary survey was made of the characteristics of the culture, the divisions between the Hinduized culture of the plains, the more caste-dominated culture of South Bali as compared with North Bali, and the variations in complexity between the mountain villages and the plains villages. The village of Bajoeng Gedé was chosen for its isolation, its size (approximately 500 people),[1] and for the peculiar feature that many of the clay walls that traditionally surround each household courtyard in a Balinese village were unfinished, with loosely constructed fences through which it was easy to see what was taking place. As keeping track of the daily life of the village is always part of my field-work routine, a village in which it was not necessary to make a formal entrance to each household in order to see what was going on inside was sure to be a great economy. As it later developed, the unfinished walls could be attributed to the general low level of achievement in Bajoeng Gedé, the tendency to simplify every pattern without losing the formal essentials, which could in turn probably be attributed to the prevailing hypothyroidism of the area.

Once the village was chosen, a house site obtained, a house built, a household organized, the salient features of the community were mapped. Work on the language with our Balinese assistant, I Made Kaler, had already been going on for two and a half months; the grammatical forms had been identified, a large number of texts worked over, and a working vocabulary in some areas acquired.[2] In mapping such

[1] This approximate statement of size is because there is always some movement in and out of such a village, not because I do not respect exact numbers.

[2] Balinese is a very difficult language to learn to speak, as there are many shades of vocabulary difference dependent upon the relative caste and status positions of the speakers—we identified 17 such shades—and because the language is extraordinarily rich in specific words and poor in general-purpose words.

a community, a scale map is made, each house is given a number, the personnel of each household is recorded, with their age, sex, and relationships to each other, and by means of connecting genealogies the relationships of the individual members of the household to other households in the village are indicated. Considerable preliminary work has to go into surveying the social forms in order to know which categories of status are so important that they should be included in the household mapping. For Bajoeng Gedé these were: membership in the village civil hierarchy; membership in the village religious hierarchy; types of landholding; location of the field house (*pondok*) where animals were kept and from which some farm work was done; and membership in temple clubs. Sets of cross-referencing records, by name of householder, by name of wife, and so on, are then set up for use.

The daily routine of life has to be explored so that allowance can be made for it. In Bajoeng Gedé this meant knowledge of the market days when members of the village went to Kintamani to market and knowledge of the way in which families and parts of families migrated back and forth between their field houses and their town houses. The rituals of *rites de passage* have to be explored so that a preliminary framework can be set up, within which each ceremony as it occurs can be placed. In Bajoeng Gedé this involved the series of ceremonies for an infant; the end of the first taboo periods; the 105th-day ceremony; the 210th-day ceremony; the ceremony for ear-piercing; the entrance of youth or maiden into the village youth groups; the ceremonies attendant on marriage; payment of a cow to the village herd; purification of a newly married pair; the ceremonies celebrating later periods in marriage; and finally the sequence of ceremonies at death. The ceremonial round has to be established. In Bajoeng Gedé there was a series of feasts associated with the lunar calendar that included feasts at each new and each full moon and feasts associated with planting and harvesting. A second series of feasts was geared to the observance of recurrences in the 210-day-year calendar, associated with temples, with special deities, and with the life cycles of individuals. Calendrical system and individual *rites de passage* met in a system by which individuals ascended the religious hierarchy by a series of feasts associated with their elevation, and also included a series of more personal observances, elaborate because of the village status of the participants.

Every ceremony in Bali, even the simplest, involves some hundreds of ritual items; a series of gestures, postures, a set of "offerings," complexly arranged objects that vary from a single folded leaf containing a copper penny to objects ten feet high themselves containing hundreds of individual, named, stylized items of fruit, flowers, cooked food, and so on (*Balinese Character,* Plate 4). It was necessary to explore enough of the ceremonial usages to establish the categories, so that the appropriate observations could be made at each ceremony and a division of labor worked out between I Made Kaler and myself for routine verbal recording.

This basic anthropological task of ordering the observed detail of a new culture in terms of the existing cross-cultural categories is routine for any proper anthropological investigation and lies back of any statement about a relationship or a ceremony made in any publication on the field work. It is necessary to stress this in some detail, as many students of other disciplines seldom read anthropological monographs and have very little idea of what studying a whole culture—by modern methods of field work—involves.[3]

But the anthropologist has a second task beyond that of ordering his material in already recognized categories. Each culture is valuable not only because it provides new versions of behavior already observed elsewhere, but also because it is a source of new categories that once abstracted, can be used in the study of other cultures and for the enrichment of our general observational apparatus. While the anthropologist is collecting and classifying, he must be continually alert for the new, the unexpected, the never previously guessed-at aspects of behavior.[4]

A third area of work is relating oneself to the life of the village, which begins with the choice of a house site, the choice of what sort of

[3] The series of publications on the Arapesh (see Appendix 3, Part III) is almost a complete account of the work done, except for an account of the men's sacra and for a series of feasts attended outside the base village of Alitoa, which Reo Fortune has never published. But a glance through the American Museum series should give the student some idea of the areas that are included. On larger and more complex cultures, certain aspects have to be blocked out, but the detail not filled in, or one has to depend upon the work of others for part of the detail, as, for example, in music our Balinese field work simply took account of the work Colin McPhee was doing. (See Appendix 3 for bibliographical notes.)

[4] For the discussion of one such amplification of former cross-cultural categories, see Bateson, Gregory. "Bali, the Value System of a Steady State." For the way in which insights based on the study of a different culture may be used to expand, or qualify, a hypothesis, see his "The Frustration-Aggression Hypothesis." For the amplification of a hypothesis based upon the study of a new culture by the re-examination of material collected *previously* on a different culture, see Mead, Margaret. *Male and Female,* p. 71, and p. 392, where Manus material is used to amplify the definition of reciprocity as given by Bateson, Gregory. "Morale and National Character." For full references, see Appendix 3.

household one will assemble—as houseworkers and various sorts of assistants—and the choice of points of observation. The practice of a large amount of routine simple clinical medicine has been an inevitable accompaniment of our field work in the Pacific, so that simultaneously with mapping the village, learning the language, establishing the main lines of the culture, and setting up relationships to people, we had to acquaint ourselves rapidly with the vocabulary of illness, the principal recognized complaints, and the taboos and observances connected with such matters as exuviae, purges, bloodletting.

Additionally, in my particular type of field work I follow a large number of children very closely, and relationships must be established with them and their households as quickly as possible so as not to miss essential stages. As it was, failure to recognize early enough that the Balinese, who invoke so many calendrical systems with such specious facility, are utterly inaccurate about ages—so that if I missed a child's 210th-day ceremony I would never know its age—considerably reduced the number of children of about the same age who could otherwise have been included in this study.

One has to work out an etiquette that makes it possible to attend ceremonies in other people's homes, and this is done under guidance from one's native assistants, who will stipulate for every type of formality. It is important to stress that the anthropologist is never the particular type of "participant observer" that is becoming fashionable recently in some researches in our society, in which the research worker poses as a patient or a high-school student, falsifying every human relationship as he does so. The anthropologist has always been conspicuous—not because of a universal recognition of the ethical and scientific implications of falsification, but simply by virtue of being of a different race and a conspicuously different cultural level from the people he studies. The establishment of a *modus vivendi* between the anthropologist and the people as to when invitations have to be issued, when presents may or must be given, when the people enter the anthropologist's house and when the anthropologist enters theirs, has to be worked out anew in each piece of field work. In the course of developing the style of interrelationship, a great deal of valuable understanding is of course built up.

Even a working day of fifteen or sixteen hours is a very short period in which to get all these things done. Plans are continually interrupted by unexpected events that must also be attended to—accidents, illnesses, births, elopements, deaths, quarrels. Any attempt to schedule home visits to the infants who are being systematically observed is quite hopeless, as the family of each child is itself subject to the same pulls toward ceremonies or other events in the village. Plans to photograph a ceremony are annulled because the practitioner cannot be found until after dark, or the chicken that was to form part of the offering cannot be caught. The fieldworker's working day is an attempt to divide time between learning more about the culture; improving one's linguistic skill (and in Bali, with a Balinese assistant who kept Balinese records, this included going over each record that he kept, identifying new words and concepts); attending ceremonies; watching events; treating the sick; following up details of past events; making check-up calls on children being followed; holding sessions with individuals who have special knowledge of technology, the calendar, or midwifery; writing up and analyzing records to be sure nothing has been missed that should be followed up on the spot; bargaining for, cataloguing, and classifying objects being collected (in Bali these were principally objects of contemporary art work, carvings and pictures). A diary has to be kept in which all of the different activities, photography, records of scenes, births and deaths, receipt of letters and theoretical papers from the outside world, illnesses, and so on are recorded, so that the exact conditions of an observation can be ascertained later—whether something occurred before or after something else, whether an observation was made before a given article was read or a given hypothesis was formed.

All observations are made against time, so that the date provides the integration between a series of still photographs, the records I kept of each request for medicine, the number of rolls of Cine film exposed, sets of observations of behavior made by any one of us (including a Balinese text account by I Made Kaler), and the diary providing the context of the particular date.

I have described the procedure of field work at some length to provide a partial answer to such questions as: Why does not the anthropologist have the proper kind of sample of 100 babies born within a week of each other, selected from different quadrants of four villages, and observed at monthly intervals? It took a year's work by three people, and several months in the next two years, to get the longitudinal series of photographs of eight children with known ages. To get a hundred would, I think, take about five years' work by one person who, after all the preliminary work on the language and culture, styles of contact and field work, had been done for him, would do practically nothing else.

Instead of the type of selection and standardization, the repeated observation under controlled conditions that is possible in an American city, the anthropologist uses exploration in depth. The child is not observed at exact monthly intervals, but when it is observed it is securely placed in the event matrix within which it has been living. The actual selection of individuals is subject to a great number of considerations; contiguity to the anthropologist's house, temperament of parents, which infants survive, and so on. But once a given individual child is chosen and enough observations are accumulated, the anthropologist working intensively in a small village with a homogeneous culture has a knowledge of that child which is very different from that available in urban American clinics, even when therapy is involved. The two methods are, however, incomparable in many ways, and when we developed the final plans for this book, one reason why there was no attempt to place Gesell photographs side by side with the Balinese ones was that such a method would have obscured the differences in the conditions under which they were collected.

I include here, for illustration, a sample page from my diary and a sample page from an observation, that made at the delayed *otonin* ceremony for I Sepek on April 30, 1937, from which so many of the photographs are drawn.

## *Sample Page of Notes*

(Italicized comments in brackets added June 1951, for clarity of presentation)

May 1, 1937
[*date of writing up*]

April 30, 1937
[*date of event*]

OTONIN FOR I SEPEK
(deferred, real *otonin* Feb. 23, 1937)

| [*Children present*] | [*Adults present*] | [*Photography*] | [*Themes*] |
|---|---|---|---|
| I Sepek<br>I Degeng<br>I Leket<br>I Njawa<br>I Bikoel Njawi<br>(unnamed Njawi baby)<br>I Njawi | N. Degeng<br>M. Degeng<br>N. Leket<br>M. Leket<br>M. Njawi<br>M. Roenka | Cine ½ roll<br>Leicas e-j<br>(no text) | Balance before walking, all fours, family groups, exhibitionism of second child, holding new baby, behavior to real and adoptive father, dog eating feces, urinating, bathing, eating, comparative boys' and girls' behavior |

I Degeng came for us a little after three and we had a three-hour wait before Do Adji [*religious officiant from Salat, father's village*] came, so I sent MK [*our Balinese assistant, I Made Kaler*] home and there is no text of this whole scene.

3:25

Men Leket and Nang Leket about, Men Leket and Men Roenka and Men Degeng inside the house. I Degeng and I Leket running about outside with N. Degeng and N. Leket. Offerings all finished. Mat spread for us outside. I Leket with a long rib of *ron* [*leaf*] very happy and gay (has been well for over a month now). I Leket given a toy, which he has dropped, a wooden field knife.

I Leket moved about carrying the knife under his arm.

L. [*Leket*] walks off, puts knife in mouth, out of mouth, and under arm again (position of the Boedoeh's [*mild insane man who lived in our kitchen*] carving, except not supported by other hand).

Exhibitionistically dances about. N. Leket immediately says, "Be a *djanger* dancer." (I say, "Don't. Let him alone." But actually this was probably not done entirely for us, but might nevertheless have made the child self-conscious.)

Then N. Leket says, "Stay still." I Leket stands, finger deep in mouth. Then puts corner of blade of wooden knife into his mouth too.

Leket sits down and exhibits a cut in his toe to N. Leket; does this over and over.

Degeng beside his father, watching the Cine.

Degeng looking through Cine camera.

I Leket dances about holding his penis.

END OF A FILM
GB LOADING

D. looks through Cine again.

Leket smiles, flirts with us, then cuddles down beside his father in sudden shyness. (I say, "Bring Sepek out," and he is sent out by Degeng).

N. Degeng takes Sepek.

3:36

I Leket starts shouting a series of nonsense syllables.

CINE

(I say to make Sepek crawl [*creep*]. Degeng tries to attract him and fails, then MK furnishes chain and fountain-pen top.) Sepek, on mat, reaches, goes on all fours, squats, keeps balance, standing, smiles. Picked up, stands up, stands, almost falls, and himself recaptures his balance.
Held, and I Leket gets inside closer to holder.

(This page gives a fair picture of the way notes were organized and the extent of stimulation it was necessary to introduce if Balinese children were to be photographed in action. See Plates XV and XVI, and also Plates I, Fig. 4; XXI, Fig. 2; XXII, Fig. 2; XXIII, Fig. 3; XXIV, Fig. 1; XXV, Fig. 6; XXVI, Fig. 2; XXVII, Fig. 1; XXIX, Fig. 3; XXX, Fig. 5; XXXII, Fig. 4; XXXIV, Fig. 4; XXXVI, Fig. 1; XLII, Fig. 1; LII, Fig. 7, and LVI, Fig. 4.)

*My Diary for the Same Day*
April 30, 1937

Cockfight in Toekade [*ravine between Bajoeng Gedè and Peloedoe*]
N. Degeng *ngotonins* I Sepek (2 months late)
N. Patera *metjaroe* [*special purification offerings – village cycle*]
Cine–Bathing I Sami
Loaded cassettes 16
Dinner, 9:30

But there is a second aspect of field work that it is equally important to record; that is, the set of problems and preconceptions with which the fieldworkers began a particular piece of research. In this case, the general theoretical formulation have been published and are available to the student.[5] In particular, Bali had been selected as a culture that would be relevant to the problems of the institutionalization of the type of temperament found in the actor and the dancer, problems of photographic study of culture because of the expressiveness of the people, and problems of the relationship between culture and schizophrenia—these three theoretical interests springing from different contexts. In addition, I had been particularly interested in Jane Belo's report that Balinese children are not allowed to creep, and I suspected that Bali would prove to be a culture where analysis of total bodily movement and of the

[5] Bateson, Gregory. *Naven;* Mead, Margaret. *Cooperation and Competition among Primitive People* and *Sex and Temperament in Three Primitive Societies.*

surface of the whole body would prove more rewarding than the zonal-modal analysis that fitted the three cultures described in *Sex and Temperament.* I wanted to make some longitudinal studies of children to evaluate the relative usefulness of longitudinal and cross-sectional studies of child development.[6] I believed that if we were to make any advances in the understanding of the way in which different cultures institutionalize temperament, it would be through a detailed study of development rather than any comparison between adult constitution-temperament types and cultural forms. I accepted in general that human beings display growth patterns that have their own laws, but I had no familiarity with Gesell's theory of spiral development. I believed, however, that character is formed by continuous interaction between a growing child and others, in which formation the age and the stage of development of the child at which a given interaction occurrs may be crucial, and that such matters as whether a child is carried passively or has to hold on, how close the contact to the mother's body is, and whether the child learns by verbal admonition, by a model, or by manual teaching—that these are important.

When two years of Balinese work had been concluded, we did eight months' work among the Iatmul of New Guinea and then returned to Bali. Experience in making the same type of photographic analysis of the Iatmul was background for the last work in Bali. In the United States, the Balinese materials, especially the films and the carvings, were shown to a variety of psychologists, psychiatrists, and social scientists; the series of carvings were subjected to a detailed analytical analysis by Claire Holt; Leica rolls and Cine rolls were catalogued, many in great detail. The state of theory and understanding of Bali thus arrived at is recorded in *Balinese Character,* published in 1942.

In 1945, at the Vassar Summer Institute, I was a colleague of Dr. Frances Ilg and had an opportunity to hear her present studies of different "ages" in which she described, so vividly that my finger tips tingled, the motor-kinesthetic patterns peculiar to different stages of development. As I came to understand the spiral concept of development, how it supplements the concepts of epigenesis of Erik Erikson and reorders many of the observations on children's behavior that had been classified as regression, and how the development of a series of spiral models

[6] For discussion, see Mead, Margaret. "Researches on Primitive Children," *Manual of Child Psychology,* (L. Carmichael, editor). New York: John Wiley & Sons, Inc., 1946, pp. 667-706.

would give us a device for examining cultural specializations in terms of timing of learning, I felt that I had found something I had been looking for for the last ten years—a research device that would make it possible to explore the nexus between the rhythms of given temperaments and the way in which a culture institutionalizes these rhythms so that all individuals born within the culture, at varying cost, are also subjected to the same pattern of learning. But it seemed clear that in order to uses this Gesell-Ilg approach, ages were absolutely necessary, and much more comparable situations would also be essential, so I assumed that any use of the method would have to wait upon more field work. In early 1946 I read a paper at the Viking Fund. "On the Implications for Anthropology of the Gesell-Ilg Approach to Maturation," which Dr. Ilg discussed. My first personal contact with Dr. Gesell was when he and I delivered papers together at a meeting of the New York Neurological Society, January 8, 1946, where it was possible to discuss some of the implications of the symmetro-tonic stages of the spiral, in particular the ease with which a seven-month-old child is able to repeat a symmetrical prayer gesture.

In the spring of 1946 I met Frances Macgregor in connection with her search for comparative cross-cultural material on attitudes toward bodily disfigurement, and discussed with her her hope of using photography as a research tool in anthropological work. In the course of this discussion it first occurred to me that it might be possible, given a collaborator with sufficient sensitivity to movement and to the way in which photographs represented movement, to do at least an exploratory study of the Gesell-Ilg hypotheses by using the existing collection of Balinese photographs. I had then no idea whether it would ever be possible to enlist Frances Macgregor's interest, but my own imagination was sufficiently stirred by the possibility of doing something with the Balinese photographs to encourage me to apply to the Committee for the Study of Dementia Praecox for a grant. In the autumn of 1946, Eva Lulinsky started making the enlargments of the photographs of the Balinese children on whom we had the longest sequences.

Here it is necessary to go back to another piece of work. There are about 25,000 Balinese stills,[7] and in the field, records were kept by en-

[7] The approximate number given here is because the number of frames on a Leica film varied a little, as they were cut from bulk stock. Our method of cataloguing does not include cataloguing each frame when an entire negative is devoted to an event on which there are detailed notes, so that to get an absolute count of frames it would be necessary to count each frame.

tering on the tail of the film the time a film was put in and taken out of the camera, entering a record of any extensive photography in the diary, and keeping parallel running notes on event sequences, ceremonies, and so on. As Gregory Bateson carried his camera constantly, there were also a large number of single shots—a mother and child met in the road, a temper tantrum caught just as it subsided—taken when neither I Made Kaler or I were present to take notes. In the summer of 1939, after returning to the United States, we catalogued these 25,000 stills by films, so that if 3 films corresponded to an occasion called "Bathing the Karma children," the catalogue would read "Bathing the Karma children" for films 11 U, 11 V, and 11 W, and that was all, but if the film contained a series of short sequences, the catalogue page would run as follows:

Bajoeng 1:25, Aug. 18 to 8:38 Aug. 19, 1937
1. I Tjoengkeoh [*insane man who lived in our kitchen*] at *Meperagat* [*wedding ceremony*]
2. Temper tantrums outside *gebangan* [*watchhouse*] X 13
3. I Karsa and a bird at N. Oera's gate
4. *Metadjoek* [*ploughing*]

This means that only occasionally in the case of short special sequences that were identified from the negatives in combination with the notes do the names of individuals appear in the Leica catalogue. After this initial cataloguing, diapositives were made of all the Leica negatives. In the summer of 1940, a detailed analysis was made of all the sequences involving the Karma family—the family to which I Kenjoen (Plates III and IV) belonged. In the summer of 1941, almost all of the Balinese diapositives were projected, one by one, so as to make a selection of about 6000 frames for preliminary enlargement for *Balinese Character,* and further corrections and entries were made in the Leica catalogue at that time. Somewhat comparable operations were gone through with 100-foot rolls of Cine film; an over-all catalogue was made which referred to notes and diary record, and detailed analyses were made of a portion of the rolls, including especially those which were selected for use in lecturing and teaching.[8]

Meanwhile, in 1939, my college friend Dorothy Kraus (now Mrs. Arthur Davis) came to work on the Balinese material, and during 1940-41 she made an analytical index for each of the most important children,

[8] See list of available films on Bali, page 214

based on diary, Leica and Cine catalogues, and the running notes made by me and by I Made Kaler, so that it was possible to see just what types of material were available for any given child at any given age. Here she was dependent on the check lists of personalities that I place at the head of each write-up.[9] If there was a record, for example, of a *sangiang* dance at which someone was holding I Karba in his arms, this would only be noted if I had made a special series of notes on his behavior, or if there was a sequence of Leica or Cine shots focused on him. This is important to realize in judging the sample of stills of individual children that were used as the basis for this study. Not every picture of I Karba, but every picture of I Karba that could be caught through these various cataloguing devices, has been examined.

This index made by Dorothy Davis was the basis of 4000 enlargements made by Eva Lulinsky with which Frances Macgregor later worked.

In May 1947, when this series of enlargments was partly completed, Frances Macgregor came to talk over the possibility of collaborating with me on this research, and before there was any discussion of my hypothesis to influence her perceptions, she spent two days working over the enlargements. At that time, with no directive categories to guide or restrain her observation, she selected the mothers' hands as of key interest and wrote the following note:

> The hands of Balinese mothers, fathers, and even of child nurses, while not actively engaged in administering to the babies' needs or teaching them, commonly assume a limp, passive, and detached expression even though the child may be suckling or troubled. Not only do the hands offer little physical support (more often it is the wrist or arm), but expressions of tenderness, security, anxiety, or tenseness as conveyed by the hands are lacking.

In September 1947, Frances Macgregor began work on the project, dividing her time between it and her work with plastic-surgery patients. Dorothy Davis worked with her, placing the ages of the children in each individual frame and looking up identification materials in the notes. At no time did Frances Macgregor work directly with the notes, which, although typed, contain enough Balinese words so that considerable familiarity with the field work is necessary before they can be used easily. In the division of labor between her and myself, I asked her to

[9] *Supra,* page 195.

try to master the basic Gesell categories—sitting with support, sitting without support, standing with support, and so on—from the literature, so that she could arrange the photographs in terms of these categories, for preliminary communication with the Gesell group. I kept the responsibility for integrating her suggestions with Balinese culture. Her perceptions are, therefore, relatively free from cross references from other materials on Bali.[10]

My role was as follows: First, I was to test observations made on single pictures or sequences of single pictures of individual children against my entire knowledge of those children as I had watched them, held them, treated them when they were ill, watched them respond or fail to respond to medication, listened to the tones in their voices, and heard those tones change with circumstances and maturation. Second, I was to test each tentative finding against other aspects of Balinese culture, dance posture, carving behavior, ritual gestures. For example, we had done a long intensive study of three carvers, making a running record, a series of stills and Cines and a verbal record, of the process of simultaneous carving of three versions of the same theme. In the course of this intensive observation, we had noted how the Balinese fail to enlist the whole body, using instead just the absolutely essential amount of localized muscular effort. Findings on the pictures of the children as to the degree to which body parts are independent of each other, some being in flexion, others in extension, could be related to this other set of observations. Third, I was to test any finding against, and consider it in connection with, our organized theoretical formulations about the Balinese material. Thus the passive hands of the pupil were commented upon by Gregory Bateson, "From his dancing lesson the pupil learns passivity, and he acquired a separate awareness of different parts of his body,"[11] and I had described the Balinese child as follows: "Surrendering all autonomy and passively following the words spoken in its name [this referring to a verbal area not used in the present analysis] or the rhythm of the person who carries it [referring to an observation that can be made in real life or on moving-picture film], the child's body becomes more waxy flexible as it grows older."[12] These observations I would then integrate with the findings of Frances Macgregor and of

[10] Frances Macgregor used original Gesell publications Nos. 3, 4, 5, 7, 9, 11, 12, 13, 17, 18, 19, and 20 in Appendix 3, Part II.

[11] *Balinese Character,* p. 87.

[12] *Balinese Character,* p. 14.

the Gesell group as to low tonus and the hypothesis of the preservation of the meandering fetal tonus of the infant, and in turn with certain plastic likenesses to catatonic schizophrenia. The relative weakness of the thumb, which was related by the Gesell group to the predominance of outward rotation, the prevalence of eversion, and the ulnar emphasis, could also be related to the lack of goal orientation in Bali.[13] Or the apparent weakness of lateral eye movements, commented upon by the Gesell group, would be systematically related by them to other motor patterns, but I could relate it to the very highly controlled lateral eye movements in the dance (*ngeledet*), and relate this contrast in turn to the tendency in Bali to counterpoint the theater to real life, as discussed by Jane Belo.[14]

By November we were ready for a conference with the Gesell group. Frances Macgregor had two sets of exhibits ready, a series of photographs arranged in the basic Gesell categories, and a set of photographs that were called points of "special interest," which included photographs showing extreme distortion of body parts (Plate XXX), the little-finger position (Plate XLVIII), disassociated body parts (Plates LIV and LV), and ways of balancing (Plate XXX).

We spent two days in New Haven, going over our material with Dr. Gesell, Dr. Ilg, Dr. Ames, and some of their coworkers, and recording their responses, their discussions with us, and their discussions among themselves. During the second day they showed us their film *Prone,* and we showed them a selected series of Balinese films of the children they had seen in the still photographs. However, as the moving pictures seemed to confirm the points they had made, but not to provide new insights, we decided that the whole collaborative effort could be based on the still photographs alone. From November to March, Frances Macgregor worked on the photographs again, arranging them this time in accordance with the new insights that had developed in the conferences with the Gesell group. This rearrangement was then presented to Dr. Ilg and Dr. Ames in a two-day conference here in New York, and on the basis of their responses a final set of plates was planned.

The way our discussions went is well illustrated by a memorandum from Frances Macgregor to me after the March conference:

[13] Bateson, Gregory. "The Frustration-Aggression Hypothesis."

[14] Belo, Jane. "The Balinese Temper."

Dr. Ilg and Dr. Ames, during the November 1947 conference, pointed out the asymmetrical position of Balinese children in tantrums and symmetry in limbs; to apply what I inferred was their definition of the terms to our material was not as easy as it first appeared. Initially I attributed my difficulty as a failure in communication and a lack of specificity as to what their concept of these terms was. Our Balinese pictures of gross body postures, as well as some of the individual body parts—when not obviously symmetrical—seemd to have a quality which was more than just the opposite of symmetry; i.e., asymmetry. The extreme flexibility of the body or body parts had a unique and additional element. There was more than asymmetry; there were diverse turnings on the self; there was distortion. The extreme flexion of the Balinese, their ability to twist separate body parts in opposing directions within a plane, made any clear-cut application to symmetrical and asymmetrical positions seem (to me) unsatisfactory.

Hoping to clarify the Ilg-Ames definitions, those photographs which supposedly fitted into them were specifically marked. As these pictures were seen at the second conference (March 1948), the question was repeatedly asked by me: "Would you say this was a good illustration of symmetry (or asymmetry)? Does it belong in the category?" In attempting to answer, Dr. Ilg and Dr. Ames decided that actually the categories of symmetry and asymmetry were not satisfactory, and the over-all category of flexibility should be employed instead. This heading would include external and internal rotation, flexion, and extension, and would be applied to the gross body positions and the finer and more individuated movements of eyes, hands, toes, etc.

I want to pause here to discuss what had happened, methodologically, in comparison with what happens when the anthropologist goes into the field. First, the Balinese material was arranged in the most general of the Gesell categories, such as "standing alone," which may be regarded as having the same sort of cross-cultural usefulness as a category like "social organization." Second, Frances Macgregor made a preliminary study of the Gesell *terminology,* out of published work, which is something like the first work one does with a linguistic informant, so as to be able to communicate. Then we presented the Gesell group with our materials, (1) arranged in their categories, and (2) what seemed to Frances Macgregor to be "different." To this they responded (1) by refinement within their catagories, (2) by reacting to what was *new* in our material, and (3) by their comments on the photographs and their discussions with each other and the presentation of their film material, giving their categories meaning for us. Thus by the use of shared material, itself complex and representative of whole situations, very rapid and satisfactory communication was established. Most cross-disciplinary research falls down, I believe, because there is not a sufficiently large body of *shared* material in terms of which each worker can *show* what he means so that others can *see* or *hear* what he means.

The whole project then lay dormant for almost three years for reasons primarily external to the research—the fact that I had to assume direction of the Columbia University Research Project when Ruth Benedict died, plus a series of delays in making final publication plans without which the book could not be cast in final form. Meanwhile, also, Dr. Gesell retired and the new Gesell Institute for Child Development was organized in New Haven. In February 1951, the plates were pasted up and taken up to the Gesell group to look at again. In this conference, although no new insights were developed, the final phrasing as given in the conclusions was clarified, the order of the plates was rearranged so as to place the significant sequence from frogging through walking together,[15] a few pictures were shifted from one plate to another, and the titles of a few plates were changed. No new material was added. With slides of these plates Drs. Ilg and Ames presented at the Viking Fund, April 2, 1951, a paper on "How Knowledge of Child Development in Our Culture Can Be Useful to Anthropologists."

We may finally look at this enterprise in terms of what came out of it, as compared with the original research intent. My intent as stated in my application for a grant to the Committee for the Study of Dementia Praecox in April 1946 was as follows:

> What I have in mind now is a longitudinal study of several of our Balinese children whom we followed from infancy, illustrated with photographs and compared in detail with the developmental studies which are now available of infants and young children in our own society. It has already been suggested that one of the determining aspects of Balinese character formation, which is so strikingly like—and unlike—the character displayed by schizophrenics in our society, is the skipping of certain phases of development and special emphasis on others. The inhibition of spontaneous grasping, the confinement of the legs in the carrying shawl, the limitation of crawling, combined with the emphasis on symmetrical body movements, as in prayer and dancing

[15] The original plate order as of June 1948 was: XI, XII, I, II, III, IV, V, VI, XV, XVI, XIII, XIV, IX, X, VII, VIII, XVII, XVIII, XIX, XX, XXII, XXIII, XXVI, XXVII, XXVIII, XXV, XLII, XLIII, LVII, XXXIX, XL, XLI, XXXVIII, XXXI, XXXII, XXXIII, XXIV, XXI, XXX, XXIX, XXXV, XXXIV, XXXVI, XXXVII, L, LI, XLVII, XLIV, XLV, XLIX, XLVIII, XLVI, LII, LIII, LV, LIV, LVI, LVIII.

positions which may coincide with maturational phases, seem to be promising foci of investigation.

The contributions I expected the use of the spiral model of growth to make to anthropological research is summarized in Chapter 2. My original research plan, as outlined for Frances Macgregor, September 5, 1947, also emphasized the spiral model very heavily:

BGI Study<br>
Theoretical framework: mm September 5, 1947

The study is to be centered around the theme of spiral development as developed by Gesell and Ilg (see M.M.'s paper and statement to the Committee for the Study of Dementia Praecox attached). It will attempt to organize the Balinese material to throw *further light* upon the type of illumination the Gesell-Ilg theories throw *upon cultural development,* and to suggest ways in which those theories have to be modified in the light of materials from other cultures. The data from Bali are not complete enough, nor sufficiently comparable to the Gesell material, to provide conclusive proof of differences, but they can be very suggestive.

In going over the material, attention should be given to the following categories:

(a) Pictures outlining the *early experience of an infant,* bathing, feeding, learning to walk, etc. (after 6 mo. mostly Karbo and Kenjoen)

(b) Pictures *embodying the family frame,* mostly Karmas, *showing sibling position, parental behavior* (mother bathing Gata, father bathing Gata, etc.), *grandparent behavior, child nurse with different-aged children* (Karmi with Gata, Gati with Kenjoen, etc.)

(c) Materials which are *most like the Gesell materials*

(d) Materials which are *least like the Gesell materials* (e.g. suckling) which they may not have published, but may have

(e) Gaps in our materials, which cannot be compensated for now, but which might be discussed with the Gesell group to find substitutes in our stuff.

Then for the main theoretical problem, the spiral concept of development, attention should be paid to: *elongation or condensation, acceleration* or *retardation,* different sorts of overlap, differentiation of a different type, sex differences of a different type.

Also, cases where *cultural pressures seem to coincide with* a Gesell *observed point* on spiral (Balinese praying at *otonin*) and places where *cultural pressure* does not *coincide* or actually *works against a readiness which might be* assumed on the basis of the Gesell stuff

Also, *behavior of adults which mirrors, counterpoints,* or is tangential to the observed child behavior (e.g., FM's point about *tense and relaxed hands* in different parental contexts)

Gesell pictures (already published and suitable for comparison) should be noted for future reference, or possible side-by-side publication.

The results have not contributed heavily to our knowledge of the way in which the spiral can be used to interpret Balinese material, or of the way in which Balinese material can contribute to the spiral model, except in one respect, and that, significantly enough, is a possibility that I had not thought of in working out my paper in 1946.[16] The Balinese material suggests that shifts in amplitude of the ascending curves should be one cross-cultural dimension of the spiral, that while the Balinese children pass through the same stages, if these are looked at vertically, a different segment of the base—the fetal and early postnatal meandering tonus—is elaborated with a smaller degree of amplitude. But this is suggestive only: it is clear that for spiral analysis it is necessary to have much more detailed sequential material, taken at something like standard intervals and under somewhat more standard conditions.

There are two main findings of importance:

First, that within the same developmental analysis as that used by Gesell, and using his categories, it is possible to distinguish both similarities and significant differences in the culturally patterned development of Balinese children.

Second, that in focusing upon children within whole situations in which the older child or adult is included, these categories help to discriminate the specific interaction between infant and others through which the major cultural learnings are transmitted to the child and maintained in the adult.

Although the three plates that illustrate this theme of child-other interaction (Plates XXXIX, L, and LI) were completed in June 1947, my appreciation of the way in which this interaction can be analyzed has been very much sharpened, on the one hand, by subsequent sessions of the Macy Foundation Conferences on Cybernetics, which provided a model for thinking of cultural learning as a feed-back system involving adults as well as children, and on the other hand, by participation in current controversies over the role of child-rearing practices in character formation, which have intensified with the publication of some of the results of Columbia University Research in Contemporary Cultures,[17] especially Geoffrey Gorer's hypotheses about pre-Soviet Russian

[16] Mead, Margaret. "On the Implications for Anthropology of the Gesell-Ilg Approach to Maturation."

[17] Mead, Margaret. "Research in Contemporary Cultures," *Groups, Leadership and Men, Research in Human Relations,* (Harold Gutzkow, Editor), Pittsburgh: Carnegie Press, 1951, pp. 106-18.

character.[18] These developing lines of theory[19] have undoubtedly influenced my final integration of these materials.

This research venture has also demonstrated several points about cross-disciplinary research: (1) the importance of an adequate amount of shared visible or audible raw material—complex and not reduced by any form of analysis beyond the recording—in integrating the insights of a team whose members use different sorts of imagery, different levels of abstraction, and different backgrounds of experience; (2) the greater ease with which it is possible to communicate when both approaches are systematic, so that working with the Gesell group proved much easier than working with some of the other specialists who have been good enough to look at the Balinese materials; (3) the way in which exact ages of a few children act as a key to a whole body of material on children whose ages are only approximately known. This should serve to alert fieldworkers to the importance of using all possible clues to establish at least a few exact ages.

Finally, I believe that cross-disciplinary work can be done only when the workers are drawn together by a spontaneous interest in the problem, or in each others' methods of work, as identified individuals, not as representatives of "other disciplines" on some problem with which only one of them—usually the project director—was originally concerned. In this undertaking, each of us was activated by primary research interests, so that each of us provided part of the necessary momentum for the group research to proceed with great speed and flexibility toward the development of new hypotheses about growth in culture.

[18] Gorer, Geoffrey, and John Rickman, M.D. *The People of Great Russia: A Psychological Study.* London: The Cresset Press, 1949, and New York: The Chanticleer Press, 1950.

[19] Summarized in part in my article in the publication of the Tenth Conference on Science, Philosophy, and Religion, "The Comparative Study of Cultures and the Purposive Cultivation of Democratic Values, 1941-49," pp. 87-108.

APPENDIX 2

# *Notes to Chapters*

For full bibliographical references, see Appendix 3, Bibliographical Note.

## PART ONE

### Chapter 1

1 Gorer, Geoffrey. "More Equal than Others," Chapter VIII in *The American People,* pp. 188-219.

2 Conducted by the Progressive Education Association under a grant from the General Education Board under the direction of Dr. Caroline Zachary.

3 Mead, M. *Coming of Age in Samoa.* 1928.

### Chapter 2

1 Dixon, Roland B. "Oceanic" in *The Mythology of All Races,* 1916, p. 13.

2 Matthew 18:3.

3 John 3:5.

4 "From Early Buddhist Books," *The Viking Portable World Bible.* 1944, p. 19 and p. 127.

5 See Mead, M. *Male and Female.* Erickson, E. *Childhood and Society.*

6 Calas, E. *Soviet Child-Training Ideals and Their Political Significance.* Studies in Soviet Culture, 1949 (unpublished).

7 See Note 5 above.

8 See Mead, M. "Some Relationships between Anthropology and Psychology," *Dynamic Psychiatry,* (Franz Alexander and Helen Ross, Editors), (to be published).

Cobb, E. "The Ecology of the Imagination in Childhood" (unpublished manuscript).

Paalen, Wolfgang. "Metaplastic," *Dynaton,* p. 7 (child's drawing showing the effect of a person-centered and a mechanical-object-centered world).

9 Mead, M. "Collective Guilt," *Proceedings of the International Conference on Medical Psychotherapy,* 1949, pp. 56-66. "Social Change and Cultural Surrogates," *Journal of Educational Psychology,* XIV (1940), pp. 92-109. "Some Anthropological Consideration Concerning Guilt," *Feelings and Emotions*: The Mooseheart Symposium, 1950, pp. 362-373.

Chapter 3

1 In the film, *Karba's First Years,* there is a 210th-day ceremony showing the whole series of ceremonial behaviors through which a Balinese baby is put.

2 This limitation of the discussion is solely a matter of practicality. It does not mean that I have changed my theoretical approach, decided that motor behavior is the only important behavior, or repudiated in any way the types of analysis used in *Balinese Character* and in *Male and Female.* This particular study is a study of motor behavior for purposes of comparison with some of the Gesell materials. The number of words and of illustrations is limited by publishing considerations.

3 McPhee, Colin, unpublished manuscript on Balinese music.

4 The interchangeability between human beings and puppets, especially in the *sangiang* dance, has been discussed by Jane Belo in "Bali: Rangda and Barong" and is illustrated in *Balinese Character,* Plates 18 and 19.

5 See note on pronunciation and orthography, p. 2.

PART TWO

Introduction to the Plates and Captions

1 Page 52

2 Definition of these terms will be found in the Index-Glossary. Although Drs. Ilg and Ames were good enough to go over the draft of the captions, the final responsibility for any misuse of the terminology is the authors'.

3 For illustrations of such sequences, see *Balinese Character,* Plates 52, 53, 64, 65, 70-72.

4 For examples of the behavior sequences in the Cine films, see *Karba's First Years* (New York University Film Library) which gives falling, leaning, dancing, and teasing sequences.

5 There are undoubtedly occasional errors in the *frame* numbers. Since this was stock film, the frames are not numbered, and the number must be derived each time by counting. Then, for purposes of enlargement, bits of thread are inserted in the edging holes of the negative. The threads are removed after the enlargement is made. As the frame numbers are useful simply for cross-referencing purposes and as the exact sequence is preserved both on the uncut negatives and the diapositives, the frame numbers in this book have been made to conform with those in *Balinese Character* when differences in the numbering of the two sets of enlargements were found.

6 See Appendix 1 for sample of notes based on this occasion.

Conclusions

1 For a comparative photographic series on methods of carrying children and the amount of activity involved, see Mead, M., "Researches on Primitive Children," *Manual of Child Psychology,* (L. Carmichael, Editor), 1946, pp. 667-706.

2 See paper given by Margaret Mead at Section H of the American Association for the Advancement of Science, December 28, 1950, "Mother and Child as an Intercommunicating System," (unpublished).

APPENDIX 3

# *Bibliographical Note*

This bibliographical note is divided into three parts, (I) a bibliography of immediately relevant publications on Balinese culture, (II) a bibliography of immediately relevant publications by the Gesell group, and (III) references to general theoretical articles or course materials either referred to in the text or relevant to problems treated in the text.

## I

### *Balinese Culture*


1. ABEL, THEODORA M. "Free Designs of Limited Scope as a Personality Index," *Character and Personality,* VII (1938), pp. 50-62.

2. BATESON, GREGORY. "An Old Temple and a New Myth," *Djawa,* XVII (September, 1937).

3.——. "Equilibrium and Climax in Interpersonal Relations" (Paper read at the Conference of Topological Psychologists, held at Smith College, Northampton, Mass., December 31, 1940–January 2, 1941).

4.——. "Experiments in Thinking about Observed Ethnological Material," *Philosophy of Science,* VIII, 1, (1941), pp. 53-68.

5.——. "The Frustration-Aggression Hypothesis," *Psychological Review,* XLVII (1941), pp. 350-355.

6.——. "Comment on 'The Comparative Study of Culture and the Purposive Cultivation of Democratic Values,' by Margaret Mead," *Science, Philosophy, and Religion,* Second Symposium (published by the Conference on Science, Philosophy, and Religion), New York, 1942.

7.——. "Morale and National Character," *Civilian Morale,* Second Yearbook of the Society for the Study of Social Issues (Goodwin Watson, Editor). Boston and New York: Houghton-Mifflin, 1942.

8.——. "Bali: The Human Problem of Reoccupation," Supplementary Material on the Exhibit. New York: Museum of Modern Art, 1942 (mimeographed).

9.——. "Cultural Determinants of Personality," *Personality and the Behavior Disorders* (J. McV. Hunt, Editor). New York: Ronald Press, 1944, II, Part V, pp. 714-736.

10.———. "Bali: the Value System of a Steady State," *Social Structure*: Studies Presented to A. R. Radcliffe-Brown (Meyer Fortes, Editor). Oxford: Clarendon Press, 1949, pp. 35-53.

11.———. (with Claire Holt) "Form and Function of the Dance in Bali," *The Function of Dance in Human Society, a Seminar Directed by Franciska Boas.* New York: Boas School, 1944, pp. 46-52.

12. Bateson, Gregory, and Mead, Margaret. *Balinese Character: A Photographic Analysis,* Special Publications of the New York Academy of Sciences, Vol. II. New York: New York Academy of Sciences, 1942 (100 plates).

13. Belo, Jane. "The Balinese Temper," *Character and Personality,* IV (December, 1935), pp. 120-146.

14.———. "A Study of Customs Pertaining to Twins in Bali," *Tijdschrift voor Ind. Taal-, Land-, en Volkenkunde,* LXXV, 4 (1935), pp. 483-549.

15.———. "A Study of a Balinese Family," *American Anthropologist,* XXXVIII, 1 (1936), pp. 12-31.

16.———. "Balinese Children's Drawings," *Djawa,* XVII, 5 and 6 (1937), pp. 1-13.

17.———. "Bali: Rangda and Barong," *American Ethnological Society Monograph No. 16* (February, 1949).

18. Eissler, Kurt R. "Balinese Character," *Psychiatry,* VII, 2 (May, 1944), pp. 139-144.

19. Goris, R. "Overzicht over de Belangrijste Litteratuur Betreffende de Cultur van Bali over het Tijdvak 1920-1935," *Mededeelingen Kirtya Liefrinck van der Tuuk,* Aflevering 5, 1936 (?).

20. Holt, Claire. "Les Danses de Bali," *Archives Internationales de la Danse,* Part I (April 15, 1935), pp. 51-53; Part II (July 15, 1935), pp. 84-86.

21.———. "Théâtre et Danses aux Indes Néerlandaises," *Catalogue et Commentaires,* XIII, Exposition des Archives Internationales de la Danse (1939). Paris: Maisonneuve, 1939, p. 86.

22.———. Analytical Catalogue of Collection of Balinese Carvings in the American Museum of Natural History, New York (unpublished).

23. Kat, Angelino de, and Kleen, Tyra de. *Mudras auf Bali.* Hagen and Darmstadt (Germany): Folkwang Verlag, 1923.

24. Lekkerkerker, C. *Bali en Lombok: overzicht der litteratuur omtrent deze eilanden tot einde 1919* (Uitgave van het Bali-Institut). Rijswijk: Blankwaardt & Schoonhoven, 1920.

25. McPhee, Colin. "The 'Absolute' Music of Bali," *Modern Music,* XII (1935), p. 165.

26.———. "The Balinese Wanjang Koelit and Its Music," *Djawa,* XVI (1936), p. 1.

27.———. "Angkloeng Music in Bali," *Djawa,* XVII, (1937).

28.———. "Children and Music in Bali," *Djawa,* XVIII (1938).

29.———. "Figuration in Balinese Music," *Peabody Bulletin* (May, 1940).

30.———. *A House in Bali.* New York: John Day, 1946.

31.———. *A Club of Small Men.* (Children's Story.) New York: John Day, 1947.

32.———. "Dance in Bali," *Dance Index,* VII, 7 and 8 (1948).

33.———. "Five-Tone Gamelan Music of Bali," *Musical Quarterly,* XXXV, 2 (April, 1949), pp. 250-281.

34. Mead, Margaret. "Public Opinion Mechanisms among Primitive Peoples," *Public Opinion Quarterly,* I, 3 (1937), pp. 5-16.

35.———. "Strolling Players in the Mountains of Bali," *Natural History,* XLIII, 1 (1939), pp. 17-26.

36.———. "Men and Gods in a Bali Village," *New York Times Magazine* (July 16, 1939), pp. 12-13, 23.

37.———. "Researches in Bali, 1936-39; on the Concept of Plot in Culture," *Transactions of the New York Academy of Sciences,* Series II, Vol. 2 (1939), pp. 1-4.

38.———. "Character Formation in Two South Seas Societies," *American Neurological Association, Transactions,* 66th Annual Meeting, June, 1940, pp. 99-103.

39.———. "Social Change and Cultural Surrogates," *Journal of Educational Sociology,* XIV (1940), pp. 92-109. Reprinted in *Personality in Nature, Society, and Culture,* (Clyde Kluckhohn and Henry A. Murray, Editors). New York: Knopf, 1948, pp. 511-522.

40.———. "Conflict of Cultures in America," *Proceedings, 54th Annual Convenvention, Middle States Association of Colleges and Secondary Schools,* November 23-24, 1940, pp. 30-44.

41.———. "The Arts in Bali," *Yale Review,* XXX (1940), pp. 335-347.

42.———. "Administrative Contributions to Democratic Character Formation at the Adolescent Level," *Journal of the National Association of Deans of Women,* IV (1941), pp. 51-57. Reprinted in *Personality in Nature, Society, and Culture* (Clyde Kluckhohn and Henry A. Murray, Editors). New York: Knopf, 1948, pp. 523-530.

43.———. "Family Organization and the Super-Ego" (read at the Conference of Topological Psychologists, Smith College, Northampton, Mass., December 31, 1940-January 2, 1941).

44.——. "Back of Adolescence Lies Early Childhood," *Childhood Education,* XVIII (1941), pp. 58-61.

45.——. "Community Drama, Bali and America," *American Scholar,* II (1941-42), pp. 79-88.

46.——. "Educative Effects of Social Environment as Disclosed by Studies of Primitive Societies," in Symposium on Environment and Education (E. W. Burgess, W. L. Warner, Franz Alexander, Margaret Mead), University of Chicago, Supplementary Educational Monographs, No. 54. Human Development Series, I, (1942), pp. 48-61.

47.——. "The Family in the Future," *Beyond Victory* (Ruth Nanda Anshen, Editor). New York: Harcourt, Brace, 1943, pp. 66-87.

48.——. "Research on Primitive Children," *Handbook of Child Psychology* (Leonard Carmichael, Editor). New York: John Wiley, 1946, pp. 667-706.

49.——. "Age Patterning in Personality Development," *American Journal of Orthopsychiatry,* XVII, 2 (April, 1947), pp. 231-40. Reprinted in *Personal Character and Cultural Milieu,* compiled by Douglas G. Haring. Syracuse: Syracuse University Press, 1948, pp. 539-546.

50.——. *Male and Female: A Study of the Sexes in a Changing World.* New York: William Morrow & Company, 1949.

51. MURPHY, GARDNER and LOIS. "Review of *Balinese Character: A Photographic Analysis,*" *American Anthropologist,* XLV, 4, Part I (October-December, 1943, pp. 615-619.

52. ZOETE, BERYL DE, and SPIES, WALTER. *Dance and Drama in Bali* (preface by Arthur Waley). New York and London: Harper & Brothers, 1939.

*Films, Recordings, and Music*

53. BATESON, GREGORY, and MEAD, MARGARET. *Character Formation in Different Cultures*: (1) *Karba's First Years;* (2) *Bathing Babies in Three Cultures.* New York University Film Library.

54. MCPHEE, COLIN. (Recording) *Music of Bali;* An Album of Six Balinese Compositions, transcribed for two pianos and performed by Benjamin Britten and Colin McPhee. New York: G. Schirmer, Inc.

55.——. (Published music) *Balinese Ceremonial Music*: (1) *Gambangan;* (2) *Pemungkah;* (3) *Taboeh Teloe.* Transcribed for two pianos. New York: G. Schirmer, Inc.

II

*Gesell Group Publications*

1. AMES, LOUISE B. "Precursor Signs of Plantigrade Progression," *Journal of Genetic Psychology* LV (December, 1939), pp. 439-442.

2.——. "Supine Leg and Foot Postures in the Human Infant in the First Year of Life," Journal of Genetic Psychology, LXI (September, 1942), pp. 87-107.

3. GESELL, ARNOLD. *The Mental Growth of the Pre-School Child.* New York: The Macmillan Company, 1926.

4.———. *Infancy and Human Growth.* New York: The Macmillan Company, 1928.

5.———. "Maturation and the Patterning of Behavior," *A Handbook of Child Psychology,* 2nd ed. revised, (G. Murchison, Editor). Worcester, Mass.: Clark University Press, 1933, pp. 209-235.

6.———. "The Tonic Neck Reflex in the Human Infant: Its Morphogenetic and Clinical Significance," *Journal of Pediatrics,* XIII (October, 1938), pp. 455-464.

7.———. "Reciprocal Neuromotor Interweaving: A Principle of Development Evidenced in the Patterning of Infant Behavior," *Journal of Comparative Neurology,* LXX (April, 1939), pp. 161-180.

8.———. "Ontogenesis of Infant Behavior," *Handbook of Child Psychology,* (Leonard Carmichael, Editor). New York: John Wiley, 1946, pp. 295-331.

9. GESELL, ARNOLD (with others). *An Atlas of Infant Behavior: A Systematic Delineation of the Forms and Early Growth of Human Behavior Patterns.* Two volumes. New Haven: Yale University Press, 1934. (3,200 action photographs).

10. GESELL, ARNOLD, and AMATRUDA, CATHERINE S. *Developmental Diagnosis.* New York: Hoeber, 1941.

11.———. *Embryology of Behavior.* New York: Harper & Brothers, 1945.

12. GESELL, ARNOLD, and AMES, LOUISE B. "The Ontogenetic Organization of Prone Behavior in Human Infancy," *Journal of Genetic Psychology,* LVI (June, 1940), pp. 247-263.

13.———. "Ontogenetic Correspondences in the Supine and Prone Postures of the Human Infant," *Yale Journal of Biology and Medicine,* XV (March, 1943), pp. 565-573.

14.———. "The Development of Handedness," *Journal of Genetic Psychology,* LXX (June, 1947), pp. 155-175.

15.———. "Tonic-neck-reflex and Symmetro-tonic Behavior," *Journal of Pediatrics,* XXXVI (February, 1950), pp. 165-176.

16. GESELL, ARNOLD, and HALVERSON, H. M. "The Development of Thumb Opposition in the Human Infant," *Journal of Genetic Psychology,* XLVIII (June, 1936), pp. 338-361.

17.———. "A Cinema Study of the Daily Maturation of Infant Behavior," *Journal of Genetic Psychology,* LXI (September, 1942), pp. 1-32.

18. GESELL, ARNOLD, and ILG, FRANCES L. (in collaboration with Louise B. Ames and Janet Learned). *Infant and Child in the Culture of Today.* New York: Harper & Brothers, 1943.

19.———. (in collaboration with Louise B. Ames and Glenna Bullis). *The Child from Five to Ten.* New York: Harper & Brothers, 1946.

20. GESELL, ARNOLD, AMATRUDA, CATHERINE S., AMES, LOUISE B., CASTNER, BURTON M., HALVERSON, HENRY M., ILG, FRANCES, and THOMPSON, HELEN. *The First Five Years of Life.* New York: Harper & Brothers 1940.

21. HALVERSON, H. M. "An Experimental Study of Prehension in Infants by Means of Systematic Cinema Records," *Genetic Psychology Monographs,* X (1931), pp. 107-286.

22.———. "Studies of the Grasping Responses of Early Infancy, I, II, III." *Journal of Genetic Psychology,* LI (December, 1937), pp. 371-449.

III

*General Articles Relevant to Problems Treated in the Text*

1. BALLOU, ROBERT O. (editor). "From Early Buddhist Books," *The Viking Portable World Bible.* New York: The Viking Press, 1944.

2. BATESON, GREGORY. "Some Systematic Approaches to the Study of Culture and Personality," *Character and Personality,* XI,1 (1942), pp. 76-82. (Re-printed in *Personal Character and Cultural Milieu,* compiled by Douglas G. Haring, revised edition, Syracuse: Syracuse University Press, 1949, pp. 110-116.)

3.———. *Naven.* Cambridge (England): Cambridge University Press, 1936.

4. DIXON, ROLAND B. "Oceanic," in *The Mythology of All Races,* (Louis Herbert Gray, Editor), Vol IX. Boston: Marshall Jones Company, 1916.

5. ERIKSON, ERIK H. Childhood and Society. New York: W. W. Norton, 1950.

6. FORTUNE, REO. "Arapesh Warfare," *American Anthropologist,* XLI (January-March, 1939), pp. 22-41.

7.———. "Arapesh," *Publications of the American Ethnological Society,* XIX (1942), New York.

8.———. "Arapesh Maternity," *Nature,* CLII (August 1943), p. 164.

9. FRANK, LAWRENCE K. *Nature and Human Nature.* New Brunswick: Rutgers University Press, 1951.

10. GORER, GEOFFREY. *The American People.* New York: W. W. Norton, 1948.

11.———. *The People of Great Russia.* London: The Cresset Press, 1949. New York: Chanticleer Press, 1950.

12. McGRAW, MYRTLE. *Growth.* New York: Appleton-Century, 1935.

13. MEAD, MARGARET. *Coming of Age in Samoa.* New York: William Morrow, 1928. (Reprinted in *From the South Seas.* New York: William Morrow, 1939.)

14.———. "The Marsalai Cult among the Arapesh," *Oceania,* IV (September 4, 1933), pp. 37-53.

15.———. "The Arapesh of New Guinea" (short summary) *Cooperation and Competition among Primitive Peoples* (Margaret Mead, Editor) New York: McGraw-Hill, 1937, pp. 20-50.

16.———. "The Mountain Dwelling Arapesh" Part One of *Sex and Temperament in Three Primitive Societies.* New York: William Morrow, 1935. (Reprinted in *From the South Seas,* New York: William Morrow, 1939.)

17.———. "The Mountain Arapesh." *American Museum of Natural History Anthropological Papers,* New York: I, An Importing Culture, Vol. XXXVI (1938), Part 3, pp. 139-349; II. Supernaturalism, Vol. XXXVII (1940), Part 3, pp. 317-451; III. Socio-Economic Life and IV. Diary of Events in Alitea, Vol. XL (1947), Part 3, pp. 163-419; V. The Record of Unabelin, (with Rorschachs), Vol. XLI (1949), Part 3, pp. 289-389.

18.———. "Anthropological Data on the Problem of Instincts," *Psychosomatic Medicine,* IV, 4, (October 1942), pp. 396-397. (Reprinted in *Personality in Nature, Society and Culture,* edited by Clyde Kluckhohn and Henry A. Murray. New York: Alfred A. Knopf, 1948, pp. 109-112.)

19.———. "Our Educational Emphases in Primitive Perspective," *The American Journal of Sociology.* XLVIII, 6 (May, 1943) pp. 633-639.

20.———. "Personality, the Cultural Approach to," *Encyclopedia of Psychology,* (Philip Harriman, Editor), New York: Philosophical Library, 1946, pp. 477-488.

21.———. "The Implications of Culture Change for Personality Development," *American Journal of Orthopsychiatry,* XVII, 4 (October 1947), pp. 633-646. (Reprinted in *Personal Character and Cultural Milieu,* compiled by Douglas G. Haring, revised edition, Syracuse: Syracuse University Press, 1949, pp. 549-563.)

22.———. "The Concept of Culture and the Psychosomatic Approach," *Psychiatry,* X, (1947) pp. 57-76. (Reprinted in *Personal Character and Cultural Milieu,* pp. 518-538.)

23.———. "On the Implications for Anthropology of the Gesell-Ilg Approach to Maturation," *American Anthropologist,* XLIX, 1, (January-March 1947) pp. 69-77. (Reprinted in *Personal Character and Cultural Milieu,* pp. 508-517.)

24.———. "Contributions from the Study of Primitive Cultures," *Problems of Early Infancy.* (M. J. E. Senn, Editor), New York: Josiah Macy Jr. Foundation, 1947, pp. 36-39.

25.———. "Collective Guilt," *Proceedings of the International Conference on Medical Psychotherapy,* III, London: International Congress on Mental Health, 1948, New York: Columbia University Press, 1949, pp. 57-66.

26.———. "Character Formation and Diachronic Theory," *Social Structure: Studies Presented to A. R. Radcliffe-Brown* (Meyer Fortes, Editor) Oxford: Clarendon Press, 1949, pp. 18-35.

27.———. "Psychologic Weaning: Childhood and Adolescence," *Psychosexual Development in Health and Disease.* New York: Grune and Stratton, 1949, pp. 124-133.

28.———. "Grownups in the Making," *Child Study,* (summer 1950), p. 76.

29.———. "The Role of the Arts in a Culture," *The Art Education Bulletin,* Yearbook Issue, The Eastern Arts Ass'n., Pa., 1950, pp. 10-16.

30.———. "Some Anthropological Considerations concerning Guilt," *Feelings and Emotions*: The Mooseheart Symposium, (Martin L. Reymert, Editor), New York: McGraw-Hill, 1950, pp. 362-373.

31.———. "L'Etude du Caractère National," *Les "Sciences de la Politique" Aux Etats-Unis* (traduit de l'américain par J.-G et P.-H. Maucorps) Paris: Armand Colin, 1951, pp. 105-132.

32.———. "The Comparative Study of Cultures and the Purposive Cultivation of Democratic Values, 1941-1949," (comments by Karl W. Deutsch, Geoffrey Gorer, Rhoda Metraux) *Perspectives on a Troubled Decade: Science, Philosophy and Religion,* 1939-1949 (Lyman Bryson, Louis Finkelstein, R. M. MacIver, Editors) New York: Conference on Science, Philosophy and Religion in their Relation to the Democratic Way of Life, Inc., 1950, pp. 87-108.

33.———. "Night after Night," a review of *Movies: A Psychological Study* by Martha Wolfenstein and Nathan Leites, Glencoe: The Free Press, 1950 in *Transformation,* I, 2, (1951) pp. 94-96.

34.———. *The School in American Culture.* (Inglis Lecture, 1950) Cambridge, Mass: Harvard University Press, 1951.

35.———. "Research in Contemporary Cultures," *Groups, Leadership and Men, Research in Human Relations* (Harold Guetzkow, Editor) Pittsburgh: Carnegie Press, 1951, pp. 106-118.

36.———. "Some Relationships between Anthropology and Psychiatry," *Dynamic Psychiatry* (Franz Alexander and Helen Ross, Editors) (in press).

37. Paalen, Wolfgang. "Metaplastic," *Dynaton,* The San Francisco Museum of Art, 1951, p. 7.

38. Ruesch, Jurgen, and Bateson, Gregory. *Communication: The Social Matrix of Psychiatry.* New York: W. W. Norton, 1951.

# *Index - Glossary*

This index-glossary follows the conventions used in *Balinese Character* with two exceptions.

1. Each individual Balinese is listed alphabetically under his or her name, not by households.
2. To enable the reader to follow a single child or adult chronologically from the earliest picture to the latest, plate numbers following personal names are in chronological order instead of plate order.

Technical terms used in accordance with Gesell terminological conventions and those especially developed for this book are included. Balinese words occurring only once in the text, and explained there, are not included. For explanation of Balinese names, see page 2. For Acknowledgments, see pp. VII-VIII.